The Book of Daily Prayer

The Book of Daily Prayer

Morning and Evening, 1999

Kim Martin Sadler

Editor

United Church Press
Cleveland, Ohio

United Church Press, Cleveland, Ohio 44115
© 1998 by United Church Press

Hymn lyrics are primarily from *The New Century Hymnal*
(Cleveland, Ohio: The Pilgrim Press, 1995); alterations copyright © The Pilgrim
Press and used by permission.

Biblical quotations are primarily from the New Revised Standard Version of the
Bible, © 1989 by the Division of Christian Education of the National Council
of the Churches of Christ in the U.S.A., and are used by permission.
Adapted for inclusivity.

All rights reserved. Published 1998

Printed in the United States of America on acid-free paper

03   02   01   00   99   98   5   4   3   2   1

Library of Congress Cataloging-in-Publication Data

The book of daily prayer : morning and evening, 1999 / Kim Martin Sadler, editor.
p. cm.
ISBN 0-8298-1260-1 (alk. paper)
1. Prayers. 2. Devotional calendars. I. Sadler, Kim Martin.
BV 245.B586   1997
248'.8—dc20   95-51065
CIP

Contents

Introduction

I recently greeted a friend with the usual phrase "How are you doing?" Her response was "I'm blessed!" Later, as I reflected on her affirmation, I was reminded how truly blessed we are.

As we begin the last year of the twentieth century, we should count our blessings! Looking back over the years, we and the world we live in have experienced births, deaths, triumphs, and tragedies. In spite of the ups and downs, our faith has sustained us. How blessed we have been! We can count our blessings and thank God for yet another year.

As you pray during 1999, share your blessings by allowing God to do a new thing in you. Increase the names and causes for which you pray. Share your faith with someone who needs to see God through you. Open your heart and home to someone from a different racial–ethnic group. Communicate with a relative to whom you have refused to speak because of past hurts. Volunteer in the nursery of your local hospital. Spend an afternoon reading to children in your local elementary school. Whatever you do, be a blessing to others.

"Behold, you will do a new and wonderful thing!" Begin and end 1999 in fervent prayer. Be a blessing to those around you, and make a change in your world.

Count your blessings!

KIM MARTIN SADLER

FRIDAY, JANUARY 1
(Read John 1:1–18)

(Morning)
All-creating God, another year is here, one that never before has been. Like
fresh white snow glittering across a wide field in the early-morning light,
it opens up, inviting me to run out into the bright future of your promising
creation. As I leap off the back porch of another year gone by, open my heart
to receive you again with a child's wise wonder.

(Evening)
All-creating God, your Word has called into being an end to this new beginning.
As I lie down in the mystery of the night, help me to trust in your Word,
the source and light and hope of all people.

With you, God, every end is a beginning; every door closed, a door opened;
every hurt, an occasion for healing; every failure, an opportunity for growth.
Give me courage in the year ahead to be a bolder witness to the warmth and
strength of your light, that more may know and receive you, that no darkness may long overshadow your truth. Thank you for shining your truth
into our world through your Word-become-flesh, Christ Jesus. I trust that
you are always with me because of what you have done in Christ.

(Morning)
As I greet the wonder and promise of a new year, give me eyes to see the signs
of your presence everywhere around me and a heart great enough to share them.
(Prayers of Intercession)

(Evening)
Grant me confidence in your love as I recall my shortcomings of the day,
that I may sleep in the assurance that you are indeed as full of grace as of truth.
(Prayers of Intercession)

May my life be a living witness to your Word-made-flesh with all to dwell.
(Pray the Prayer of Our Savior.)

(Morning)
Thank you for new life and the light
you give to live it. In Christ's name.
Amen.

(Evening)
When the light shines in the morning,
may I awaken stronger in your will.
In Christ's name. Amen.

SATURDAY, JANUARY 2
(Read Psalm 147:12–20 and Jeremiah 31:7–14)

(Morning)
As I awaken this morning, Sovereign God, pour your wisdom into my soul,
that I may be inspired and encouraged to be your servant today. Give me the
strength to speak truth to power, love to fear, and faith to cynicism.

(Evening)
As I sleep this night, Sovereign God, I thank you that though this day has not
left me blameless, you still count my life holy. Even when I have been a
damned fool, you have reminded me that I am still a redeemed child of the One
who is the source of all wisdom, including the wisdom of mercy.

Thank you, God, that your wisdom is greater even than our foolishness.
Over all our self-protective pride, our mistrusting fear, our idolatrous na-
tionalism, our self-securing greed, and even the violence in our hearts that
we harbor in your name—"over every people and nation" your wisdom
holds sway. In every age, you have entered the souls of Christ's servants,
like Sojourner Truth, Martin Luther King Jr., Oscar Romero, and countless
others, and have "withstood dread kings with wonders and signs" of your
sovereign Wisdom and her children, Love and Justice. Because of this, I
trust you enough to take risks in your service.

(Morning)
O God, guide me in the marvelous way of your wisdom.
Make me wise enough to dare to be a fool for Christ's sake.
(Prayers of Intercession)

(Evening)
Honestly, God, the world doesn't seem to be getting much better.
It is still a far cry from the realm which you have promised us in Christ.
As I lie down this night, fill me with the peace of faith.
(Prayers of Intercession)

**Just as you have led us through the deep waters of evil and trouble in every
age, lead us on in the faith of Christ Jesus, in whose name and way I pray.**
(Pray the Prayer of Our Savior.)

(Morning)	(Evening)
Today I commit myself to your service. In Christ's name. Amen.	Thank you, God, that even while we sleep, your realm of love, justice, and peace draws ever closer. In Christ's name. Amen.

SUNDAY, JANUARY 3
(Read Ephesians 1:3–14)

(Morning)
Holy One, on the second Sunday of Christmas, may my every thought and deed praise your name. In response to the innumerable blessings you have poured out on me, may my life this day be a thankful blessing to you.

(Evening)
Holy One, though some of my thoughts and deeds have been unthankful this day, I have grown in my experience of your love.
For that, I give you thanks and praise.

For everything, gracious God, I am utterly dependent on you. Without you I am hopeless. Why do I pretend by living as if I were self-sufficient, when without you I am nothing? Why do I take pride in my accomplishments, when it is you who make them possible? For everyone and everything that is good in my life, for life itself, I give you all glory. To give you thanks and praise is the beginning of any wisdom I am blessed to receive. May it always be my end.

(Morning)
O God, in Christ your eternal goodness and truth have taken form in human life. May they take form in my life this day, that my living will be a sign of your eternal choice to act for the good of all that you create.
(Prayers of Intercession)

(Evening)
O God, in Christ I have heard once again the Word of truth and the good news of salvation. As I sleep this night, mark my soul with the seal of the Holy Spirit, that I may rest and grow in the Spirit's greatest gift: your eternal, gracious love.
(Prayers of Intercession)

With thanks and praise I pray.
(Pray the Prayer of Our Savior.)

(Morning)
As I prepare to live another precious day you have given me, help me to set all my hope on you, and help me to live only for the praise of your glory. In Christ's name. Amen.

(Evening)
Now I lay me down to sleep, with trust in you my soul to keep. Thank you, God, that because of all you have revealed in Christ, I can entrust everyone and everything to you. In Christ's name. Amen.

MONDAY, JANUARY 4
(Read Acts 10:34–39)

(Morning)
Holy God, Bestower of new life, I see newness around me this morning as the world awakens. As I begin this new year, grant me newness and vitality.

(Evening)
Holy God, you give me life: breath, pulse, and thought. As I rest this night, may your rejuvenating presence be in me, so that I may awake refreshed.

God, you show no partiality. We are found acceptable to you if we fear you and do what is right. And we have an opportunity for new life because of your child, who died for us. In this new year, O God, you give me new paths to forge. Let me boldly seize this moment and pledge to be your witness.

(Morning)
Help me to discern your call amidst other voices. Open my ears, that I may clearly hear your voice calling my name and directing my steps.
(Prayers of Intercession)

(Evening)
I so often feel trapped by my behavior. Help me to find the new life that you graciously extend and give me courage to change my ways.
(Prayers of Intercession)

"We are witnesses to all that Jesus did both in Judea and in Jerusalem."

(Morning)
This year may my New Year's resolutions not be for myself alone, but may they be the product of your call to me. May I also find new and abundant life in you. In Jesus' name. Amen.

(Evening)
May this new year be a year of grace-filled living in you. In Jesus' name. Amen.

TUESDAY, JANUARY 5
(Read Psalm 29)

(Morning)
God, I arise and greet the new day. I give to you, Yahweh,
glory and praise. I worship you, who are all strength and majesty.

(Evening)
God, in closing this day, I rest confidently in your strength and power.
In ascribing to you, Yahweh, I join the heavenly host in worship.
In lying down to sleep, I prepare to arise again in the new day.

Mighty God, your voice sounds throughout the universe, from the desert to the waters, from the mountains to the forests, from the planets to the galaxies. All creation praises you, and I add my voice to their voices, which respond to your voice resounding in the world. Just as Isaiah heard your voice calling him amid a chorus of cherubim and seraphim, so I, too, join with all the company of heaven in worshiping you.

(Morning)
In my actions today, may my ears be opened to hear your voice
and may all that my mouth utters be worthy of you.
(Prayers of Intercession)

(Evening)
While I sleep, attune my body to your voice,
so that I may hear you in a persistent nudge or in a quiet whisper.
(Prayers of Intercession)

"The voice of Yahweh is powerful."

(Morning)
The voice of Yahweh thunders, breaks, flashes, and shakes, reminding us that you, O God, rule over all. God, rule over my heart today. In Jesus' name. Amen.

(Evening)
The voice of Yahweh is powerful and majestic, for you, O God, are enthroned over creation. God, grant me a portion of your strength, and may I rest in peace. In Jesus' name. Amen.

WEDNESDAY, JANUARY 6
(Read Psalm 29 and Matthew 3:13–17)

(Morning)
Your voice, Yahweh, calls to me in the light of this new morning.
Open my ears, that I may hear.

(Evening)
Your voice, Yahweh, spoke to me today in a friend's smile, in a colleague's
commendation, in the wind's rustling of leaves, in music's melodic strains.
I thank you for the constancy of your presence.

Creating God, you speak, and life springs forth. You began creation with a
Word, you delivered your people after speaking your name, and your voice
sounded from heaven at Jesus' baptism. The psalmist says, "The voice of
Yahweh is upon the waters," the waters from which we receive life. We
hear your voice in waves that splash upon the shore, in trickles of a mountain stream, and in showers that make the desert bloom. We hear your voice
in baptismal pledges and statements of faith, in covenantal promises and
affirmations. We hear your presence in water poured and feel it in hands
outstretched.

(Morning)
Today I celebrate my baptism.
May I live in the newness of life sealed by that covenant.
(Prayers of Intercession)

(Evening)
Thank you for calling me your beloved child.
Help me to live more fully in relationship with you.
(Prayers of Intercession)

"The voice of Yahweh is upon many waters."

(Morning)	(Evening)
In baptism, you take the initiative and call me as your own. May I respond in confidence and be a new creation. In Jesus' name. Amen.	In baptism, you give me a sign and seal of your love for me. May I rest securely, knowing that I am always in your care. In Jesus' name. Amen.

THURSDAY, JANUARY 7
(Read Acts 10:39–43)

(Morning)
Life-giving God, you call my name today, and I rise,
make my bed, and ready myself for a new day.

(Evening)
Life-giving God, you gave me your hand to steady my step, lifted me
to safety, and showed me opportunities today for your service.

Just as Jesus was put to death on the third day, you allowed him to rise and appear to your chosen ones. Like Peter, let me speak your Word, and give me the courage to preach and testify that Christ is the "judge of the living and the dead." For "everyone who believes in Christ receives forgiveness of sins through Christ's name."

(Morning)
Instill in me the confidence that this day is in your care. I hear you
calling me by name, urging me to rise. Give me the courage to respond.
(Prayers of Intercession)

(Evening)
Help me know that I can trust you. Deal kindly with my attempts to respond
faithfully by opening my eyes, seeing your presence, and stepping out in faith.
(Prayers of Intercession)

**"He commanded us to preach to the people and to testify that he
is the one ordained by God as judge of the living and the dead."**

(Morning)
O God, today, may I respond to your
call to preach and testify for you. In
Jesus' name. Amen.

(Evening)
When Jesus was raised, you chose
those to whom he would appear. May
the seeds that I planted today bear
fruit, so that people may again
believe in you. In Jesus' name. Amen.

FRIDAY, JANUARY 8
(Read Isaiah 42:1–9)

(Morning)
Creator, you spread forth this globe of soil, endowed with life abundant. As you originally breathed life into humankind, so also breathe life into my nostrils.

(Evening)
Creator, your hand stretches out the heavens like a tent,
bestowed with glorious life. I see your handiwork in the
twinkling stars, swirling orbits, and spinning ecosystems.

"I am Yahweh," you said through the prophet, recalling the revelation of your name to Moses. You cause to be all that is and give life where none has existed. By giving your name, you reveal yourself to us and give power to act in your behalf. May my actions bring glory to your name.

(Morning)
Your servant does not break a bruised reed and does not take advantage
of anyone close to the breaking point. When I am beaten down,
may I find such care from you. Help me be such a servant to others.
(Prayers of Intercession)

(Evening)
Your servant does not quench a dimly burning wick and does not snuff
the life out of anyone barely hanging on. When my energy is waning,
be gentle with me. Help me serve others as does your servant.
(Prayers of Intercession)

The servant "will bring forth justice to the nations."

(Morning)
Holy God, none other has your glory. Only you have perfect glory. Open my eyes to see your glory and avert idolatry. In Jesus' name. Amen.

(Evening)
Holy God, no graven image has your praise. No idol can satisfy our longings for you. Forgive my infatuation with what does not reflect your glory. Help me see anew. In Jesus' name. Amen.

SATURDAY, JANUARY 9
(Read Isaiah 42:1–9 and Acts 10:34–43)

(Morning)
God, you take me by the hand this morning and give me vision
for the day's work. Let your Spirit pulse through me.

(Evening)
God, you called me in righteousness and set me to be a light to others.
Keep me steadfastly on the path of truth.

God of justice, you have called us to roll away tombstones for those entrapped in death, to push back the blinders that limit eyesight, and to break open the walls and glass ceilings that imprison your people. Yet for all our efforts, we often fail and feel discouraged, entrapped by unjust systems. Healing God, we need your touch now. There is much weeping in our families, much wailing in our towns, much grieving in our nations. Please come to us without delay.

(Morning)
I grieve as the widows did for untimely deaths.
I dedicate myself as did Peter to bringing life this day.
(Prayers of Intercession)

(Evening)
This day reminded me how much we need your vision.
I pledge myself as did your servant to help bring forth justice.
(Prayers of Intercession)

The coastlands wait for God's law.

(Morning)
Let me be like Peter today, going where people are crying and weeping. When I am entreated to go, let me not tarry. In Jesus' name. Amen.

(Evening)
When I am overcome by the anguish of the world, remind me that you are God, who gives breath and spirit to all the earth. When I am overcome by my own grief, help me to know that you weep and grieve with me. Be my comfort this night. In Jesus' name. Amen.

SUNDAY, JANUARY 10
(Read Isaiah 42:1–9, Acts 10:36–43, and Matthew 3:13–17)

(Morning)
God, I begin my day with water, which cleanses me as do the waters of baptism.
God, purify me to be your servant today.

(Evening)
God, you chose me as your servant and gave your Spirit. In closing this day
with water, may I be cleansed from old ways to new ones.

In the waters of baptism, we signify our dying and rising with Christ. Just
as Christ died, was washed, and rose, so may I experience new birth and
cleansing. You, O God, have always chosen servants: Peter, Israel, Jesus.
May I be worthy of your call to be your servant.

(Morning)
Holy God, you sent your Spirit upon your servant Israel and upon Jesus.
Send your Spirit upon me today, that what I do and say may be from you.
(Prayers of Intercession)

(Evening)
"This is my beloved Child, with whom I am well pleased."
"Behold my chosen, in whom my soul delights."
May I be pleasing in your sight.
(Prayers of Intercession)

"I have given you as a covenant to the people."

(Morning)	(Evening)
In baptism, you covenant to be my God as I am your child. Help me live in ways that demonstrate whose I am by the newness of life you have given. In Jesus' name. Amen.	In death, the old passes away and the new appears. In baptism, the old dies and the new comes. In promises, when the old is fulfilled, the new springs forth. God, this new year, help me lay aside what is past and allow your new life to arise. In Jesus' name. Amen.

MONDAY, JANUARY 11
(Read Isaiah 49:1–3)

(Morning)
God of all creation, you have called me forth to meet this new day. You equip me with gifts of love and compassion. Help me to use them to your glory.

(Evening)
God of all creation, I rest with the knowledge and satisfaction
that we were present to each other this day.

Being a servant is not very attractive, God. It is a word fraught with a history of oppression and dehumanization—yet you call us to be your servants. Servanthood requires discipline and commitment. I need to be clear about whom I serve and toward what end. It is possible to be self-serving as well as to be used by others in the name of service. I prefer to serve you, God, and others. Assist me, God of life, to distinguish between those deeds that are done in humility and out of genuine love, and those that are selfish and motivated by greed. God, at what cost am I your servant?

(Morning)
You sustain me with your strength and power.
I am your servant as this day unfolds.
(Prayers of Intercession)

(Evening)
Bind me to others in your world.
(Prayers of Intercession)

"For God so loved the world . . . "

(Morning)
Help me to discern what it is to be of true service to you and the coming of your dominion. Place me at those places and in situations where I can truly make a difference in the lives of people. In Jesus' name. Amen.

(Evening)
While I am only a small speck of creation, I have sought to make a contribution to your plan. I have responded with love and joy to a life that is full of challenges, and I rest now with the hope that I have served you well. In Jesus' name. Amen.

TUESDAY, JANUARY 12
(Read Isaiah 49:4 and Psalm 40:1–5)

(Morning)
God of this new day, give me the strength to confront tensions
and anxieties with calm and assurance. Help me to think clearly
and to temper my words with understanding and graciousness.
Assist me in overcoming my own insecurities and fear of failure.

(Evening)
God of this new night, I have done my best to confront the fears
that lurk within me. You have provided me with the assurance
and certainty that only in you do I find true acceptance and freedom.

"We have nothing to fear but fear itself," proclaimed President Franklin D. Roosevelt. How often he must have felt afraid in the midst of his own struggle to survive his disability. However, he feared and trusted at the same time. We fear what we do not know and trust only what we can see! Roosevelt trusted in the people's capacity to rise above their fears of the moment. We trust in you, O God, whom we cannot see. We believe in events we cannot confirm. But it is precisely because of this trust that our faith is strengthened and our lives freed from the captivity of fear.

(Morning)
Provide me with the insight to make decisions that are worthy of the label
"Christian" and to further serve your purposes in the world.
(Prayers of Intercession)

(Evening)
As I approach the end of the day, I recount the many ways in which you have
challenged me to rise above the anxieties and fears that can paralyze me.
(Prayers of Intercession)

You are my rock and foundation.

(Morning)	(Evening)
Assure me, O God, that even in the face of failure, I am accepted and loved. I am part of an unending cycle of creation that is sustained and nurtured by your mercy and providence. In Jesus' name. Amen.	Praised be your name, gracious God, for all the new experiences of this day. They have deepened my understanding of your universal love and purpose. In Jesus' name. Amen.

WEDNESDAY, JANUARY 13
(Read Isaiah 49:5–7)

(Morning)
Sovereign God, I feel as if I have a purpose to my day—
to be actively engaged in your world and to share life in ways
that demonstrate your love and concern for all your children.
May I find ways in which justice and righteousness are made concrete.

(Evening)
Sovereign God, the evening news may not bring "good news,"
but I know you are present in the midst of suffering, pain, and agony.

God, it is so difficult to feel that I can make any difference in the world. The global problems seem so overwhelming—homelessness, hunger, poverty, economic injustice, countless uprooted persons, and the daily destruction of your creation. Yet I must care and respond with a sense of responsibility and urgency. As a Christian, I am part of a larger global community of faith, which is united by your love and committed to your mission. The future does not depend on my actions alone but on the collective activity of the body of Christ, which, with others of good will, transforms evil into good, division into harmony, and death into life.

(Morning)
May my witness to your goodness be grounded in the knowledge
that you, gracious God, are the Author of the universe
and that your Spirit converts, transforms, and heals.
(Prayers of Intercession)

(Evening)
May your healing power be present around the world.
(Prayers of Intercession)

"Therefore, I make you a light to the nations."

(Morning)
May I seek to make myself available as a vehicle of healing and understanding to all those who may find themselves in despair and gloom this day. In Jesus' name. Amen.

(Evening)
Grant me your peace even while I contemplate and remember those who experience very little peace this night. In Jesus' name. Amen.

14

THURSDAY, JANUARY 14
(Read Psalm 40:6–11)

(Morning)
God, I approach today with fresh openness and make myself available
to you. May my deeds and actions praise your name and be
genuine expressions of all that is good and acceptable in your sight.

(Evening)
God, set my mind upon those things that unite me
with the world and grant me your peace.

The psalmist proclaims "glad news of deliverance"! South Africa is free
from the captivity of apartheid and seeks to build an open and free society.
Led by Nelson Mandela, a man of vision, South Africa has emerged into
the dawn of a new day. The former Yugoslavia, however, suffers from deep
divisions that emerge from religious and ethnic differences. Where is the
glad news here, God? The president of Serbia instituted ethnic cleansing in
order to achieve his objectives. How is it that two such very different models of human society can exist side by side and during the same period of
history? Is it us? Is it you? What is it within us that compels us to huddle in
corners of hatred and mistrust rather than seek out your gift of diversity?

(Morning)
It is as blessed to receive as it is to give.
(Prayers of Intercession)

(Evening)
Blessings upon all those who have honored your name
by giving and sharing life with one another. Let me join those
who resist the natural forces of division and see unity in you.
(Prayers of Intercession)

"I delight to do your will, O my God."

(Morning)
The presence of your Spirit is evident
wherever we truly understand what it
means to share life. In Jesus' name.
Amen.

(Evening)
Surround us with your love and protect
us with your presence, now and
always. In Jesus' name. Amen.

FRIDAY, JANUARY 15
(Read 1 Corinthians 1:1–9)

(Morning)
God, with a grateful heart, I rejoice in the opportunities that will present themselves this day. May I seek out the Christ in everyone I meet and in whatever situation I encounter. I pray that your transforming power will be present to the hearts and souls of those with whom I relate and engage.

(Evening)
God, from a distance I can now bring a measure of understanding
and thanksgiving to this day's journey.

A young woman in Sarajevo is shot by a Serbian sniper. She is Serbian. The man who comes to her aid is also Serbian. Who is the enemy? North Koreans die from hunger due to famine and isolation from the rest of the world. A newspaper columnist asks, "Should South Korea feed an enemy who vows to destroy it but who is also its neighbor?" Who is the enemy? Life often places before us impossible choices. God, you are there as a source of strength and courage. Often our choices will put us in personal peril, but you call us to obedience and sacrifice.

(Morning)
Help me, God of grace, to face the unpleasantness
of life with creativity and skill.
(Prayers of Intercession)

(Evening)
I have sought to meet the challenges of this day
with determination and grace. Offer me, God of hope,
the rest that will refresh my spirit and restore my energy.
(Prayers of Intercession)

"I always give thanks to my God for you."

(Morning)
May the choices I make today be acceptable in your sight, Sovereign God of forgiveness and mercy. In Jesus' name. Amen.

(Evening)
I give thanks for those around me—family, friends, and coworkers, who sustained me and were present to me this day. This circle of humanity, which I call community, is sacred. I ask your blessing, God of life, upon us all. In Jesus' name. Amen.

SATURDAY, JANUARY 16
(Read John 1:29–34)

(Morning)
Gracious One, send down your Spirit upon me, that I may witness to your
glorious deeds! Fill me with all measure of goodness and righteousness,
so I may be a vehicle of your unity and mission.

(Evening)
Gracious One, my heart yearns for patience and understanding.
In the shadow of your mercy, I take my rest. Forgive my misdeeds,
bless my attempts to witness to your love, and grant me your peace.

In Vietnam, a church delegation visits the site of the My Lai massacre.
This is the place where hundreds of Vietnamese men, women, and children
were slaughtered in a ditch. The delegation stands by the ditch in meditation and prayer. A small boy on the other side of the ditch watches curi-
ously. After the brief service, a senior member of the delegation blows up a
balloon, walks into the center of the ditch, and offers the balloon to the
smiling child. Reconciliation and the hope of new life take place in the
ditch where fear, tears, and blood were shed. God, your Spirit once again
has descended and offered a new beginning.

(Morning)
All things are possible in and through your love for us.
You sacrificed yourself on a cross so that we might be offered new beginnings.
Help me respond and create those opportunities this day.
(Prayers of Intercession)

(Evening)
While I may not have finished all the tasks of the day or done anything
terribly miraculous, I might very well have planted
the seed or set the stage for your transforming Spirit to work.
(Prayers of Intercession)

"Here is the Lamb of God who takes away the sin of the world!"

(Morning)
Reconciliation is the act that repairs
brokenness and restores wholeness. I
wish to be an instrument of your
reconciliation and to heal the brokenness in my life and with those where
there is relationship-building to be
done. In Jesus' name. Amen.

(Evening)
Gather me into your fold, great
Shepherd, where I might rest and be
refreshed by the everlasting glow of
your Spirit. In Jesus' name. Amen.

SUNDAY, JANUARY 17
(Read John 1:35–42)

(Morning)
God, I follow in the footsteps of many who have journeyed after you.
The journey is long and hard. I am searching for the One who offers life
and hope. May this day bring me closer to the One who is love and peace.

(Evening)
God, this day I have seen ways in which your will is revealed and how often
opportunities for growth are missed. Forgive my awkwardness.

We are called to be your disciples, God. We must give up our "rootedness"
and journey with you. As a great historian once declared, "If you don't
know where you came from, you will not know where you are going."
Adjustment to new environments is a way of life, and yet when I ask someone "Where are you from?" the answer will begin to define who that person is. Our roots are important, and yet, as people of faith, we are people
on the move. Our identity is more than a place, more than immediate family, more than race and ethnicity. Identity is integrity, convictions, commit-
ments, and sacrifice for those principles that most closely reflect your will.

(Morning)
When considering who I am this day, may my devotion to love
and justice be primary in answering that question.
May your will, not mine, be done.
(Prayers of Intercession)

(Evening)
Followers of yours, God, get tired. Tired of all the talk, competition,
and pettiness. Release me from this debilitating consequence
and grant me moments of quiet reflection.
(Prayers of Intercession)

**"When Jesus turned and saw them following, he said to them,
'What are you looking for?' "**

(Morning)
Provide me with energy for the journey, strength to complete the tasks of
the day, and the courage to be all that
one who claims to be a disciple of
Jesus can be. In Jesus' name. Amen.

(Evening)
In seeking you this day, I have
discovered anew the burdens of
discipleship. I rejoice in the fact that I
am not alone but share life with many
others who claim the same God. In
Jesus' name. Amen.

MONDAY, JANUARY 18
(Read Isaiah 9:1–4)

(Morning)
O Faithful One, remembering your promises,
I anticipate the coming day and whatever it holds.

(Evening)
O Faithful One, the constancy of your promises once again has sustained me.
I remember my childhood prayer, "Now I lay me down to sleep . . . ,"
and intend to be constant in my trust in you.

In the routines of my everyday life, I seek awareness of your promises and presence. Whatever my surroundings, whether gloom or joy, may I be focused on your promises and expectations. As with the faithful who are visually impaired, may my seeing of you transcend light and darkness. Indeed, may I know you in moments of anguish and joy, in times marked by routine and surprise, in periods of entrapment or oppression, and in knowing I am released from bondage and lifted up in freedom.

(Morning)
Your promises are real, whether I feel myself to be between a rock and a hard place or rising up on eagle's wings. Keep me sustained in that knowledge.
(Prayers of Intercession)

(Evening)
Now this day is ending, but never-ending is my trust in you.
(Prayers of Intercession)

**My words join the words of faithful ones through the ages,
who both comfort and strengthen me even now.**
(Pray the Prayer of Our Savior.)

(Morning)
For each new day, no matter what it holds, your promises hold secure. Bless me, that I might live this day embodied and emboldened in their truthfulness. In Christ's name I pray. Amen.

(Evening)
Where I have faltered today, sustain me anew. Where my faith in your promises has sustained me to help my friends and neighbors, thank you. In Christ's name I pray. Amen.

TUESDAY, JANUARY 19
(Read Psalm 27:4–9)

(Morning)
God, in thankfulness may I begin this day, remembering a delight, offering up a joyous song, anticipating once again the gifts I already have received from you. May I keep aware of my safe dwelling place in your promises.

(Evening)
God, on this very day, as I have walked with you and talked with you, I am so grateful that you live even in my neighborhood, even attending my daily life.

O Present One, what comfort it is to know that you chose to pitch your tent among your people. O Embodied One, how I celebrate that you keep choosing to live even in my neighborhood and to hear my feelings and concerns about the people and events of my everyday life. My dwelling place can be in you, for you have chosen to dwell with your creatures. And so I am sheltered; I am safe; my head is lifted up. I am with you.

(Morning)
As your promises are real and embodied, not vague,
so may I live out what I have promised to do and to be today.
(Prayers of Intercession)

(Evening)
Even here and again today, you have sought me. I so want to be found, lifted up.
I dare to sing my joy in relating to you. I seek you; find me now.
(Prayers of Intercession)

What comfort to remember and to hope in the name of Jesus.
(Pray a phrase or prayer particularly important to you.)

(Morning)
What amazing grace that you live in my neighborhood! I will look for you today, your presence and your expectations for how you would have me live here—today. In Christ's name I pray. Amen.

(Evening)
Another day, dear Jesus, I have sought you and found you and missed you and let you down. In all, I am thankful for this day and for my coming rest. In Christ's name I pray. Amen.

WEDNESDAY, JANUARY 20
(Read 1 Corinthians 1:10–13)

(Morning)
Creator of all humankind, may your desire that we might all
be one live freshly within me. Help me to listen as well as to speak
and to be open to learn what I can from other voices.

(Evening)
Creator of all humankind, help me to celebrate the variety of persons who were
in my life today. Strengthen my wholeness in you, so that I can receive those
who are different and seek with them to deepen our understandings of you.

Your world is so full of a number of things—colors and voices, stories and
happenings, temperatures and elevations, sizes and heights and depths—
and so much more. May I be so centered in you that I do not have to be the
center around which I expect persons in my life to revolve. May I be so
grounded in your promises that I am not thrown asunder when I experience
practices unfamiliar to me. May I be so resilient—in being buoyed up by
you—that I can bounce back when my feelings are hurt and can initiate
overtures toward forgiveness when enmity has appeared to triumph. One
God. One humankind. May your intent become mine.

(Morning)
May I see each person I meet today as a person of dignity,
created by you. May the words of my mouth and
the reflections in my heart and head bring honor to you.
(Prayers of Intercession)

(Evening)
Help me to discover daily and nightly the peace that is possible
when I trust that you are tented here, even now, reminding me
of past blessings received and promised blessings to come.
(Prayers of Intercession)

Free me to live in your promises, O Holy One.
(Pray the Prayer of Our Savior.)

(Morning)
Our oneness in you is both a given
and a task. This day, keep me listening for your promises, that I may hear
others also seeking after you. In
Christ's name I pray. Amen.

(Evening)
May my rest, like my tasks, lie in the
open arms of your promises. Your
peace sustains through the divisions of
day and night and seasons. Even now
abide with me. In Christ's name I pray.
Amen.

THURSDAY, JANUARY 21
(Read 1 Corinthians 1:14–18)

(Morning)
Savior God, whatever this day may hold, may I be present
in its movements, with its peoples, in the midst of its tasks.
And may my presence be gospel-grounded, however humble,
and my words meet needs, however less than eloquent their expression.

(Evening)
Savior God, within the processes of my daily living, I have been
and am being sustained by your power.Help me to understand
my daily pilgrimage as bearing your transformative power.

God, on some days I get it, and on others I simply miss it. For I know that
your power is not the power to triumph over others. Rather it is the power
to receive others even onto the cross. But on some days, oh how I want to
win! To be firmly in control! To triumph with my wisdom and my righteousness! Guide me in your wisdom, O Gracious One, that I may distinguish between folly and foolishness and learn to live in the powers of the
cross.

(Morning)
Be my wisdom as you are my Creator, Redeemer, Friend.
May your presence be embodied as I am present with others on this very day.
(Prayers of Intercession)

(Evening)
Abide with me. In the sufferings and joys of nights past and nights to come,
free me to remember you, both Crucified and Risen One.
(Prayers of Intercession)

**I pause in silence—with my memories and hopes.
I pray a prayer of familiarity and comfort to me.**
(Pray the Prayer of Our Savior.)

(Morning)
Sunrise, sunset, all times in between—
I anticipate occasions to thank you
anew for blessings, persons, and
participation in your salvation processes. In Christ's name I pray. Amen.

(Evening)
Sunrise, sunset, all times in between—I remember occasions when I
felt your presence, embodied your
hopes, and was less than you would
have had me be. Yet at all times, I am
yours, Redeemer and Holy One. In
Christ's name I pray. Amen.

FRIDAY, JANUARY 22
(Read Matthew 4:12–17)

(Morning)
O God who remembers your promises, O Creator who remembers
your creatures, remember me as I receive and respond to this day.
And as you do, may I remember you, so that your commands
and promises will empower me.

(Evening)
O God who remembers and promises, as this day is ending—
whatever it has held—I now remember your promises to my ancestors
and how they trusted that they would be fulfilled. May I so trust,
even in my present wanderings, even in this dwelling place.

O God, do remember me. Such solace it brings to know that I am not forgotten by you. Such glimpses of hope come alive in me even when I despair. For I remember what it has meant to me in the past to trust your
presence. When I sit in despair or depression, may your presence glow
warm within me. Or if I am defeated and isolated, open me to the newness
of relationship with you and others who share my journey. May I be faithful in seeking and remembering you.

(Morning)
How perfect is Jesus' trust as he prays and acts.
May that integrity guide me in my prayers and actions.
(Prayers of Intercession)

(Evening)
Night and day I seek your way. For your creatures and your creation now I pray.
(Prayers of Intercession)

Living in the promises of Christ, my Savior, I live, I pray, I sing.

(Morning)
I will be aware of your promises and
seek to trust in you as this day
unfolds. May I be a part of the
coming of your dominion. In Christ's
name I pray. Amen.

(Evening)
As I reflect, I delight in the places
where you found me today. Where I
missed you, I know you have not
forgotten me, and in this blessed
assurance I come to my rest. In
Christ's name I pray. Amen.

SATURDAY, JANUARY 23
(Read Matthew 4:18–22)

(Morning)
Here I am, Jesus. My name is [your name]. Like Mary and Martha,
Andrew and James, I want to follow you into this day—whatever it holds.

(Evening)
Here I am, Jesus. This day I have sought to know your intent for me.
In the midst of vocation and avocation, please know, O Holy One,
that I have tried. I both celebrate and pledge to persevere.

You promise that your dominion is at hand! I would follow you toward that
place of justice—that promised land of a whole and fulfilled humanity.
Strengthen me to follow you through stonings and downsizings, through
refusals and disillusionments. I remember the fishermen and the difficulties that beset their way. Yet as they experienced your peace that surpasses
understanding—even when their histories did not turn out as they had hoped
and expected—I would join them, even in my vulnerability and finitude.

(Morning)
Help me to remember that many of the others with whom I will share
this day also seek to follow you. And help me to remember to invite
others to follow you, even as I myself was once invited—and said yes.
(Prayers of Intercession)

(Evening)
I pray that my desire to follow you was communicated
to others on this day, even to those who view me as leader.
May they view me, first of all, as your follower.
(Prayers of Intercession)

**I follow you, knowing that you will not turn away from me
no matter what occurs.**

(Morning)	(Evening)
May I mend my nets and weave my tapestries to your glory. May I dance in circles and ascend in elevators as your follower. In Christ's name I pray. Amen.	Whether sleeping by the sea or sleeping in a tent in the city, I have sought to do my work in your name and with your blessing. Please let me rest in your peace. In Christ's name I pray. Amen.

SUNDAY, JANUARY 24
(Read Psalm 27:1)

(Morning)
God, I approach this day seeking strength in the midst of the fear
and trembling that often accompany my journey. I turn to you,
and my approach to the day is stronger in your presence.

(Evening)
God, this day has now been lived, its fears encountered through your strength,
and its leftover tasks to be let go now. For you will accompany me through this
night and be my stronghold tomorrow.

Creator God, it is good to have places of memory where we can rest securely. And it is good to have poems and stories to help in our interpretations and tasks. But it is even better to hold to some scriptural passages that have sheltered us in the past, that call to mind your previous presence with us, that anticipate what is promised to us and what we believe is real. It is strengthening to call to mind those promises that help us hold on and those we may not always freely share with others: "Jesus loves me—this I know"; "For God so loved the world"; "Neither life nor death nor things in the heavens above or the earth below"; "You are my light and my salvation, the stronghold of my life. Whom shall I fear? Of whom shall I be afraid?"

(Morning)
I remember not only your promises but that I actually can count on
them as I face the experiences of this day.
(Prayers of Intercession)

(Evening)
Sometimes I make it, and sometimes I don't. But you are always my light,
my salvation, my stronghold. Be with all for whom I pray.
(Prayers of Intercession)

In my dwelling place, you are here. In your dwelling place, I am there.
(Pray the Prayer of Our Savior.)

(Morning)
Your promises are not for just a week
or even a lifetime. Surely I can count
on them today. In Christ's name I
pray. Amen.

(Evening)
Another day. May I now rest without
fear. Why should I be afraid? For you
are near—always. In Christ's name I
pray. Amen.

MONDAY, JANUARY 25
(Read Micah 6:1–5)

(Morning)
Dear God, you have not wearied me. I have wearied you.

(Evening)
Dear God, as the sunset fades and shadows fall, relieve my mind of worries.

God, in Genesis we are told that you created the sun to rule the day and the moon to rule the night. Then, as an afterthought, the text reads, "and the stars." If this story were told today, how would we speak of the stars? There are billions of them, reaching into outer space for millions of light years' distance. If we were writing the story today, would we change the text and say, "God made the earth also?" Yes, through endless ages, you fashioned our earth home with limitless care and patience. Its beauty and grandeur grow as we contemplate the vast miracles of its richness and beauty. God,you have been so very patient.

(Morning)
Be patient with me and help me to be patient, too.
(Prayers of Intercession)

(Evening)
Through eons of time, you have loved our planet earth.
Help me care for it for my trust-appointed time.
(Prayers of Intercession)

I now pray the prayer that Jesus taught.
(Pray the Prayer of Our Savior.)

(Morning)
The clocks of time have many hours. May I use them well. I pray in Jesus' name. Amen.

(Evening)
The day is done, gone the sun. All is well, safely rest. God is nigh. I pray in Jesus' name. Amen.

TUESDAY, JANUARY 26
(Read Micah 6:6–8)

(Morning)
Savior God, you ask us to do justice, love kindness, and walk humbly
while the prophet names my deepest need: to tame my wants and ego.

(Evening)
Savior God, help me to find the peace and joy of humility.

Creator God, how strange it is that through all the ages of human history,
humans have assumed themselves to be the centerpiece of all creation. With
their self-endowed egos, people could strut, preen, fight, and dominate at
will. They owned our planet earth and its skies, and even laid first claim to
heaven. Surely, today a new and profound humility should come to temper
our pretensions. Instead of a license to dominate, exploit, and rule the earth,
we have been given a stewardship, a garden planet, entrusted to our care
for a time.

(Morning)
God, help me to listen intently and to speak softly.
(Prayers of Intercession)

(Evening)
God, help me to be patient with the loud voices I heard today.
(Prayers of Intercession)

I now pray the prayer that Jesus taught.
(Pray the Prayer of Our Savior.)

(Morning)
Help me to understand true humility,
to find that giving is greater and
worth more than receiving. I pray in
Jesus' name. Amen.

(Evening)
I gave money to a homeless girl today.
She was very grateful. I would like to
do more. I pray in Jesus' name. Amen.

WEDNESDAY, JANUARY 27
(Read Psalm 15)

(Morning)
Savior God, the high road always calls for selfless giving,
even the making of loans without interest. Is that just an archaic idea?

(Evening)
Savior God, your hand in mine and your love in my heart
are what I need to measure up and "not be moved."

Savior God, "Who may abide in your tent? Who may dwell on your holy hill?" Let me also walk blamelessly, speak the truth, do no evil, and not take up reproach against my neighbors. Empower me to do these things so that I will never be moved.

(Morning)
O great Sovereign of the seas, open my eyes to see
the other little boats on the oceans of my life.
(Prayers of Intercession)

(Evening)
Thank you for calming the winds.
(Prayers of Intercession)

I now pray the prayer that Jesus taught.
(Pray the Prayer of Our Savior.)

(Morning)
Give me greater understanding and trust in your mighty power. In Jesus' name I pray. Amen.

(Evening)
Bless all the folks and friends I met today. In Jesus' name I pray. Amen.

THURSDAY, JANUARY 28
(Read 1 Corinthians 1:18–31)

(Morning)
Creator God, your love is the strength of my life in every way and day.

(Evening)
Creator God, help me to understand the wisdom of faith and the power of truth.

God, your Word tells us that you will destroy the wisdom of the wise and the discernment of the discerning. Help me to know my call so that my source of life is that of the Christ. The voice, the Word, the truth of Christ call us to a faith that goes beyond wisdom.

(Morning)
My fishing nets are empty, too. Help me to learn
to let them down again and again and again.
(Prayers of Intercession)

(Evening)
Precious God, you have been my insight and power today
to overcome doubts and weakness.
(Prayers of Intercession)

I now pray the prayer that Jesus taught.
(Pray the Prayer of Our Savior.)

(Morning)
I have many duties today. Help me
overcome doubt and believe the
impossible. I pray in Jesus' name.
Amen.

(Evening)
My heart is warmed, and my mind is
gladdened by your Word and presence.
I pray in Jesus' name. Amen.

FRIDAY, JANUARY 29
(Read Matthew 5:1–5)

(Morning)
Dear God, how can happiness come from a lowly, mourning, and meek spirit?

(Evening)
Dear God, today I found joy in sharing tears.

God, so often we see the disparities before us—wealth and poverty, the haves and have-nots, those living in comfort and those living in the hardness of the streets. Thank you for your blessings to us, the poor in spirit, for us who mourn and for us who are meek.

(Morning)
Help me find the power and meaning of shared agony and grief.
(Prayers of Intercession)

(Evening)
Pour out your blessings, O Mighty One, on both the servants and the served.
(Prayers of Intercession)

I now pray the prayer that Jesus taught.
(Pray the Prayer of Our Savior.)

(Morning)
Forgive my sins of doubt and grant me the strength of your presence. In Jesus' name I pray. Amen.

(Evening)
I will remember this day for its discovered truth and strange kind of joy. In Jesus' name I pray. Amen.

SATURDAY, JANUARY 30
(Read Matthew 5:6–8)

(Morning)
Ever-knowing God, thirsting for righteousness calls for an undivided heart.

(Evening)
Ever-knowing God, as I have shown forgiveness, have mercy upon me.

God, as we travel life's pathways, we are prone to wander a bit. We see eyes that are cast down. We see those who are worried in spirit. Life has become a treadmill. We can wake up and greet the dawn each day with gladness because of your blessings. You bless us with your mercy. You bless us with your grace. And you bless us with your peace. Thank you.

(Morning)
Merciful God, forgive my weakness and sin.
(Prayers of Intercession)

(Evening)
Purity of heart and mind is my desire. I need your presence and help.
(Prayers of Intercession)

I now pray the prayer that Jesus taught.
(Pray the Prayer of Our Savior.)

(Morning)
Bless me this day, O God of high callings. Show me the trails of truth and purity. In Jesus' name I pray. Amen.

(Evening)
With your blessing, I am happy. I am ready for pleasant dreams. In Jesus' name I pray. Amen.

SUNDAY, JANUARY 31
(Read Matthew 5:9–12)

(Morning)
God, should I be glad when others hate me? Impossible!

(Evening)
God, good heavens! Today I discovered a friend who had misunderstood me.

God, your gospel relates Jesus' words: When we are offering our gifts at the altar, if we remember that our neighbor has something against us, we should leave our gift before the altar and go and be reconciled to our neighbor. Then we may come and offer our gift. In sixty years of ministry, I have never seen a pile of gifts left at the altar while donors seek reconciliation with their accusers, tormentors, enemies, or persecutors. The usual course of events multiplies tension and hatreds. Yet Jesus promises greater blessings to those of us who forgive, forget, and go on in peace.

(Morning)
Help me find common ground, dear God, with those who have hated me.
(Prayers of Intercession)

(Evening)
My mind has found some peace even though my accusers still revile me.
(Prayers of Intercession)

I now pray the prayer that Jesus taught.
(Pray the Prayer of Our Savior.)

(Morning)
Help me, O God, to forgive and forgive and forgive. In Jesus' name I pray. Amen.

(Evening)
The spirit of your peace passes all understanding. In Jesus' name I pray. Amen.

MONDAY, FEBRUARY 1
(Read Isaiah 58:1–4)

(Morning)
God, I wake seeking ways to know and teach according to your profound truths.
Help me to know your Word and act on it with joy today.

(Evening)
God, thank you for this day to live and act according to your discerned truths.
Thank you for helping me to find my way.

God, I want to continue to work to make this world a better place. But rather than work, I perform. I find myself acting on the expectations of others in order to please and be liked. I become more interested in my good reputation than in acting according to your truth. Creator God, help me to take the time to discern fresh and positive directions to take my life. Help me, through my actions, to inform and transform in a positive, nurturing way. Let me be less concerned with what others think of me and more concerned with doing your work of promoting peace and justice.

(Morning)
God, keep me from wasting time on empty forms
and show me new light toward actions that will inform.
(Prayers of Intercession)

(Evening)
Loving God, help me to risk without resentment my comfortable life
in order to help those who have fewer material goods.
(Prayers of Intercession)

I fall into silent prayer.

(Morning)
I am sure of your love. Let me find it enough to keep me through this day. In Jesus' name I pray. Amen

(Evening)
I end wrapped in your loving arms, O God, knowing that I will find the right path. In Jesus' name I pray. Amen.

TUESDAY, FEBRUARY 2
(Read Isaiah 58:9b–12)

(Morning)
God, let my actions come from my heart and be acceptable to you,
no matter how small or pointless they may feel to me.

(Evening)
God, thank you for being there for me when I was
frustrated and for showing me your love.

God, you know that when I am centered, I can see the path. But often it is so hard to be centered. Often I run around trying to accomplish too much and end up ignoring those around me. I take on heavy responsibilities, get very busy, and find less and less time to take care of those closest to me, including myself. Soon I am without sleep; I stuff junk food into my mouth; and I run from one task to another. God, this is when I need to be reminded that you are the One who refreshes and nourishes me. Time is a precious commodity, but some of it must be used to stop and reflect. Only then will I know what it is to have my needs satisfied in those parched places that I hit so often. And only through you will I be able to find my path again.

(Morning)
God, please clear the fog of my busyness and make a clear path
evident for me and for those with whom I work.
(Prayers of Intercession)

(Evening)
Loving God, from you I can gather a sense of proportion, helping me see how
much I can accomplish, helping me not to commit to more than I can do.
(Prayers of Intercession)

I pray silently, taking the time to relax all my muscles.

(Morning)
God, help me to know that it is only through knowing you better that I accomplish anything. In Jesus' name I pray. Amen.

(Evening)
As I enter the rest of sleep, O God, may I become relaxed and joyful. In Jesus' name I pray. Amen.

WEDNESDAY, FEBRUARY 3
(Read Psalm 112:1–9)

(Morning)
God of the righteous, help me to know the wonder of being centered in your truth. Help me to use the peace that I find to make this a better world for all.

(Evening)
God of the righteous, thank you for making clear your truth and helping me to find others with whom I can do your work each day.

To be righteous is to follow the way that Jesus, your child, taught us. I celebrate so many in my community—near and far—who have lived that righteousness. In particular, I raise up the life of Fay "Honey" Knopp— first, through her work in the civil rights movement and, second, in her prison ministry. She did support work for sex offenders. For years she worked with these troubled people, unconcerned to have her efforts honored and always ready to encourage others in this work or similar work. God, to be with Honey was to be drawn into your nurturing love. Since her death, many miss her warm smile and wise words, but she remains an example of what it means to live a righteous life.

(Morning)
God, you are my comfort. Continue to be there for those who help me to discern truth and live righteously.
(Prayers of Intercession)

(Evening)
O God, may the light of your truth overwhelm the ocean of darkness that surrounds us so often.
(Prayers of Intercession)

I pray silently, bringing into my mind the faces of those who are examples of righteousness.

(Morning)
Jesus, I need only look to your example to know the true path. In Jesus' name I pray. Amen.

(Evening)
Dear God, thank you for sending Jesus as your example. May I be, in some small way, a human model of your true way. In Jesus' name I pray. Amen.

THURSDAY, FEBRUARY 4
(Read Psalm 112:10)

(Morning)
God, I see so much suffering around me. I must not
sink into the despair that makes me angry and judgmental.

(Evening)
God, when I see evil, please help me to speak out
against the acts and not the people who commit them.

It is so easy to divide the powerful and the oppressed and then to judge the former wicked and the latter innocent. God, is it not the task of the faithful to raise the consciousness of the wicked rather than to judge and condemn them? Such faithfulness requires one to see clearly the evil and help the oppressed to speak out against it from their own experience. As soon as we judge, we create an opening for hatred and violence. How much better it is to help each group view the situation through the eyes of the other! Through such understanding come forgiveness and peace.

(Morning)
God, let me act on the foundation of your eternal love for all creatures.
(Prayers of Intercession)

(Evening)
May the various peoples of this earth move
through these times of hate into the embrace of your love.
(Prayers of Intercession)

Silently I pray for all the creatures of God's beautiful earth.

(Morning)
Let me find a way to help one person
see another in love this day. In Jesus'
name I pray. Amen.

(Evening)
Thank you, God, for allowing us to
see your love through the beauty all
around us on earth. In Jesus' name I
pray. Amen.

FRIDAY, FEBRUARY 5
(Read 1 Corinthians 2:1–12)

(Morning)
O God, let me know your true wisdom—not by my own logic
or the words of others, but by my quiet waiting upon the Spirit.

(Evening)
O God, thank you for the daily peace I have
by knowing you better and having a glimpse of your truth.

Savior God, though sometimes I would rather figure it all out by myself, I know that I must take time to come into that silent place where I can find your wisdom. Often it is hard for me to slow down long enough to find that place. Yet as I rush from deed to deed, accomplishment to accomplishment, I seek to be your vessel. My most important work comes when I am in that place of peace where I can listen, reflect, and be your hands, ears, and eyes.

(Morning)
Let me learn to pray in a way that opens me to the wisdom
of the Spirit and through a true understanding of Jesus' life and work.
(Prayers of Intercession)

(Evening)
Let me rest in confidence that through your child,
Jesus, I can come closer to knowing you.
(Prayers of Intercession).

I humbly wait upon God in silent expectation.

(Morning)
Jesus was sent to us as an example in order for us to understand something above human wisdom. Through his words and actions, O God, we can see you reflected. In Jesus' name I pray. Amen.

(Evening)
Let me know that only to your judgment am I subject. Those who wrongly judge me can do me no harm. I sleep in your arms, loving God. In Jesus' name I pray. Amen.

SATURDAY, FEBRUARY 6
(Read 1 Corinthians 2:13–16)

(Morning)
God, I give thanks for the model of Jesus; for in his communicated
thoughts and actions on earth, we can see your light.

(Evening)
God, may I know my gifts, so that I may act with others to heal the world.

God, my gifts are to empower people to work with others cooperatively
and provide them with some of the resources they need. But sometimes
this work seems not enough, and it is so slow. The world is filled with the
message that if one thinks with great brilliance, discovers the one correct
answer, and enlists the right people, one can instantly change the world.
The politicians, gurus, and corporate leaders tell us that they have the answer. Vote for them, join their community, buy their products, and all will
be well. How easy it would be to plod along and work with my simple gifts
for the instant answer. But God, it is even harder to stick with the way
Jesus taught.

(Morning)
God, give me and those around me who try to work
through the Spirit the patience to stick with our work,
though it may seem slow and ineffective at times.
(Prayers of Intercession)

(Evening)
God, thank you for helping me and those around me to live in your light.
(Prayers of Intercession)

I sit silently, pondering Jesus' example.

(Morning)
It is your love I seek to spread, O God.
May my hands and mind do your will.
In Jesus' name I pray. Amen.

(Evening)
May I rest knowing that my simple
gifts are those that spread the Spirit.
In Jesus' name I pray. Amen.

SUNDAY, FEBRUARY 7
(Read Matthew 5:13–20)

(Morning)
Dear God, may I have the strength to make your light
and love shine throughout the world while working with others.

(Evening)
Dear God, thank you for being present to me today
as I struggled to know your truth and act on it.

Loving God, we study the law of our ancestors and what Jesus taught, yet some truths are hard to discern. Even as a faithful community, we often are confused. For instance, what is the righteous action when one faces unwanted pregnancy or an abusive marriage where children are involved? What would Jesus have done? How do we know the truth in these situations? There are still gray areas, even if we work hard within our spiritual communities trying to discern your truth. God, give us the strength not to shrink from teaching your truths, even when they are unpopular.

(Morning)
God, please help those facing gray areas to choose the right path,
so they, too, can reap the harvest of a righteous life.
(Prayers of Intercession)

(Evening)
May your wisdom be revealed through my prayers.
(Prayers of Intercession)

**"Be patterns, be examples. . . . Then you will come to walk cheerfully
over the world, answering that of God in everyone."**

(Morning)
The task is great. Help me stay with it
this day. In Jesus' name I pray.
Amen.

(Evening)
God, how happy I feel to work hard,
love a great deal, and rest at the end of
the day! In Jesus' name I pray. Amen.

MONDAY, FEBRUARY 8
(Read Exodus 24:12–18)

(Morning)
God, thank you for inviting me into your presence one more time.

(Evening)
God, thank you for keeping me close to you this day.

God of love, you have set before us the way. You have given us light for our journey. You have provided us with food, drink, shelter, garments, and love. You have cared for our every need. And you have given us a place to wait on your love. Caring God, you have given us a place in your heart. Hear us this day as we live our lives as monuments to you.

(Morning)
God, as I face the challenges of this day,
be with me and let me know that you are there.
(Prayers of Intercession)

(Evening)
God, I ask for forgiveness if, in my haste,
I missed your intent for my life today.
(Prayers of Intercession)

In a state of grace I pray.
(Pray the Prayer of Our Savior.)

(Morning)
I pray for the power of patience to heed your call—when you call, and not when I want to hear. In Jesus' name. Amen.

(Evening)
You were more patient with me than I was with you. Forgive me, and help me to do better tomorrow. In Jesus' name. Amen.

TUESDAY, FEBRUARY 9
(Read Psalm 2)

(Morning)
Loving God, I awake into a sinful and hateful world.
Please help me to show your love to someone new today.

(Evening)
Loving God, thank you for guiding me past the
hidden dangers that lay in wait for me today.

God, I just want to say thank you to you, who in your expressions of might can hold all life in the palm of your hand, yet in your expression of love smiled on me this day. You rule with authority, yet you are not brutish like us, your children. I declare to you, you who inhabit the heavens, that my heart is open to rest in you. Visit me in your Holy Spirit and dwell within me, so my soul will always shout and sing praises to you.

(Morning)
Saving God, help me to withstand the evil that I will confront this day.
(Prayers of Intercession)

(Evening)
Thank you, God, for not letting me be overcome by the enemy today.
(Prayers of Intercession)

In a state of thankfulness I pray.
(Pray the Prayer of Our Savior.)

(Morning)
God do not laugh at me today. Fill me with your Holy Spirit, so all that I do is pleasing in your sight. Without you, what reason do I have to be? In Jesus' name. Amen.

(Evening)
You found me lacking in faith this day, yet you still watched over me. You found me unable to witness with my whole life, yet you still allowed me to take refuge in you. I have no words other than "thank you." In Jesus' name. Amen.

WEDNESDAY, FEBRUARY 10
(Read Psalm 99)

(Morning)
Sovereign God, guide me this day. Show me the way that I should go.
Entrust me to your charge, and do not let me stray.

(Evening)
Sovereign God, thank you for guiding me this day. You kept me safe,
and I will praise you for having mercy on a sinner like me.

God, you are mighty, and you are all powerful. Sometimes in my arrogance, I think that you need me. Thank you for showing me that it is you who are to be exalted, and not me. Loving God, I am but a speck in all of the universe, yet you know me by my name. It is not because of me, but because of your love for me, that I am able to achieve success in life. God, I praise your name. I exalt your name, and I will worship you—not just with my mouth, but with my life. Praise be to your blessed and holy name.

(Morning)
God, I look for your pillars this day—not of smoke, but of those
you have placed in my life who are God-filled and Spirit-led.
(Prayers of Intercession)

(Evening)
My day was cluttered with the voices of deceitful people, but through
all of the clamor, I heard you call me by name. Thank you.
(Prayers of Intercession)

In a state of awe I pray.
(Pray the Prayer of Our Savior.)

(Morning)
God, allow me the privilege to pray at
your feet today. In Jesus' name. Amen.

(Evening)
God, you heard my cries this day and
lovingly responded. In Jesus' name.
Amen.

THURSDAY, FEBRUARY 11
(Read 2 Peter 1:16–21)

(Morning)
Jesus, this day let me live in the knowledge of your being.

(Evening)
Jesus, I saw your power in action as you helped me through this day.

Loving God, once more I was blessed by your grace. When I was feeling sad, I saw you in the smile of a stranger. When I was feeling hurt, I was comforted in the arms of your angel. When I was angry, you sent a ray of sunshine through my window. God, I was an eyewitness to your mercy today. Gracious God, thank you for being my God. Thank you for being real in my life.

(Morning)
As you love Jesus, please love me as well.
(Prayers of Intercession)

(Evening)
I did my best today to be found pleasing in your sight.
Help me again tomorrow to serve you with my all.
(Prayers of Intercession)

In a state of love I pray.
(Pray the Prayer of Our Savior.)

(Morning)
Jesus, be with me this day so I may hear your voice calling to me. In your name. Amen.

(Evening)
I found solace today by standing on the mountain of your love. I need you, and I thank you for caring for me. In Jesus' name. Amen.

FRIDAY, FEBRUARY 12
(Read 2 Peter 1:16–21)

(Morning)
God, as I awaken to the sounds of life, may I hear your Word in all that I see.

(Evening)
God, when I thought I knew more than you today,
your light shone through to correct me.

Patient God, today as I was going astray in my thoughts, your Holy Spirit entered and guided me back on the right track. How foolish I am, sometimes replacing your will with mine! How selfish of me to think that I am the only one who understands you. I have but a piece of the truth. Savior, keep me in your arms, so I can share the truth I know with the truth you have shared with others.

(Morning)
God, let me read your Word anew today.
(Prayers of Intercession)

(Evening)
I was upheld by your Word today. It has never failed
to help me in times of difficulty.
(Prayers of Intercession)

In a state of believing I pray.
(Pray the Prayer of Our Savior.)

(Morning)
Savior, I offer you my life today.
May it be worthy of your use.
In Jesus' name. Amen.

(Evening)
God, without you, I would have failed
to show love to a stranger today who
needed my help. Thank you for not
letting me pass by unnoticing.
In Jesus' name. Amen.

SATURDAY, FEBRUARY 13
(Read Matthew 17:1–9)

(Morning)
God of light, shine. God of light, shine. God of light, shine through me.

(Evening)
God of light, I pray that I was used today to
show someone who was lost the light of Christ.

God of wonder, I pray for your healing touch today. My body is racked
with the pain of a world that does not know you. Heal me, so I can go and
proclaim your Word by the witness of my life. Transform me from my selfish state to a state of Christ-centeredness. This day, Savior Christ, control
every aspect of my life according to your holy will.

(Morning)
It is good to be found in the land of the living.
May I live today in new ways that show your love in my life.
(Prayers of Intercession)

(Evening)
This was a great day. All day long, I knew that you were with me.
(Prayers of Intercession)

In a state of expectation I pray.
(Pray the Prayer of Our Savior.)

(Morning)
Savior, today cover me with your
Spirit, so all that I do is a reflection of
my life in Christ. In Jesus' name.
Amen.

(Evening)
Thank you, God, for speaking through
me today when I did not have the
words to comfort someone in need. In
Jesus' name. Amen.

SUNDAY, FEBRUARY 14
(Read Matthew 17:1–9)

(Morning)
God, no one has a greater love than you.
You loved me enough to give and redeem my life.

(Evening)
God, you showed me how much you loved me today
when you picked me up from my fall.

God, give me voice today to proclaim to the world that Christ has taken control of my life. Lead me away from sinful desires. Guide me in a way that will cause others to follow you into all truth. Let the power of your resurrection fill my body. Renew me in the power that can come only from you. Let me show my love for you through the ways I show my love to others.

(Morning)
Precious God, this day let me comfort someone
who has lost a loved one by pointing them toward you.
(Prayers of Intercession)

(Evening)
Blessings unto you, loving God. May I praise your name forever.
(Prayers of Intercession)

In a state of renewed hope I pray.
(Pray the Prayer of Our Savior.)

(Morning)
Help me, God, to build a lasting monument to your steadfast love. Mold me in your image, so all can see what you can do—even with someone like me. In Jesus' name. Amen.

(Evening)
Thank you, Jesus, for rising from the grave. When the gravity of sin is pulling me down, I know that I believe in a God who believes in getting back up. In your name I pray. Amen.

MONDAY, FEBRUARY 15
(Read Joel 2:1–2, 12–17 or Isaiah 58:1–12)

(Morning)
Abundant God, prepare my heart for the day of your reckoning.
As this day dawns, let me stand ready for your judgment.

(Evening)
Abundant God, may your search of my inner workings find me
accepting of your guidance, your vision, and your love. O God,
like those who struggled in fields plagued by locusts and drought,
so we find ourselves plagued by feelings of doubt and fear. These
emotions cause us to lose sight of your efforts to help us and love us.

Yet you continue to surround us with words of strength and comfort, even
in the midst of despair. How great is God, who through ancient prophets
advises, "Return to . . . your God, for God is gracious and merciful, slow to
anger, and abounding in steadfast love, and relents from punishing."

(Morning)
All-knowing God, make me ready today for the blessings you send.
(Prayers of Intercession)

(Evening)
All-knowing God, I rejoice for the events of this day,
sure in the knowledge that I rest in your care.
(Prayers of Intercession)

**"Yet even now, says God, return to me with all your heart, with fasting,
with weeping, and with mourning; rend your hearts and not your clothing."**

(Morning)	(Evening)
As you called for the sounding of trumpets in Zion, loving God, may the sound of my rejoicing for you resound in my being this day. In Christ's name. Amen.	At close of day, loving God, may the sound of your name resound in my soul. Amen.

TUESDAY, FEBRUARY 16
(Read Psalm 51:1–17)

(Morning)
Merciful God, pour out your love on me this morning.
Let me know that I greet you with each breath I take.

(Evening)
Merciful God, take all my actions made this day
and wipe away each transgression I may have made.

God, you know my heart as no other, and unlike any other, you forgive the sins of my heart and the wrong deeds I fashion with iniquity. Hear this day, this hour, this moment, the timeless plea I make for your salvation. Sovereign God, search my heart, my soul, my total being, so you may find the sorrow I feel when I stray from your path.

(Morning)
Remind me, God, through your mercy, of the newness
of this day and the newness I can find with the dawn.
(Prayers of Intercession)

(Evening)
May I hear joy and gladness echoing in my ears with the waves of blissful
sleep sent by your loving, forgiving hands, God, Creator of us all.
(Prayers of Intercession)

**"Create in me a clean heart, O God, and put a new
and right spirit within me. Do not cast me away
from your presence, and do not take your Holy Spirit from me."**

(Morning)
May every action I make this day be
acceptable to you, O God, as the
sacrifice of a contrite heart. Amen.

(Evening)
May every action I made this day
have been acceptable to you, O God,
for my actions were done with a
contrite heart. Amen.

WEDNESDAY, FEBRUARY 17
(Read 2 Corinthians 5:20b–6:10)

(Morning)
O God, thank you for filling my heart with joy this morning!

(Evening)
O God, thank you for filling my heart with certainty
this evening—sure of the salvation you bring!

How gracious is God! How patient is God with each of us. In our human-ity, we place barriers between ourselves and the ministry of Jesus Christ—barriers of hesitation, of doubt, of fear, of confusion—any excuse we can give to put off declaring to the world, "I love God!" Yet with the gift of grace, we are empowered to be like the early Christians; we are empow-ered to be "servants of God."

(Morning)
Let me meet any obstacle this day with renewed
assurance of your grace, dear God.
(Prayers of Intercession)

(Evening)
Through every difficulty of this day,
I stood in the power of your righteousness, dear God.
(Prayers of Intercession)

"See, now is the acceptable time; see, now is the day of salvation!"

(Morning)
God, I stand as your servant and seek your grace. Through this grace, may I possess a loving spirit, worthy of your ministry. Amen.

(Evening)
God, I bow and thank you for your grace. Through your Holy Spirit, I rest as one possessing all that is needed for peace. Amen.

THURSDAY, FEBRUARY 18
(Read Genesis 2:15–17, 3:1–7)

(Morning)
Thank you, God, for the gift of choice you gave to all children,
women, and men of your creation. May I use this choice wisely
on this day and be pleasing in your sight.

(Evening)
Thank you, God, for the gift of choice you gave to all children,
women, and men of your creation. May the choices I made
this day have been acceptable in your sight.

Yes, it is a fact: I am sometimes easily swayed from the truth. There are
times when I am like the first humans of God's creation—Adam and Eve—
listening to the whispering of temptation, even in the midst of plenty. How
much is enough? How much is too much? What do I say when I hear a
racist remark or see an abused child? Do I walk away, or do I take a stand?
May God continue to guide me as I struggle between good and evil.

(Morning)
O God, may I choose this day to follow you and be strong in the face of entice-
ment. Let me choose to call on you, dear God; let me choose to call on you.
(Prayers of Intercession)

(Evening)
O God, thank you for allowing me to follow you today.
Thank you for strengthening my resolve. I rejoice that I called
on you, dear God; I rejoice that I called on you.
(Prayers of Intercession)

"Let my eyes be open, with the truth only God can provide."

(Morning)
Let me not fall prey to wickedness, to
temptation, to sin. Amen.

(Evening)
In the whirlwind of this day, I
searched for you, God, and found
peace in the eye of the storm. Amen.

FRIDAY, FEBRUARY 19
(Read Psalm 32)

(Morning)
I rose with a smile on my lips, happy for God's forgiveness!

(Evening)
I sleep secure, meditating on God's goodness!

What joy can be compared to the forgiveness of God? What joy can compare to God's grace? How blessed I am, how blessed are all who confess their sins to a loving Creator, one who waits like a mother or father for children to see the error of their ways. How forgiving are parents who can say, "Ah, they learned from their mistakes."

(Morning)
God, I dared to do wrong, and in your infinite love, you dare to trust me again.
Let me be worthy of your trust! Let me be worthy of your love!
Let me be worthy of your grace!
(Prayers of Intercession)

(Evening)
I sleep in peace, thankful for God's teachings!
(Prayers of Intercession)

"You surround me with glad cries of deliverance."

(Morning)
Thank you, God, for removing the streak of stubbornness I possess. Thank you for the blessing of your continued teachings. Amen.

(Evening)
Thank you, God, for rescuing me from every snare today. Thank you for adding my voice to those who trust you and long to do your will. Amen.

SATURDAY, FEBRUARY 20
(Read Romans 5:12–19)

(Morning)
Rejoice this day! Rejoice, for death has met its end!

(Evening)
Rejoice this night! Rejoice, for death has met its end!

Thank you, God, for keeping your promises to the children of Adam and Eve. Thank you, God, for keeping your promises to the children of Moses and Zipporah. Thank you for keeping your promises to me and mine. Thank you for forgiving all our trespasses against you and your will. Thank you for the gift of Jesus Christ, who taught us when praying to call upon you.

(Morning)
God, with what wonder I am able to approach you,
with your assurance of pardon.
(Prayers of Intercession)

(Evening)
God, such peace I find whenever I think about
the gifts you have given me today and every day.
(Prayers of Intercession)

"Therefore, just as one person's trespass led to condemnation for all, so one person's act of righteousness leads to justification and life for all."

(Morning)
As I move into the morning, let me reach the heavens with prayers of thanksgiving—for grace, for love, for forgiveness of all. Amen.

(Evening)
As I move into the still of night, let my inner prayers and thoughts continued to be blessed. Amen.

SUNDAY, FEBRUARY 21
(Read Matthew 4:1–11)

(Morning)
Free me, God; free me this morning from inner torments and demons.

(Evening)
Gracious God, you stood by me today; stand by me this evening, I pray.

If I were offered all the realms of the world, would I have the strength to look to God? If I were offered all the splendor the world had to display, would I have the strength to look to God? O gracious and holy God, give me such strength. O gracious and forgiving God, give me the wisdom to follow you. O gracious and loving God, give me your peace.

(Morning)
Guide my feet, God; let me worship only you.
(Prayers of Intercession)

(Evening)
Guide my soul, God; let me worship only you.
(Prayers of Intercession)

"Worship . . . your God, and serve only God."

(Morning)
O Christ, I remember you this morning, withstanding the temptations of evil and staying true to God. May I follow your example today, Jesus; may I follow you. Amen.

(Evening)
May my soul feast upon the words of God, giving me unimaginable joy and peace. Amen.

MONDAY, FEBRUARY 22
(Read Genesis 12:1–4a)
(Read or sing "The God of Abraham Praise" or another familiar song)

(Morning)
God of all journeys, it's time to begin a new day. One can only wonder—
will this be a day of familiar happenings, or will it bring the event that
may change my life and the lives of others? Let me be ready
for what the day may bring. Be with me.

(Evening)
God of all journeys, how did I do? It was your day, and now it is your night.
As you were present with me during the day, be with me now in the night.

God, we can only imagine how difficult it was for Abram, Sarai, and their
family to pick up stakes and begin to journey to a new land. It was your
command and promise that sustained them and compelled them to go. God,
your words to us are not sweet nothings. Sometimes they are calls and
commands to "Move out!" "Move on!" If Moses, Deborah, Abram, Esther,
Jonah, Mary, Lydia, and Paul were among those who were called to begin
a new journey, I should not be totally surprised when the call comes to me:
"Get up! Move out! A new land, dream, challenge, person, task is awaiting
you."

(Morning)
God of the pilgrimage, understand my inertia. I may want to stay home even
when I am called to move. Keep me from being trapped by the homely
and the familiar. Let me be stirred by the call to journey.
(Prayers of Intercession)

(Evening)
You know how tired I am. As you have goaded me to life during the day,
refresh me in this time of rest. Put your wings over me
and let me nestle in your care, without fear.
(Prayers of Intercession)

And now I will rest in your blessing.
(Pray the Prayer of Our Savior.)

(Morning)	(Evening)
Thank you for the challenge of this new day. Today I may meet the love of my life, the hope of my tomorrow, the turning point of my existence. Hold my hand as you guide me, God of my life. In Christ's name. Amen.	My body and spirit need to be refreshed and renewed. Let my dreams be filled with hope and my subconscious filled with faith. Greet me when I awake. In Christ's name. Amen.

54

TUESDAY, FEBRUARY 23
(Read Psalm 121)
(Read or sing "Unto the Hills We Lift Our Longing Eyes" or another familiar song)

(Morning)
God of the morning, I open my eyes and see a new day. I search for you. I pray
that you will come down to the valley to be with me this day.

(Evening)
God of the evening, today there have been "mountaintop" experiences when I
have felt very close to you. It was good to sense your presence even in the
boring moments of the day. You helped to redeem them and give them life!

From time to time, God, either you would descend from the mountain or a
courageous person would climb the mountain with the hope and fear of
confronting you. Even if one didn't climb the mountain, it was comforting
to look to the distant hills and know that you were there. Most of my life is
spent in the valley, wrestling with problems of the commonplace. It is both
startling and wondrous to suddenly feel you, Divine One, breathing down
my neck and summoning me to deal with the ordinary from a mountaintop
perspective. I never could make it in the valley unless I sometimes could
be refreshed by a journey to and from the mountain.

(Morning)
God of the mountains and valleys, keep me from becoming lost in the valley.
There are small hills that I will be forced to climb this day; may they give me a
better view of the mountain and of you.
(Prayers of Intercession)

(Evening)
I am weary, yet I am still restless. Calm me, that I may be unafraid. From your
high mountain, never lose sight of me. Protect me throughout the night.
(Prayers of Intercession)

And now I will rest in your view.
(Pray the Prayer of Our Savior.)

(Morning)
Whatever the day may bring, you will
watch over me, through joys or
sorrows, failures or victories. I may
be brilliant or I may be stupid,
compassionate or churlish. Forgive
me and guide me. In Christ's name.
Amen.

(Evening)
Thank you for being with me through
the ups and downs of this day. Even
when I stumbled and fell, I could look
and know that you were still with me.
Greet me when I awake. In Christ's
name. Amen.

WEDNESDAY, FEBRUARY 24
(Read Romans 4:1–5)
(Read or sing "My Faith, It Is an Oaken Staff" or another familiar song)

(Morning)
God of yesterday, today, and tomorrow, be with me this day, that my faith in you
and the endless possibilities will be as obvious to those with whom I am in
contact as is my physical presence. Let them see, hear, taste, and smell my faith!

(Evening)
God of yesterday, today, and tomorrow, I am happy that my mark on this day
will be the impact of faith, not that which I have tried to accomplish. I am sure
that your presence will shape this day in history.

"What did Abraham gain according to the flesh?" Paul asks. Was Abraham
put on good terms with you, God, because of his good works? Am I? No,
says Paul; Abraham is known because of his badge of faith, not because of
his badge of works. This is not news to me, but I still try to make myself
acceptable to you by the things I do. What a waste of time! A strong faith
will carry me through everything. My faith, a gift from you, is as much a
part of me as the air I breathe. I need to name it and depend upon it.

(Morning)
Let me go forth boldly in this new day, O God of faith, bearing your gifts of
hope and promise. Let it be evident to the persons whose paths will cross mine.
May they perceive that they are crossing paths with a person borne by faith.
(Prayers of Intercession)

(Evening)
Some parts of my flesh are tattered and torn. Since you are the trustee of my
faith, O Holy One, it is whole and without blemish. Keep me in the faith, even
when my belief in you may waver. Holy One, your belief in me never wavers.
(Prayers of Intercession)

And now I will rest in your gift of faith.
(Pray the Prayer of Our Savior.)

(Morning)
I put on the "whole armor of God"; its
name is faith. God, I depend upon your
presence to guide me as a "pillar of fire
by night and a cloud by day"; its name
is faith. I journey today with faith. In
Christ's name. Amen.

(Evening)
Even when I sleep, the gift of faith is
present. Even when I dream, the gift
of faith permeates me. Even when I
stir with restlessness, the gift of faith
calms me. The gift of faith will
awaken me. In Christ's name. Amen.

THURSDAY, FEBRUARY 25
(Read Romans 4:13–17)
(Read or sing "Amazing Grace")

(Morning)
God of the unfettered, I am going to try to live this day without a rule book.
For this day, I pray that the rule of love, not law, will determine my behavior.
Your amazing grace will always accompany me.

(Evening)
God of the unfettered, in a grace-filled day, I am constantly surprised! The
serendipity of life constantly amazes me. So much good has come to me this
day, not because I deserved it but because of the "grace notes" of life.

The belief that the Hebrews' faith was based on a rule of law, says Paul, is
a perversion of theology and history. Even Abraham was directed by faith,
not law. The promise of the future comes to us as grace and envelops both
those who live by faith and those who live by the law. Grace is the true gift
from you. Our future is less dependent on what we do than on what you
have done.

(Morning)
Even as I prepare for the day, O God of grace, let me be open to the moments
when you will intrude upon my plan and take me in a different direction. Let me
run wild on the fields of life with the sound of music and the song of grace.
(Prayers of Intercession)

(Evening)
There have been "grace notes" throughout this day. I have basked
in them and cherished each of them. Now as I come to the time of rest,
let your gift of grace sustain me and nurture me.
(Prayers of Intercession)

And now I will rest in your gift of grace.
(Pray the Prayer of Our Savior.)

(Morning)
With a skip and a jump, a lilt and a
laugh, I face this day with an eye out
for the unexpected, an ear tuned to the
surprising which I face this day. Help
me to find your face of grace in the
day before me. In Christ's name.
Amen.

(Evening)
I carry the tune of other people in my
head this night. They sang odes of joy,
chorales of praise, the blues, and
marching songs. Their rhythm, beat,
and tone invaded my mind and soul.
Grace notes, God, the music of angels.
In Christ's name. Amen.

FRIDAY, FEBRUARY 26
(Read Romans 4:18–25)
(Read or sing "Great Is Your Faithfulness")

(Morning)
God of the future, you have a long view of history. What we do today will affect the lives of so many future generations. Help me to realize the ways in which I am connected to others, both in the present and in the future.

(Evening)
God of the future, the relationship with others nurtured me this day. I have sensed the presence of my brother Jesus as we struggled for the good of our true family. I sensed Jesus in some whom I met on the Jericho road this day.

Abraham did not begin his journey of faith because of self-interest. It would have been much easier and less stressful simply to remain with the familiar and the comfortable. Journeys are arduous events for old bones! God, Abraham pulled up stakes to do his part to fulfill the promise of a better world for his descendants. We also want to help shape a world fit for our children. Similarly, your child, Jesus, did not die on a cross for personal glory; it was done for others! And my family and I are among those others.

(Morning)
Give me the eyes of recognition, O Mother God, to see my sister or brother in the faces of coworkers and others whom I will meet this day.
(Prayers of Intercession)

(Evening)
I hear the call of the children this night, O Father God. I hear the cries of the hungry, homeless, dispossessed, unappreciated. Who will be with them this night? Let them know that they are not alone. I lift my prayers for them, that you may be with them to comfort them as you are with me.
(Prayers of Intercession)

And now I will rest in your promise of a better world.
(Pray the Prayer of Our Savior.)

(Morning)
Feed the hungry. Comfort the afflicted. Embrace the scorned. Rescue the perishing. Find the lost. We are family, together. In Christ's name. Amen.

(Evening)
On the Jericho road today, among the lonely, hungry, and afflicted wanderers I met, I wonder which was the Christ incognito. I pray that they may know I tried to relate to them as I would to the Christ. In Jesus' name. Amen.

SATURDAY, FEBRUARY 27
(Read John 3:1–17)
(Read or sing "God Loved the World" or another familiar song)

(Morning)
God of love, the knowledge that I am loved enables me to begin this new day.
Sometimes human love is fleeting, but when you enfold me, I know that it is
unconditional, permanent, and real. Let me bask in that love this day.

(Evening)
God, so many times today I needed to be reminded of your gift of love. There
were moments when I was beaten and discouraged, but then your love lifted me.

Creator God, Nicodemus asks the tough question, "How can anyone be
born after having grown old?" Jesus' answer points not to biological birth
but to a new birth of the spirit. And how many times have I felt the need of
that? How many times have I sensed that my spirit was dying or dead? The
promise is: I can be lifted out of the mire of death not by anything I do but
rather by what you, O God, have done for me through your child, Jesus. I
need only to accept this in the love in which it is given.

(Morning)
I pray for new births of the Spirit this day. As I feel the wind on my face, may I
feel the Spirit in my heart. But let me not keep it there. I need to be the vehicle
by which that love and Spirit are made known to others.
(Prayers of Intercession)

(Evening)
Come, Holy Spirit, come. Come as the fire and burn. Come as the wind and
refresh. Come as the rain and cleanse. Come to convict, convert,
and convince me of the way of love.
(Prayers of Intercession)

And now I will rest in your assurance of love.
(Pray the Prayer of Our Savior.)

(Morning)
"Love divine, all loves excelling, joy
of heaven on earth be found. Fix in us
a humble dwelling, all your faithful
mercies crown; Jesus, you are all
compassion; pure unbounded love
impart. Visit us with your salvation,
enter every trembling heart"(Charles
Wesley). In Christ's name. Amen.

(Evening)
"Come, Almighty, to deliver. Let us all
your life receive. Suddenly return and
never, nevermore your temple leave.
You we would be always blessing, love
you as your angels love. Pray and
praise for your unfailing, wounded
arms outstretched above"(Charles
Wesley). In Christ's name. Amen.

SUNDAY, FEBRUARY 28
(Read Matthew 17:1–9)
(Read or sing "Jesus, Take Us to the Mountain" or another familiar song)

(Morning)
O Beloved, with Peter, James, and John, I will follow Jesus, who gives me a vision of all people. How will I change today? Can I truly journey with Jesus and share his vision and commitment? I pray that I may be among the beloved.

(Evening)
O Beloved One, even as I climb the mountain with Jesus, I must descend to the world below. I pray that some of the radiant light from atop the mountain will continue to light my path, even in the shadows of the world and of the night.

O God, the gospel stories tell of Jesus' struggle to accept and fulfill your promise—even if it meant the way of the cross. Several times Jesus withdraws from the world to confront himself and draw upon your strength. Not only are his resolve and vision strengthened, but he is transfigured. The Mount of Transfiguration corresponds to Mount Sinai, where you descended and touched humanity.

(Morning)
Take me up to the high mountain, O Holy One. Let me hear the words of the beloved. Let me know that I am not alone. There is a glory that may shine through me in what I say and what I do this day.
(Prayers of Intercession)

(Evening)
To know that I have been called "beloved" is the fountain of my life. There is peace and surety, warmth and challenge in the security of being loved. I bask in it this night, as I rest in your being. Holy One, you are the lover of my soul.
(Prayers of Intercession)

And now I will rest in the experience of being the beloved.
(Pray the Prayer of Our Savior.)

(Morning)
I journey today up on a mountaintop. What am I to see there? What am I to hear there? What am I to learn there? Who will be with me there? I do not know. I climb with Jesus. In Christ's name. Amen.

(Evening)
I was in God's presence today. Like Moses, I was frightened by the thunder and lightning. Like Elijah, I could hear the still, small voice. Like Jesus, I could hear the voice in a bright cloud. God has purpose for me. I am beloved. In Christ's name. Amen.

MONDAY, MARCH 1
(Read John 4:5–42)

(Morning)
God, as I arise to this new day that you have made,
I rejoice and trust my life to you.

(Evening)
God, allow my heart and soul to reflect your everlasting love for me.

Good and caring God, allow us to quench our thirst and our hunger for justice and peace through your Word. Intervene with your power in those places that deny dignity and wholeness to your children. Fill us with your life-giving water, so we can spread your ministry of peace and justice every day of our lives.

(Morning)
When I thirst for justice, help me to recognize your living waters in others.
(Prayers of Intercession)

(Evening)
It is well with my soul because you, my Creator God, have delivered me from my enemies. I am overflowing with the presence of your love.
(Prayers of Intercession)

**"God is spirit, and those who worship God
must worship in spirit and truth."**

(Morning)
Praising God, make my days joyful. Shower us with your power, so that your people can worship your greatness in deed and in spirit. In Jesus' name. Amen.

(Evening)
In others we find the way to our own wellness. Thank you, God, for the challenge of this day and the joy of life. In Jesus' name. Amen.

TUESDAY, MARCH 2
(Read John 4:5–42)

(Morning)
O God, thank you for your child, Jesus, and for the privilege of living a new day. May the harvest of this day be pleasing to you.

(Evening)
O God, I have planted seeds of your love in many places today. Many "crops are now ready to be harvested" by the power of your Holy Spirit. Let it be done.

Creator God and supreme Authority over all creation, hear our prayers. Men, women, and children find themselves in fields of anger, hatred, racism, and death. God, lift them out of this misery and plant in their lives love and mercy, so they can reap a harvest of justice and peace. Hear our prayers, loving God. Use us as your workers in the field by empowering us with your Holy Spirit.

(Morning)
Jesus the Christ is the Savior of the world. This I believe and trust.
(Prayers of Intercession)

(Evening)
As we plant fields for justice in your name, our eyes may never see the harvest. However, all praise be given to you, for your everlasting love.
(Prayers of Intercession)

"One person plants, another person reaps."

(Morning)
Allow your will to be done in our lives and in the world. Be with us all our days. In Jesus' name. Amen.

(Evening)
In peace I rest and trust that your blessings will awaken me to new experiences and perhaps some harvest. In Jesus' name. Amen.

WEDNESDAY, MARCH 3
(Read Exodus 17:1–7)

(Morning)
God Almighty, Creator of heaven and earth, Giver of all that is good and
wonderful, guide my footsteps and the words I use to address others.
As your humble servant, open my eyes to know your will.

(Evening)
God Almighty, Creator of heaven and earth, teach me
how to please you in every place. May all that is good
and pleasing in your sight be raised to you in worship and praise.

God, at times we find ourselves in a desert, feeling hot and thirsty, because
of wrongs done to us or because of our own guilt and sin against you and
others. Forgive us if we have sinned against you, and forgive those who
have sinned against us. At times we put you to the test. Forgive us if we
have become cynical and forgetful of the times when you have endured our
shortcomings and led us to victory! Praise be to you, God Almighty! Gloria
a Dios!

(Morning)
There is no mountaintop or desert, no waters, or any place in creation over
which you, our God, have no dominion. God, you will be with me always.
(Prayers of Intercession)

(Evening)
Human we are, and we must rest to regain energy and enjoy silence. Meanwhile,
O God, prepare us to continue our journey and speak to us in our dreams.
(Prayers of Intercession)

"Is God with us or not?"

(Morning)	(Evening)
Loving and wise God, you have provided for my needs, and for this I am grateful. Help me to continue to trust in your goodness and love. In Jesus' name. Amen.	Teach me to trust in you more each day and to believe in your miraculous powers. In Jesus' name. Amen.

THURSDAY, MARCH 4
(Read Psalm 95)

(Morning)
Creator God, receive our worship today by allowing it to manifest into loving and caring behavior toward all whom we may encounter in our world.

(Evening)
Creator God, we kneel before you in thanksgiving for all the good you have provided us. We pray that our worship is pleasing in your sight and is your will.

From the depths of our thoughts and hearts, we can hear your tender voice telling us that all is well. You have made your Word flesh in Jesus Christ, which clarifies all other words. We pray that in our faith journey you will continue to speak to us and clarify your Word to us. Precious is our dialogue with you, for you are our Creator and Savior.

(Morning)
God, you make my days joyful.
(Prayers of Intercession)

(Evening)
God, thank you for today's challenges.
(Prayers of Intercession)

"Humble ourselves and listen today to what God says."

(Morning)
O God, who scatters the proud, who fills the hungry, and sends the rich away empty, receive this morning joyful songs of praise. In Jesus' name. Amen.

(Evening)
There is no God greater than you! You have watched over us when our good intentions have gone astray, when our ears have not heard and our tongues have not spoken. We plead for your forgiveness and for a depth of faith that will make a difference in us and in the world. In Jesus' name. Amen.

FRIDAY, MARCH 5
(Read Romans 5:1–11)

(Morning)
God, how great is your love for us! You sacrificed your child, Jesus Christ,
to die for us knowing that we were still sinners. Thank you for giving us your
peace and a relationship that has no end.

(Evening)
God, your love is with us always.
May our dreams be of you and our rest for your service.

O God, we know that there is nothing in this world that can separate us
from your love. You have baptized us with your Holy Spirit, and you shield
us with your love and peace. Teach us, loving and caring God, to do what is
just and righteous, to show constant love, and to live in humble relationship with you.

(Morning)
God, use my body as a vessel for your Holy Spirit.
(Prayers of Intercession)

(Evening)
Thank you for giving us your peace.
(Prayers of Intercession)

"Christ died for us."

(Morning)
Use my body as a vessel for your
Holy Spirit to spread the good news
of Jesus the Christ. In Jesus' name.
Amen.

(Evening)
The greatest gift was given to us
through your child, Jesus Christ, while
we were still sinners. God is good all
the time! And all the time, God is
good! Gloria a Dios! In Jesus' name.
Amen.

SATURDAY, MARCH 6
(Read Romans 5:1–11)

(Morning)
O hallelujah, wisdom is for us! Ours is a union now won in Jesus.
Ours is a union now won in Jesus. O Redeemer Power, hallelujah, God.

(Evening)
O hallelujah, wisdom is for us! Your victory over death
is my hope and salvation every day of my life.

May your reign on earth be seen in our church. Kindle your Word in us to make your children wiser. Grant us your victory though good and bad times. Glory be to you, our God, our discerning power. Wisdom from on high is ever with us. O hallelujah, our faith in you has made us free!

(Morning)
I will walk with my Jesus in victory all day long.
(Prayers of Intercession)

(Evening)
What a friend I have in Jesus, who cares for me all day and night.
Guide my dreams, strengthen my body, and awaken me to your tender care.
(Prayers of Intercession)

"In knowing Jesus as your Savior, you are united to God your Creator."

(Morning)
Holy Spirit of God, abide in me. Teach me your ways. Glory and honor are yours alone. In Jesus' name. Amen.

(Evening)
Speak to my heart, O Holy One. You are my great Parent, and I am your child. Reside in my dwelling, and I become one in the Spirit with you. In Jesus' name. Amen.

SUNDAY, MARCH 7
(Read Psalm 95)

(Morning)
Protector God, walk with us. Provide us with words of courage and clothe us
with your love. Let a new song stir my heart.

(Evening)
Protector God, praise and glory for your saving actions.

Praise be to you, O God! When I think of the wondrous gifts of love you
have given freely and unconditionally, I humbly kneel before you, my Creator. I lift up my hands to give you glory and praise! Rule over our lives;
you are our Maker. Let the world sing a new song unto you.

(Morning)
God is ruler of all heaven and earth.
(Prayers of Intercession)

(Evening)
You have provided for my every need, for this I thank you.
You, my God, care and give joy to my heart.
(Prayers of Intercession)

"God is mighty, sing joyful songs of praise."

(Morning)	(Evening)
Holy Spirit of God, glory and honor	Speak to my heart and reside in me. In
are yours. In Jesus' name. Amen.	Jesus' name. Amen.

MONDAY, MARCH 8
(Read John 9:1–23)

(Morning)
O God, in the warm brilliance of the sunshine, your name is to be praised!

(Evening)
O God, in the cool shadows of twilight, your name is to be praised!

Eternal God, I confess to you my meager vision, my limited discernment and awareness, my lack of expectation and hope. I turn away from the light that would give growth and meaning to my life. Open my mind and my heart to the surprises of your healing grace and mercy, that I may rejoice in your works which are revealed day by day. In your mercy, transform my despondency into joy and affirmation.

(Morning)
Today, O God, help me to be aware of those about me
who do your work and who reveal your divine purposes.
(Prayers of Intercession)

(Evening)
Thank you for the evidence I have witnessed today of your grace,
which overcomes hopelessness and despair.
(Prayers of Intercession)

"O send out your light and your truth; let them lead me."
(Pray the Prayer of Our Savior.)

(Morning)
In this new day, open me to perceive
and to receive your leading
and your will. In Jesus' name.

(Evening)
Grant me rest, O God, this night, in
the confidence of your encompassing
love. In Jesus' name. Amen.

TUESDAY, MARCH 9
(Read John 9:24–41 and Mark 2:13–17)

(Morning)
God has made this day; I will rejoice in it.

(Evening)
God's name is to be praised as the sun goes down.

Dear God, how well you must know my illusions. I imagine that I am competent, that I have everything under control and all figured out, that my intelligence and achievements will assure me favor in your sight. Help me, O God, to cast away my illusions, that I may see myself more clearly as I really am. Grant me the courage and honesty to admit my faults and to open my eyes to see my daily need for your redeeming mercies.

(Morning)
This morning help me to remember with gratitude all those who, although perhaps despised and at risk, faithfully witness to the realm of God.
(Prayers of Intercession)

(Evening)
Help me at the close of the day to see myself, as with all of your children in all places of your creation, within the bonds of your love.
(Prayers of Intercession)

"Just as I am, without one plea but that your blood was shed for me" (Charlotte Elliott).
(Pray the Prayer of Our Savior.)

(Morning)
In this new day, God, have mercy. Christ, have mercy. God, have mercy. In your Child's name I pray. Amen.

(Evening)
At bedtime, God, have mercy. Christ, have mercy. God, have mercy. In your Child's name I pray. Amen.

WEDNESDAY, MARCH 10
(Read 1 Samuel 16:1–7)

(Morning)
O God, all creation rejoices in you this morning!

(Evening)
O God, all creation rests in you this night!

Eternal One, you know how much we rely on outward appearances, how much we judge one another by culture, skin color, and social class, and how dazzled we are by success and celebrity. Help me to understand more clearly what is really important and to repent of my reliance on the superficial. Grant to me the mind of Christ, that I may see beneath the surface and find in all your children the enduring worth which is valuable in your sight.

(Morning)
Grant me this day, O God, deeper insight into what is really important in life.
(Prayers of Intercession)

(Evening)
Cleanse the thoughts of my heart, that I may see your way and follow in faith.
(Prayers of Intercession)

**God, you know the innermost thoughts and secrets of my heart,
and yet you do not turn away from me. How wonderful!
Amazing grace!**
(Pray the Prayer of Our Savior.)

(Morning)
Help to me go forth confident of your love, O God. In your Child's name I pray. Amen.

(Evening)
Grant rest and peace this night to me and to all those whom I hold dear. In your Child's name I pray. Amen.

THURSDAY, MARCH 11
(Read 1 Samuel 16:8–13)

(Morning)
"Morning has broken, like the first morning" (Eleanor Farjeon).

(Evening)
"Day is dying in the west; Heaven is touching earth with rest"
(Mary A. Lathbury).

Great and wonderful God, you are not silent but speak, calling forth those who are to do your works of love, justice, and reconciliation in the world. Help me to hear your voice and to know my calling according to your will. Anoint me with your Holy Spirit, that I may faithfully be Christ to my neighbors and fulfill the high calling you have for all your people as partners with you in the work of healing and redemption.

(Morning)
Open my ears this day, O God, to hear your call.
Give me a grateful heart for all those who, in all walks of life,
are committed to your service.
(Prayers of Intercession)

(Evening)
Grant to me, at the close of the day,
a deeper sense of your purpose for my life, O God.
(Prayers of Intercession)

**"Jesus calls us, o'er the tumult of our life's wild, restless sea,
'Christian, follow me' " (Cecil F. Alexander).**
(Pray the Prayer of Our Savior.)

(Morning)	(Evening)
Grant me the presence of the Holy Spirit throughout this day. In your Child's name I pray. Amen.	Grant me a restful night, that in the new day I may awaken to your service. In your Child's name I pray. Amen.

FRIDAY, MARCH 12
(Read Psalm 23 and Isaiah 40)

(Morning)
"Comfort, O comfort my people, says your God."

(Evening)
"God gives power to the faint, and strengthens the powerless."

How astonishing, O Holy One, that you would be our gentle shepherd—to cause us to rest in verdant pastures, to lead us beside still waters, and to restore our souls! This faith is a great comfort to me, O God, in the midst of the anxieties of my life. I often feel pulled in many different ways; help me to cleave to the center. As you comfort me, help me to comfort others, that the peace of Christ may more and more be abroad in the world.

(Morning)
I remember before you, O God, all those who are anxious and troubled,
who live in the midst of turmoil, strife, and violence.
(Prayers of Intercession)

(Evening)
Forgive me, dear God, for my thoughtlessness and lack of consideration toward
others, which may have only added to their troubles during this day.
(Prayers of Intercession)

**"Those who wait for God shall renew their strength, they shall mount up
with wings like eagles, they shall run and not be weary."**
(Pray the Prayer of Our Savior.)

(Morning)
In the bustle of this day, help me to
find a quiet place of repose in my soul.
In your Child's name I pray. Amen.

(Evening)
Into your hands, O Shepherd, I
entrust myself for tranquil sleep. In
your Child's name I pray. Amen.

SATURDAY, MARCH 13
(Read Psalm 23 and Romans 8:35, 37–39)

(Morning)
O God, "I will sing aloud of your steadfast love in the morning."

(Evening)
O God, "The night is as bright as the day, for darkness is as light to you."

Eternal and holy God, you lead us even in the most shadowy times of our lives, or perhaps especially then. I want to believe your Word, that nothing can separate us from your love, revealed to us in Christ Jesus—not hardship or distress, not persecution or famine, not even death or anything in all creation. Help my unbelief; strengthen me in this faith. Deliver me from the fear of evil.

(Morning)
Be present with me this day, O God, that I may radiate
more clearly the love you have for us, in Christ.
(Prayers of Intercession)

(Evening)
Give me a restful night, dear God, confident that your goodness
and mercy shall follow me all the days of my life.
(Prayers of Intercession)

"If God is for us, who is against us?"
(Pray the Prayer of Our Savior.)

(Morning)
New every morning are your mercies,
O God! Thus may it be forever. In
your Child's name I pray. Amen.

(Evening)
Whether awake or asleep, help me to
live in the confidence that I shall dwell
in your house my whole life long. In
your Child's name I pray. Amen.

SUNDAY, MARCH 14
(Read Ephesians 5:8–14)

(Morning)
Dear God, as every Sunday recalls Resurrection day, help me this day to witness
to the triumph of life and to awaken to renewal.

(Evening)
Dear God, prepare me now through refreshing and restful sleep to greet the
coming new day as a day of service to you, with joy and thanksgiving.

On this Sabbath, O God, help me to reflect upon all that is good and right
and true, and to repent of my unfruitful works which are not pleasing in
your sight. Through the power of the Holy Spirit, awaken me from my
moral slumber, that the light of Christ may shine upon me and, through me,
upon all whom I know.

(Morning)
At worship this day, O God, help me to hear
your redeeming and renewing Word, that more and more
I may live my life in ways that are pleasing in your sight.
(Prayers of Intercession)

(Evening)
I am mindful this night, dear God, of how far we are from your realm; of how
wrong, falsehood, and injustice seem to rule in many places. I pray for all who
suffer under the yoke of injustice, that they may know your compassion; and I
pray for those who harm others, that they may repent and turn from their ways.
(Prayers of Intercession)

**"This little light of mine, I'm gonna let it shine, let it shine,
let it shine, let it shine" (traditional spiritual).**
(Pray the Prayer of Our Savior.)

(Morning)
As I awaken to the day you have made,
O God, awaken me to turn toward the
light of Christ. In your Child's name I
pray. Amen.

(Evening)
"All praise be yours, my God, this
night, for all the blessing of the light;
Keep me, kind Maker of all things,
beneath the shelter of your wings"
(Thomas Ken). In your Child's name
I pray. Amen.

MONDAY, MARCH 15
(Read Ezekiel 37:1–10)

(Morning)
God of breath and life, I arise this morning as if from the grave
and breathe anew your living breath. Fill me, that I may truly live.

(Evening)
God of breath and life, how fresh is the air of the Spirit!
Make me ever aware of your life and my own dryness without you.

God of promise, by your Spirit and will, dry bones live. It is not by my own breath that I come to life but by the divine breathings of your Spirit. My efforts end in a heap of death; even with sinews and flesh, without your Spirit, I am dead. Yet by your Spirit I arise, I am filled, these dry bones live! God, fill every crevice of this temple, that I, like Ezekiel, may be "brought out by the Spirit," moved and driven by you alone. Fill all your people, for only as you fill us may we know you. We then will arise at your command and call forth your Spirit, saying, "Come from the four winds, O breath, and breathe upon these slain, that they may live." And by your Spirit, it is done.

(Morning)
Let your glory now fill your temple, O God. May your life fill your people.
(Prayers of Intercession)

(Evening)
For new mercies, for divine breathings,
for the quickening of soul, I praise you, Most High.
(Prayers of Intercession)

"I will cause breath to enter you, and you shall live."

(Morning)	(Evening)
Come, Spirit, fill me until there is nothing left of me, but all and only you. In Christ. Amen.	I praise you that it is not by might, nor by power, but by your Spirit that we live. In Christ. Amen.

TUESDAY, MARCH 16
(Read Ezekiel 37:11–14)

(Morning)
God of hope, may I see you anew this day
and walk in the wonder of your presence.

(Evening)
God of hope, though once in the grave,
I now live because of your love and faithfulness.

Let your glory endure forever, O God. Let your hope fill your people! May your people rise up and call you blessed. May our eyes be opened and our ears comprehend the awesome wonder of your deeds. For we were cut off, but now we are united in you. We were dead and hopeless, but now you are our life and our hope. Oh, may we see! May we believe! By our risen lives, may we know that we are your people and you are our God, because you have opened our graves and brought us up from them. Yea, you have breathed your Spirit into us and caused us to live. Let us live to proclaim to the dying that you, O God, are loving; you, O God, are faithful and true.

(Morning)
Life-giving God, let your presence so fill us
that everything we touch comes alive.
(Prayers of Intercession)

(Evening)
Maker of our hearts, you are worthy of all our praise and lives.
(Prayers of Intercession)

**Make my heart after your heart, O God,
a life filled with your own life.**

(Morning)
Come, Holy Spirit, and make my mind,
heart, eyes, and ears as new and pure
as when they were first born. In Christ.
Amen.

(Evening)
Ever-faithful One, thank you for
drawing my heart to you. In you I
know you; in you I live. Praise be to
you, O Christ. Amen.

WEDNESDAY, MARCH 17
(Read Psalm 130)

(Morning)
O God, as I rise this morning from the depths of sleep, I call to you as deep
calls to deep. Come, Savior Jesus, fill the chasm of my soul.

(Evening)
O God, I wait in your presence until you rise over me
like the sun over the land and every moment is new like the morning.
Forgiveness floods every space. I rest in peace.

"Forgiven!" That's what you proclaim as I stand before you. "This one is
mine, bought at a price!" How could I wait for any but you, Redeemer
God? Only you bring full redemption. You paid the price yourself—on the
cross! I fall again at your feet and cry from my depths in repentance. Oh,
that I would not offend you but lift holy hands in honor and praise. For you
do not disappoint. I wait for you. This is my sole purpose and the purpose
of my soul. I wait more than those who watch for the morning, and you
appear more faithfully than the morning. Where can I go from your Spirit?
If I go to the depths, you are there! Great is your faithfulness! Unfailing is
your love!

(Morning)
God, hear my voice.
(Prayers of Intercession)

(Evening)
Great Redeemer, I wait for you alone, for you redeem me from all my sins.
(Prayers of Intercession)

"For God so loved the world that God gave God's only begotten."

(Morning)
Forever I am grateful, for you stun me
with your love. In Christ. Amen.

(Evening)
Only you, perfect Sacrifice, can fully
redeem. I live for you alone. In Christ.
Amen.

THURSDAY, MARCH 18
(Read Romans 8:6–11)

(Morning)
God of righteousness, teach me to set my mind on the Spirit,
that I would walk in peace and life and please you in every way.

(Evening)
God of righteousness, I live because you live in me.

What faith it takes to believe the mystery! You are in me. Reign in me. Move through this body. Move through your entire body, God, and by your Spirit, raise the dead. May we live to proclaim your life. That's who you are: Life. If I dwell on the things of the flesh, even the "good" things, I am dead. Yet so often I work in the flesh for the righteousness that is only by your Spirit. Oh, the death of me! I surrender! Draw me continually and help me to focus on the Spirit. If I live in the light of your righteousness— your righteousness and not my own, which is death—then I shall truly live, by the power of the Spirit who raised Christ Jesus from the dead, who dwells now in me.

(Morning)
Have your way with me, God. Make yourself at home in me.
(Prayers of Intercession)

(Evening)
Most High, it pleases you to dwell in your people.
How could we think of anything else?
(Prayers of Intercession)

**But you are not in the flesh; you are in the Spirit,
since the Spirit of God dwells in you.**

(Morning)
Nothing compares with you, precious God. You are peace, life, righteousness. Praise your name forever. In Christ. Amen.

(Evening)
You dwell in me, and I am yours. In your righteous name. Amen.

FRIDAY, MARCH 19
(Read John 11:1–16)

(Morning)
God of glory, lead me to the life that brings you glory.

(Evening)
God, teach me to trust you for who you are instead of how I think
you should respond to my circumstances, for you live by a higher plan.

I wait for you, Jesus, your perfect timing. I send my message: "The one
you love is ill." Does it dawn on me that you already know this—that in
some incomprehensible way, it will bring you more glory for that one to
"fall asleep"? And then you soothe: "This illness does not lead to death.
Rather, it is for God's glory, that the Child of God may be glorified through
it." On that day you delayed your trip, allowed Lazarus to die so you could
raise him, that we would believe. In that moment, who could understand?
You even foreshadowed your own death and resurrection, that "this illness"—the sin that destroys—would not lead to death, because of your
death on the cross and because you, the Light of the World, are with us and
in us. May we believe as we wait for you, our Savior.

(Morning)
May we live according to your way and your glory.
(Prayers of Intercession)

(Evening)
Grant us the eyes of your heart, God, that we may see
above our longings and stand on your unfailing promises.
(Prayers of Intercession)

What are you praying, God? Lead us now into your prayers.

(Morning)
God, may we move when you move
and not before,
walking in your light. In Christ.
Amen.

(Evening)
God, increase our faith. In Christ.
Amen.

SATURDAY, MARCH 20
(Read John 11:17–37)

(Morning)
Good morning, God. Today, may I live in faith that with you,
all things are possible.

(Evening)
Good evening, God of all comfort. You move me with your tears.

Four days, Lazarus lay corroding in the grave. There was reason to weep. "Lord, if you had been here," his sisters said, "he would not have died." Jesus, did you weep then for those mourning? Did you weep for your own loss? Did you weep for what you knew you would go through just a few weeks later? All were moved, all led to the place of desperation; for you had healed the sick, you had opened the eyes of the blind. And then you spoke. "Your brother will rise again." You said, "I am the Resurrection and the Life. Those who believe in me, even though they die, will live, and everyone who lives and believes in me will never die." And then the question to us: "Do you believe this?" Martha believed. And Mary, the one who anointed your feet with perfume and wiped them with her hair, wept, her tears on your skin. For this you wept. Yes, Jesus, I believe.

(Morning)
Lead me to the ones who need to know you as resurrection life.
(Prayers of Intercession)

(Evening)
O Jesus, move me until I weep for the things that move you to tears.
(Prayers of Intercession)

You are the Christ, the Child of God, who has come into the world!

(Morning)
Have every way with me, precious Jesus. I trust completely in you. In Christ. Amen.

(Evening)
I praise you that even as I sleep, you hold me and keep me. In Christ. Amen.

SUNDAY, MARCH 21
(Read John 11:38–44)

(Morning)
God of the morning, as I hear you call in the rustling of leaves,
I rise and come forth.

(Evening)
God of the evening, whose voice conquers death,
I praise you that you have stirred me to life.

We face two issues. There is the faith of those you call to remove stones and unbind the dead. And there are the dead responding to your call to "come out." Yes, you say again and again, if we would believe, we would see your glory. So we have no choice but to obey when you tell us to move the stone that separates us from the stench of death. We have little choice but to believe you will do the impossible. And I, like the one dead, emerge from the tomb, because you have called me by name. And I stand waiting for the others to take off the grave clothes, to unbind me, that I in turn may move the stones in another's life and unbind another from the wrap of death. In both cases I respond, "Yes. Jesus!"

(Morning)
Jesus, I pray for an eager heart and sensitive ears,
to hear your call and respond in faith.
(Prayers of Intercession)

(Evening)
I pray for the bound, that they may be free.
(Prayers of Intercession)

When all seems impossible, we wait for God.

(Morning)
Lead me where you desire, God, that I would roll back stones and humbly share in your plan to set people free. In Christ's name. Amen.

(Evening)
I rest in peace, knowing that you, God of life, long ago conquered death. In Jesus. Amen.

MONDAY, MARCH 22
(Read Matthew 21:1–11)

(Morning)
O loving God, grant me today the joy of victory
over the mortal battles of existence.

(Evening)
O loving God, thank you for the assurance
that in your presence there is always joy.

God, in our world of constant disappointments and often warring spirits, help us ever to recall the peace and victory that come to all who call upon your name. Enable us to keep your example of humble love, that we may be empowered to live in that wondrous peace. Please allow us to grasp the hope that you offer in exchange for our despair. When our faith has become tired and weary from the weight of this earthly care, please help us to find new energy and spiritual confidence in the miracle of faith.

(Morning)
Spirit of victory, help me to know that I am never defeated
as long as I am in your care. Give me visions of possibility.
(Prayers of Intercession)

(Evening)
Grant me, O Redeemer, the boldness and the joy of witness,
that others may know of your wondrous love.
(Prayers of Intercession)

"Help me to make each day a day of hope and victory."

(Morning)
Help me to find a new and fresh blessing of joy. Loving Creator, keep my spirits renewed by your ever-present peace and love. In Christ's name. Amen.

(Evening)
As day draws to a close, I recount the great and wonderful works of God. Even with the setting sun, my spirit cries "Hosanna!" In Christ's name. Amen.

TUESDAY, MARCH 23
(Read Psalm 118:1–2, 19–29)

(Morning)
Gracious God, as I rise I am thankful that your steadfast love is ever present.
Help me to remain alert to realize even more your enduring mercy in my soul.

(Evening)
Gracious God, praise belongs to you. I can rest in peaceful expectation
knowing that your love endures forever.

It is good to know, dear God, that the gates to secure spiritual dwelling are
ever open to the faithful. As the fears of this life often chase us with anxiety, please keep those doors to your perfect peace ever open to us. We need
to dwell on plains of faith and to maintain a sense of victorious living.
Even when we feel cast aside and rejected, we rejoice that we are yet precious in your sight. Help us to be joyful and expectant.

(Morning)
I will give you praise and thanks because of the promises
and the blessings that are made new with each day.
(Prayers of Intercession)

(Evening)
Thank you for opening the gate to salvation and for hearing our prayers.
(Prayers of Intercession)

**"The Creator has made this wonderful day.
Our spirits rejoice with thanksgiving."**

(Morning)
Open my eyes to behold the wonderful blessings of joy that are before
me. Dear God, I see new opportunities, and I am glad. In the name of
Jesus I pray. Amen.

(Evening)
You are indeed worthy of praise at all
times, O God. During these evening
hours I still recall your steadfast love,
and my heart continues to rejoice. In
the name of Jesus I pray. Amen.

WEDNESDAY, MARCH 24
(Read Isaiah 50:4–9a)

(Morning)
Sovereign God, I arise to the sobering truth of your redemptive grace. Please help me to keep this spiritual certainty within my heart throughout the day.

(Evening)
Sovereign God, in the stillness of the night, I recall, in wonder, our gift of salvation. Help us never to forget it.

Dear God, we rejoice in the knowledge that you sustain us when we become weary by granting us refreshing touches of mercy. It is good to know that there is power in your never-failing grace. When we are distressed, help us to know that we are empowered by the available resources of grace. I never can be defeated when you are near to help me.

(Morning)
Loving Spirit, help me to remind others that your help extends to all who seek relief from the pains of life.
(Prayers of Intercession)

(Evening)
O God, may we always know the words of assurance and faith, that we may be ever mindful of new possibilities.
(Prayers of Intercession)

"With a determined spirit, I face the world."

(Morning)
It is good to know that you lead us through the rough times in our lives. Please keep me filled with a countenance of faith and strength. In the name of Jesus I pray. Amen.

(Evening)
Loving God, I rest in the certainty of your love for us. I always will be humbled by the remembrance of your sacrificial acts of mercy. In the name of Jesus I pray. Amen.

THURSDAY, MARCH 25
Read Matthew 26:14–27)

(Morning)
Loving Creator, as the new day dawns with new challenges,
I seek the strength and nourishment that come from the living bread.

(Evening)
Loving Creator, I now rest in the comfort of your love. It is good to know that
the sustaining bread of heaven continues to feed our hungry souls.

Merciful One, I want to be loyal to you in every way. Please help me not to become disloyal to your cause. Help me as I strive to serve you in earnest. Please forgive me when I betray your cause by my own lack of faith or weak example of discipleship. If there are opportunities to witness against injustice and prejudice, help me not to sell out to prevailing forces but to remain strong in Christian love. Please keep us filled with the spiritual foods of peace and assurance.

(Morning)
May my life become a total loyalty to Christ's cause.
(Prayers of Intercession)

(Evening)
May I find true meaning in the body of Christ.
(Prayers of Intercession)

"Nothing is as refreshing to our spirits as the bread of heaven."

(Morning)	(Evening)
Help me, I pray, to keep always the feast of your love. There is a great joy to be filled with your glory. In Christ's name. Amen.	Spirit of comfort, I draw near to you in loyalty and in faith. I have a great confidence in knowing that you will never betray the faithful. In Christ's name. Amen.

FRIDAY, MARCH 26
(Read Matthew 27:41–50)

(Morning)
O loving God of eternal joy, I recall your wondrous sacrifice for me
on the cross. I tremble as I reflect on the depth of your love.

(Evening)
O loving God of eternal joy, help me to be ever mindful
of the never-ending flow of grace.

O you in whom my soul takes delight, I pause to survey the cross on which
you died for humankind. As I stand in my spirit around Calvary, there is a
perpetual reminder of the amazing gift and power of love. This gift enables
me to stand in awe and adoration of the miracles of mercy. I am filled with
praise to know that no problem in this life can defeat your powerful love.
Help me to live in the redeeming shadow of Calvary's tree. The debt of
love that I owe to you cannot be imagined. Yet I offer you my thanks, my
praise, and my life.

(Morning)
Loving God, I will always remember your sacrifice,
which continues to make a difference in my life.
(Prayers of Intercession)

(Evening)
In the spirit of sacrifice, help me to impart gifts of love to others.
(Prayers of Intercession)

"Divine love means that we never will be forsaken."

(Morning)
"When I survey your wondrous cross, the cross on which my Savior died, my gains I count but loss, and pour contempt on all of my pride" (Isaac Watts). In Christ's name. Amen.

(Evening)
"If nature's realm were mine, that would be a small present. Amazing love so divine demands my whole soul and life" (Isaac Watts). In Christ's name. Amen.

SATURDAY, MARCH 27
(Read Psalm 31:9–16)

(Morning)
Creator of all things, renew my earthly hope;
restore my soul in the presence of your joy.

(Evening)
Creator of all things, even in uncertain moments, I trust in your care.

My refuge and strength, I am grateful that I can find new mercies and fresh joy in your presence. I confess the distress and uneasiness that lurk in my soul at times. There are times when I feel afflicted in spirit and become defeated by the enemies of doubt and fear. Nevertheless, I find a renewed joy through your guidance. Thank you for the promise of revival. Even in my moments of lament, I lay claim to an unfaltering trust in you. This helps me to live in precious expectation of your grace.

(Morning)
Loving God, help me to know that you are always near,
even in times of my distress.
(Prayers of Intercession)

(Evening)
Loving God, please remove my anguish and renew my faith.
(Prayers of Intercession)

"But I will always trust in you, Sovereign God; you are my Redeemer."

(Morning)
When the enemies of life are present to test my faith. I rest upon a solid trust in your promise of hope. Please help me to be patient and to wait for your sure renewal. In Christ. Amen.

(Evening)
As day draws to an end, I am reminded that God's faithfulness is ever great. Thank you for allowing me to witness your steadfast love today. I pray for increased awareness of the renewing strength that you offer to all. In Christ. Amen.

SUNDAY, MARCH 28
(Read Philippians 2:5–11)

(Morning)
O Risen One, you have given us the gift of eternal victory.
We praise you for life's triumphs.

(Evening)
O Risen One, we give praise that we can face the future
with confidence. Your name be ever praised.

Spirit of joy, I am grateful for the gift of salvation. Even though you, in humble suffering, delivered us, victory was inevitable. Give me a deeper awareness of this power as life challenges me from day to day. I am ever blessed to know that no force can defeat the power of that blessed name which calms our fears. Help me to abide in this grace and to live each day in resurrection victory. Keep me humble in my own self, Spirit, but exalt me in the desire to serve you and to witness to all the power of your name.

(Morning)
Loving God, please give me the spirit of triumph in the realization
that your living presence is near.
(Prayers of Intercession)

(Evening)
Help me to know that the awful pains that you endured
defeated life's graves. Therefore, we have new life.
(Prayers of Intercession)

**"Jesus' name is above all other names in heaven and in earth.
In Jesus we have new life."**

(Morning)
It is good to know that I have the promise of life's victorious power. Thank you for the assurance of this power by the finished act of redemption and love. Your name gives me direction and grace. I am a victor. In Christ's name. Amen.

(Evening)
Help me to be ever mindful that the reality of spiritual death cannot destroy the reality of redemption. Loving One, I give you thanks for new and living hope. In Christ's name. Amen.

MONDAY, MARCH 29

(Read Jeremiah 31:1–6)

(Morning)
Savior, I thank you because I can start this new day
confident of your everlasting love for me.

(Evening)
Savior, because of your everlasting love,
I was able to get through the trials of this day.

Loving God, just as the remnant of Israel was saved by your everlasting love, I am thankful that you have extended that same unchanging love to all generations. Your loving-kindness has drawn me to you, and I rejoice this day that I am a part of the families of Israel. Your grace shall sustain me as I seek your will and direction for this day. Because of your love, I have been able to survive the sword and the wilderness experiences of this day. You will rebuild in me what the routine of the day has stripped away. I will be an example of praise and adoration to you.

(Morning)
As I continue to experience your love this day,
allow your love to flow through me as I encounter others.
(Prayers of Intercession)

(Evening)
As I look back on this day, I pray that my commitment to love others
has been a reflection of your love for me.
(Prayers of Intercession)

"God loves each of us as if there were only one of us" (Augustine).

(Morning)
Allow me to go about my day loving others as you have loved me. In the name of the Christ. Amen.

(Evening)
As I come to the close of this day, I pray that I have loved others as you have loved. In the name of the Christ. Amen.

TUESDAY, MARCH 30
(Read Psalm 118:1–2)

(Morning)
God, as I rise this morning I thank you
for your goodness and mercy, which endure forever.

(Evening)
God, as I come to the close of this day, I am grateful that your goodness
and mercy have sustained me throughout the day.

O God, because of your goodness and mercy, I have found strength to face each day. And when I have yielded to the temptations of the day, your mercy endures forever. Forgive me, God, for I have sinned. But because of your goodness, you have brought me out of my sinful state with salvation. I will make known among the people your merciful deeds and how you have sustained me. I desire to walk uprightly and tell of your goodness and mercy, which will follow me all the days of my life.

(Morning)
As your goodness and mercy follow me,
let others see the wonderful works of your hand in my life.
(Prayers of Intercession)

(Evening)
Give me the desire to extend your goodness and mercy
to others as you have extended them to me.
(Prayers of Intercession)

**"O give thanks to God, for God is good!
Because God's mercy endures forever."**

(Morning)
Dear God, your goodness and mercy are new every morning, and I thank you for allowing me to live another day. In the name of Jesus I pray. Amen.

(Evening)
Dear God, as I lie down to rest, I am confident that because of your mercy, I will arise to see a new day. In the name of Jesus I pray. Amen.

WEDNESDAY, MARCH 31
(Read Colossians 3:1–4)

(Morning)
Dear God, as I arise this morning
I will strive to set my mind on heavenly things.
I will keep my mind fixed on you.

(Evening)
Dear God, the day has brought so many earthly distractions,
forgive me if I strayed from those things that are not pleasing to you.

As I go about my daily routine, I am bombarded with thoughts of discouragement and despair. It is so easy to become distracted by the things of this world. But you have raised me as your child, with Christ, and I can set my mind on things that are not of this world. I must put to death those carnal things that separate me from you, God. Mold me, God, into your image. Direct my mind and my desires as I await your appearance, so that I may also appear with you in glory.

(Morning)
Forgive me, God, for any uncleanness,
and help me to walk uprightly as I await your appearance.
(Prayers of Intercession)

(Evening)
Forgive me, God, for allowing this world to distract me from you.
Restore me to yourself, that I might be prepared for your return.
(Prayers of Intercession)

**As your child, guard my mind so that I
can set my affections on heavenly things.**

(Morning)
God, cleanse my mind of carnal things. I desire to sit in heavenly places with you. In the matchless name of Jesus. Amen.

(Evening)
God, as I look back on my day, I realize that I must put to death those things that distract me from you. Forgive me, God, and guard my mind. In the matchless name of Jesus. Amen.

THURSDAY, APRIL 1
(Read Acts 10:34–43)

(Morning)
Dear God, I thank you for showing no partiality towards me,
for you have accepted me.

(Evening)
Dear God, I have tried to walk uprightly this day
to proclaim that you are God of all.

God, because of your impartiality toward me, you have saved me and others who fear you and walk uprightly. You have anointed me with the same Holy Spirit and power that raised Jesus. You have anointed me to do good and heal those who are oppressed. I will preach and testify of you, so that others might believe and receive remission of their sins. It is only by the power of your Holy Spirit that I am able to proclaim your peace through Jesus Christ, who is Sovereign.

(Morning)
Father God, let those whom you have sent forth to proclaim your peace
not judge others, but give hope to those who are oppressed.
(Prayers of Intercession)

(Evening)
Mother God, let your Holy Spirit empower us to go about doing good and
healing those who are oppressed.
(Prayers of Intercession)

"Soul-winning is not the art of bringing people from down where they are up to where you are. It is to bring them to Christ" (George L. Smith).

(Morning)
God, as I rise this morning, let me not start this day judging others, but showing impartiality as you have shown me. In the Savior's name. Amen.

(Evening)
God, as this day comes to a close, I pray that your grace abounded through me and that others received salvation and healing. In the Savior's name. Amen.

FRIDAY, APRIL 2
(Read Matthew 28:1–10)

(Morning)
O God, as I rise this morning to greet you,
I thank you for laying down your life for a sinner like me.

(Evening)
O God, as I come to the close of this day, I pray that my life has been lived as a
sacrifice unto you, having laid down my life for others as you have done for me.

Dear God, some seek Jesus among the dead, but let us who have witnessed
the resurrection in our hearts proclaim that Jesus is not dead but alive! The
world needs to know that you raised Jesus from the dead so that we might
have life more abundantly. I pray that I do not shrink from telling others
that we have a risen Savior, who is the Christ. I will rejoice and worship
Jesus as Sovereign, who is seated on your right hand, interceding on our
behalf. I want to be an instrument of hope as I proclaim that the same power
that raised Jesus can also raise us from our sins.

(Morning)
I pray that as I start this day, the power of your resurrection resides in me.
(Prayers of Intercession)

(Evening)
I am confident that this day was guided by the power
of the Holy Spirit, which resides in me.
(Prayers of Intercession)

"This Jesus God raised up again, to which we are all witnesses."

(Morning)
Hear my prayer, O God, that I may
start my day mindful of your awesome power in the universe. In Jesus'
name I pray. Amen.

(Evening)
Again, hear my prayer, O God, that I
have witnessed your awesome power
in the universe today. In Jesus' name I
pray. Amen.

SATURDAY, APRIL 3
(Read Psalm 118:14–24)

(Morning)
O God, as I start this day, I depend on your strength to help me face it.
As I start the day, place a song in my heart, so I can praise you.

(Evening)
O God, your strength has brought me through this day.
The song that you placed in my heart has sustained me.

Dear God, you have been my strength, my song, and my salvation, and I will rejoice in your presence. I will go throughout this day declaring your wondrous works in my life. For I will be a testimony of your righteousness. And when I fall, I will accept your chastening as a sign of your love for me. For whom you love, you chasten. I desire to bear the fruit of your righteousness. I will exalt you because you have become my salvation. I thank you for being the chief cornerstone and foundation upon which I can stand.

(Morning)
God, allow me to find strength to rejoice in the face of the trials of this day.
I thank you for each experience.
(Prayers of Intercession)

(Evening)
God, I rejoice as I finish this day in your strength.
All that I have experienced today has drawn me
even closer to your salvation.
(Prayers of Intercession)

"This is the day that God has made; we will rejoice and be glad in it."

(Morning)
Precious God, take my hand and lead me by your strength to overcome all that I will encounter this day. In the mighty name of Jesus. Amen.

(Evening)
Precious God, I thank you for your strength as I stumbled through the day. Your valiant right hand has guided me through the snares of this day. In the mighty name of Jesus. Amen.

SUNDAY, APRIL 4
(Read John 20:1–18)

(Morning)
God, as I start this day, roll away the stones in my life,
that I may arise going about this day victorious.

(Evening)
God, you did not allow the stones of the day to hinder me
from carrying out your will for my life this day.

Jesus, some went to the tomb seeking you among the dead and saw that you were not there. They left weeping in despair and disbelief. Some went to the tomb seeking you among the living and saw that you were not there. They left believing and rejoicing, for you had risen. You had ascended to God and are seated on God's right hand. Because I saw and believed in the power of your resurrection, you have given me a victorious and abundant life. You have made me an instrument of hope and peace in a world of hopelessness and despair. I will tell others that you have risen, so that they may believe and receive salvation through you. As we celebrate your resurrection, let us be your witnesses throughout all the world.

(Morning)
O risen Savior, let me go about my day in the power of your resurrection.
(Prayers of Intercession)

(Evening)
O risen Savior, I pray that those whom I touch received the hope
of your resurrection in their lives.
(Prayers of Intercession)

**"I am ascending to My Parent and your Parent,
and to My God and your God."**

(Morning)	(Evening)
Savior, I thank you for laying down your life for me. In your name I pray. Amen.	Savior, I will praise you for laying down your life for me. In your name I pray. Amen.

MONDAY, APRIL 5
(Read Acts 2:14a, 22–28)

(Morning)
God of imagination, pour out your Holy Spirit upon me,
that I might be filled with gladness.

(Evening)
God of imagination, you have shown me gladness today.
Thank you for your presence today.

How easy it is to look at my suffering and my pain and forget the foundation of my faith. When my days are filled with suffering, help me remember the Easter story and fill me with its hope. The power of life is greater than the power of death. Help me to live in the hope of the resurrection.

(Morning)
Life-giving God, your world sees so much suffering.
I pray this morning for a world that has known suffering.
May the Easter message of hope prevail.
(Prayers of Intercession)

(Evening)
Life-giving God, if I have missed an opportunity to share a word of hope today,
forgive me. Like Peter, may I be a faithful witness to your Easter promise.
May I pray for new and renewed life.
(Prayers of Intercession)

**"For I know that my Redeemer lives, and that at the last
the Savior will stand upon the earth."**

(Morning)
Risen Christ, as your Holy Spirit inspired Peter to proclaim the story of our faith, may I boldly proclaim the same story of hope. In Christ's name. Amen.

(Evening)
Risen Christ, you have not abandoned me today. Thank you for your presence and for helping my soul to sing and my tongue to rejoice. In Christ's name. Amen.

TUESDAY, APRIL 6
(Read Acts 2:29–32)

(Morning)
God of all history, you have been fully present through the night.
Be present with me today.

(Evening)
God of all history, you bring me to the close of the day.
Thank you for being present with me.

Just as David's tomb reminded our ancestors in the faith that their pilgrimage through life would be brief, so the tombs of our own day suggest our temporary existence. What sign of life can we bring to the world today, Savior God? Can we, with David's confidence, believe that you will use us today to bring good news to the world? May we be a living reminder of your eternal care.

(Morning)
Living and present God, deliver your people from the shadows of death
which corrupt and separate them from your love.
May I be a witness to the life you give.
(Prayers of Intercession)

(Evening)
As the shadows of the night surround us, I think of the day
and pray for those who have not known life. Surround them, living and present
God, with your Spirit and give to them a holy rest.
(Prayers of Intercession)

"I am the resurrection and the life."

(Morning)
Living and present God, let me be a witness to your promise for life. In Christ's name. Amen.

(Evening)
God of history, you did not abandon Jesus Christ to death, you brought him through the darkness and into your glorious light. You have not abandoned me. Thank you for keeping me safe. In Christ's name. Amen.

WEDNESDAY, APRIL 7
(Read Psalm 16:1–6)

(Morning)
My heart sings this morning. You are my God!
Guide me and protect me throughout the day.

(Evening)
My heart sings this evening. The day is behind me, and you, O God,
have protected me. Protect me and surround me throughout the night.

God, why have I chosen you? Do I feel safe with you? How am I loved by you? How have you served me? How have I served you? Who am I apart from you? Loving God, it is strange how often we take your gifts for granted. Do we believe that we have always been your followers? Sometimes we need to pause and ask ourselves, "Why do I believe?" Today is a good day to ponder my heritage and my future with you.

(Morning)
Holy One, I have chosen you above all other gods that stir the waters
and blow across the barren land. Safe in your mighty arms,
I will pray for those who struggle to know your love.
(Prayers of Intercession)

(Evening)
Many have multiplied their sorrows because they have not known your love.
May you fill them with wisdom and understanding.
(Prayers of Intercession)

God, you are my hiding place.

(Morning)
Protect me, O God, for in you I take refuge. May my day be filled with your presence. In Christ's name. Amen.

(Evening)
You, O God, are my Chosen One. You have shown me what is good. My day has been filled with your presence, and for this I give you thanks. In Christ's name. Amen.

THURSDAY, APRIL 8

(Read Psalm 16:7–11)

(Morning)
O God, the light of your new day has awakened me.
May I keep you always before me today.

(Evening)
O God, you have blessed me through the day. Now as I lie down to rest, counsel
me through my dreams and bring me to a new tomorrow.

When I awaken, I will go through the tasks, jobs, or projects that need to be
addressed during the day. Just as we go through the tasks, jobs, or projects
in our minds, the Scripture invites us to give our faith equal time. Creator
God, what is good about this new day that you have given me? What would
you want me to do today in the context of my work and play? In what way
can I imitate Jesus Christ? Let our faith guide us and let the Scripture inter-
pret our response to the challenges of this new day.

(Morning)
Present God, my heart is glad today because I have known you.
I will pray for those who are sad and alone.
May they know the gladness I have known because of you.
(Prayers of Intercession)

(Evening)
Present God, you have shown me the path of life.
Tonight I will pray for those who have lost their way.
(Prayers of Intercession)

Your Word is a light unto my path.

(Morning)
Through the night I have rested
securely. Today, show me the path of
life. In Christ's name. Amen.

(Evening)
My heart is glad and my soul rejoices,
for you have not forsaken me. In
Christ's name. Amen.

FRIDAY, APRIL 9
(Read 1 Peter 1:3–9)

(Morning)
Living Christ, I rejoice in your glorious name!
May I be a living witness to your indescribable and glorious joy today.

(Evening)
Living Christ, you have protected me today.
Now as I lie down to rest, protect me through the night.

God, in the midst of my daily struggles, I am confident that I can inherit a living hope through the resurrection of Jesus Christ. When I weep for those who have known injustice, I am confident that I can inherit a living hope through the resurrection of the Savior. When I walk in the darkness of disappointment, I am confident that I can inherit a living hope through the resurrection of Jesus Christ. In all that I do, help me to know the living Christ.

(Morning)
God of living hope, I pray for a faith that can believe
and love without proof of sight or sound.
(Prayers of Intercession)

(Evening)
God of living hope, I pray for the faith and salvation
of the souls who have not yet known your love.
(Prayers of Intercession)

**"O how foolish you are, and how slow of heart to believe
all that the prophets have declared."**

(Morning)
Blessed God and Creator of living hope! By your mercy you have given me this new day; may I proclaim hope. In Christ's name. Amen.

(Evening)
Blessed God, thank you for giving me this day to proclaim hope. May I rest this night, confident of your unfading presence. In Christ's name. Amen.

SATURDAY, APRIL 10
(Read John 20:19–23)

(Morning)
Risen Christ, stand with me today and breathe your living Spirit into my heart.

(Evening)
Risen Christ, you have stood with me throughout the day.
May your peace remain with me throughout the night.

Comforting God, I have known locked doors. I have known fear. I have known loneliness. I want to welcome the light of Jesus Christ into my heart, and I want to know the peace that the disciples knew when they received the Holy Spirit. Today is an opportunity to find life in my death, hope in my despair, and joy in the daily living of life. I want to call upon the risen Christ and receive the Holy Spirit, which Christ breathes across the barriers of time. May this day bring newness to my tired soul.

(Morning)
Amazing God, may those who struggle in life know your peace today.
(Prayers of Intercession)

(Evening)
Amazing God, may your people rejoice
and accept your peace as a word of grace.
(Prayers of Intercession)

"God of grace and God of glory, on your people pour your power"
(H. E. Fosdick).

(Morning)
Spirit God, may the words of the risen Christ be heard in my heart today. May I know the peace that you give to me. In Christ's name. Amen.

(Evening)
If I have harbored the memory of anyone's sins, please help me know, so that I might also forgive them. Bring me to a peaceful rest, and may tomorrow bring another opportunity to forgive. Thank you, Spirit God. In Christ's name. Amen.

SUNDAY, APRIL 11
(Read John 20:24–31)

(Morning)
Jesus, Child of God, may I not doubt your presence today.

(Evening)
Jesus, Child of God, as I shut my eyes, may I know your presence
and dream of a new tomorrow with you, my risen Savior.

Unless I see the mark of the nails in his hands and put my finger in the mark of the nails and my hand in his side, I will not believe. Thomas's statement is like a statement from us. We want the concrete. We want to know beyond doubt that what we profess is true. Trusting is hard to do. Children do this better than adults. Faith is not reasonable, nor is it rational. Faith is a feeling of trust that is accepted by us as unconditionally as you, loving God, love us. Today may be a good day to be like a child and trust in you.

(Morning)
Faithful God, may I pray for myself and those who cannot trust.
Help me to trust.
(Prayers of Intercession)

(Evening)
Faithful God, for those who have not trusted today and
for the times I have not trusted, I pray for a deepening faith.
(Prayers of Intercession)

**"Trust and obey, for there is no other way to be happy in Jesus,
but to trust and obey" (J. H. Sammis).**

(Morning)
Living Christ, may I know today the peace that you breathed upon the disciples. In Christ's name. Amen.

(Evening)
Living Christ, I have known your peace. May I rest tonight, so that I may share your peace tomorrow. In Christ's name. Amen.

MONDAY, APRIL 12
(Read Acts 2:14a, 36–41)

(Morning)
O God, thank you for the gift of newness you have promised in the Easter story.
I pray that it will continue to be real in my life this day and throughout my life.

(Evening)
O God, this night in quietness I come to you to reflect
on the wonder of the life you give, again and again.

I want to be a faithful servant of your good news, O God. But I confess that sometimes your Word has become so familiar that I am not "cut to the heart." Help me not to let the familiarity of your Word blind me to its radicalness, to its cutting edges, to its hope for my own life and for the world.

(Morning)
I pray that through the noise and din of war and the pain and suffering of the
bruised and broken, the good news of Easter may be heard.
(Prayers of Intercession)

(Evening)
I thank you, O God, for the good that has come to me in this day.
Help me never to forget the needs of so many others who know not your Word.
(Prayers of Intercession)

I pray the prayer Jesus taught his disciples.
(Pray the Prayer of Our Savior.)

(Morning)
Use me as an instrument of your good
news this day, I pray in Jesus' name.
Amen.

(Evening)
I entrust to your never-failing mercy
and grace all that I am and all that I
have done and thought this day. I pray
in Jesus' name. Amen.

TUESDAY, APRIL 13
(Read Acts 2:38–41)

(Morning)
Creator God, each new day is a gift you give.
Help me to use this day well.

(Evening)
Creator God, as the evening shadows lengthen,
I bring to you what I have done this day. I ask for your mercy.

O God, I have repented. Too often I do not see my need to repent—again and again and again. Again grant me the gift of your Spirit. Make new again the baptism to which my parents brought me and which I confirmed, so that this day and in the days to come, I may be an instrument of your grace and truth.

(Morning)
Your love is from everlasting to everlasting. Look with tender mercy upon your children who are lost, confused, twisted, and hurting. Help me, with all of your children, to open our hearts and minds to the flowing of your Spirit, that we might know the forgiveness and truth and mercy that lead to life.
(Prayers of Intercession)

(Evening)
I come in penitence for myself and for this broken world,
for we have not done well with this day.
(Prayers of Intercession)

I pray the prayer Jesus taught his disciples.
(Pray the Prayer of Our Savior.)

(Morning)
I go into this day with trust and hope,
O God. I pray in Jesus' name. Amen.

(Evening)
I ask for your mercy, as I lay this day before you, that you will grant me rest and renewal. I pray in Jesus' name. Amen.

WEDNESDAY, APRIL 14
(Read Psalm 116:1–4)

(Morning)
O God, sometimes the day breaks forth with sunlight,
and sometimes it opens with dark clouds and rain.
They are all gifts from you. Help me to be thankful
for each new day that you give.

(Evening)
O God, I have tried to be an instrument of your love this day.
Forgive me for my failures.

Today help me to love you because you are you, awesome God, Creator of the heavens and the earth. Author of life, so often I wait until you have acted in my behalf. And when you have not done what I have asked, I have doubted your love. Let my love be unconditioned as your love is unconditioned, so I may know the freeing power of your saving love.

(Morning)
Sometimes it is hard for me to make my prayers of intercession.
The hates and the hurts in the world go on and on. Loving God,
forgive me, and help me to persevere.
(Prayers of Intercession)

(Evening)
Bless those whom you brought into contact with me today.
And bless your bruised and broken children all over the world.
You have asked us to pray for the coming of your realm. So this I do.
(Prayers of Intercession)

I pray the prayer Jesus taught his disciples.
(Pray the Prayer of Our Savior.)

(Morning)
Help me to be an instrument of your love this day. I pray in Jesus' name. Amen.

(Evening)
Trusting in your unconditioned love, I lay to rest this day. I pray in Jesus' name. Amen.

THURSDAY, APRIL 15
(Read Psalm 116:12–19)

(Morning)
Eternal God, I ask that as the days pass,
I will not let the glorious and eternal hope of Easter fade.
Let me live with hope this day.

(Evening)
Eternal God, the burdens of my own brokenness and sinfulness are more than I
can carry. And the burdens of the brokenness and sinfulness of the world are
more than I can carry. I thank you that I can come to you—you, whose mercy
and love are larger than all that I can fathom and the world can contain.

How shall I repay you for all your goodness toward me, O God? When I
think of the bounty of your love, I can only bow in humble thanks. I ask
that you use me as an instrument of your creation: for healing where there
is brokenness, for hope where there is hopelessness, for peace where there
is anger.

(Morning)
Today, I pray for my family and the church. Each of us has his or her own
special burdens. And I pray for our president and all those who are leaders of
nations. They carry such awesome burdens.
(Prayers of Intercession)

(Evening)
Have mercy on me and on your broken humanity.
We seem unable to find our way to your peace and wholeness.
(Prayers of Intercession)

I pray the prayer Jesus taught his disciples.
(Pray the Prayer of Our Savior.)

(Morning)	(Evening)
Today let me be a witness to you and to your ways. In Jesus' name I pray. Amen.	Gracious God, I entrust this day to your grace. In Jesus' name I pray. Amen.

FRIDAY, APRIL 16
(Read 1 Peter 1:17–23)

(Morning)
O God, I wake this day with all the life it can contain.
I claim the enduring promise that you will walk through it with me.

(Evening)
O God, I have tried to live according to your truth today.
I know I have not done well. Forgive me, loving God.

Sometimes I feel it would be a lot easier if I did not have to deal with you, O God, because your judgment is true. Sometimes I feel out of sync with the world in which I live, and that's not very comfortable. Yet, I have come to this holy place again because, in Jesus, you come to me with a love that cuts through all my fears and pretensions. Help me to be obedient to your truth, that I may be an instrument of your love for my own sake and for the sake of this bruised and lost world.

(Morning)
O God, it's so easy to get stuck on the little things that surround me
that I lose touch with your larger truth.
Help me to open my heart and mind to the flowing of your Spirit.
(Prayers of Intercession)

(Evening)
Have mercy on your children,
who keep forgetting the true grounding of our lives.
(Prayers of Intercession)

I pray the prayer Jesus taught his disciples.
(Pray the Prayer of Our Savior.)

(Morning)
Let me not be a part of the things that negate your truth this day. I pray in Jesus' name. Amen.

(Evening)
Trusting in your never-failing mercy and goodness, I lay this day before you, O God. In Jesus' name I pray. Amen.

SATURDAY, APRIL 17
(Read Luke 24:13–27)

(Morning)
O God, shadows hover over some of my days.
I ask you to lead me through the shadows to your light.

(Evening)
O God, I thank you for the experiences of this day.
I have learned, and I have grown.

You have already told me your story, O God. But so often I am so overwhelmed by life's issues, its disappointments, its failures, and its despairs, that I forget the story. The world is so messed up, I sometimes begin to feel that there is no future. Help me to hear the story again, that I may hope.

(Morning)
I bring to you all those who have come to disappointment,
to the place where hope is undercut, to the place
of wondering where to go next.
(Prayers of Intercession)

(Evening)
I thank you for those who have taught me faith and courage and hope.
I bring to you all those who have little faith and courage and hope.
(Prayers of Intercession)

I pray the prayer Jesus taught his disciples.
(Pray the Prayer of Our Savior.)

(Morning)
Help me to use this day well, O God.
In Jesus' name I pray. Amen.

(Evening)
I thank you that you are in the midst of the mornings and the evenings, in the midst of good times and hard times. So, with confidence, I trust in your never-failing love. I entrust this day to your care. In Jesus' name I pray. Amen.

SUNDAY, APRIL 18
(Read Luke 24:28–35)

(Morning)
O God, who created the sun and the moon, the days and the nights,
I thank you for this day. Help me to use it well.

(Evening)
O God, I thank you for the opportunities that have come my way to be an
instrument of your good news. Forgive me for the times when I failed.

How can I recognize you, O God? I wait and hope for the signs and wonders you show me. You have already told me your story, but my mind and
heart are sometimes closed. You do come, but sometimes so unobstrusively:
in a lover, in a parent, in a child, in a teacher, in a student, in a friend, in a
broken one, in a crisis, in an opportunity, in the breaking of bread. Help me
to open my eyes, my heart, and my mind, that I may receive anew your
life-giving Word, that I may be a sign of your loving presence for another.

(Morning)
There is so much death in the world, O God, that hope is hard. I bring to you all
those who live in the midst of death, hoping that the good news of Easter will
come to them as the Word of life.
(Prayers of Intercession)

(Evening)
For all those who have come to the close of this day with the heavy burden of
sorrow, pain, fear, and want, I pray your mercy, O God.
(Prayers of Intercession)

I pray the prayer Jesus taught his disciples.
(Pray the Prayer of Our Savior.)

(Morning)
Let my heart be warmed this day, that
I may tell the good news that Christ is
alive and, therefore, we may have
hope and life. In Jesus' name I pray.
Amen.

(Evening)
This night I pray for your reign to
come upon our lost and broken
humanity. In you are our hope and our
peace. In that faith I rest this night. In
the name of Jesus Christ I pray. Amen.

MONDAY, APRIL 19
(Read Acts 2:42–47)

(Morning)
Gracious God, from whom all blessings flow, I thank you for this day.
May I use it to glorify and magnify you and your holy name.

(Evening)
Gracious God, I thank you for every task and activity that I performed during
this day. May you allow me to carry the good thoughts of today in my heart
while I give the bad thoughts to you.

I wait upon you, O God, to display your many signs and wonders. May I be
of one accord with other believers and strive to serve those in need. May
my possessions and material goods become less important and my human
relationships become more significant from this day forward. Continue to
lead me, guide me, and show me the way, both now and forevermore.

(Morning)
May I commit this day to serving others with the gifts, skills,
and attributes with which you have blessed me.
(Prayers of Intercession)

(Evening)
Dear God, as I end this day with a spirit of peace and joy, may I continue to
acknowledge the many signs and wonders that you reveal to me.
(Prayers of Intercession).

**As you increase the numbers of those who are saved,
may I always hold sacred the Prayer of Our Savior.**
(Pray the Prayer of Our Savior.)

(Morning)
With a sense of joy, I wait upon Jesus
today. In your name I pray. Amen.

(Evening)
Jesus Christ, anoint me with the
things that you have taught me today.
In your name I pray. Amen.

TUESDAY, APRIL 20
(Read Acts 2:42–47)

(Morning)
Blessed Creator, Maker of all things that are good,
I give you praise and honor today.

(Evening)
Blessed Creator, this day and all that is in it are gifts from you.
As I end this day, I commit to you all that I have done.

Dear God, those who came before me gathered in the temple, and they remembered you with praise as they ate their daily meals with glad and generous hearts. As I partake of my meals today, may I give you all the honor, the glory, and the praise, remembering that each morsel I consume is a manifestation of your love for me. God, I pray for those who dwell among us who have no food to eat. May you give me a heart of compassion that encourages me to take some action to contribute to alleviating hunger and homelessness. My hands are your hands, my feet are your feet, my voice is your voice. May I be a voice for the faceless, voiceless, nameless sufferers who exist in our midst everyday.

(Morning)
God, I commit this day to doing things that contribute positively to humankind.
(Prayers of Intercession)

(Evening)
Magnificent God, I acknowledge that you are my God
and that I am one of your people.
(Prayers of Intercession)

I am saved.
(Pray the Prayer of Our Savior.)

(Morning)	(Evening)
With a sense of joy, Jesus, I wait upon you today. In your name I pray. Amen.	Jesus Christ, anoint me with the things that you have taught me today. In your name I pray. Amen.

WEDNESDAY, APRIL 21
(Read Psalm 23)

(Morning)
My God, may the people bow down to you,
my Shepherd and my Provider.

(Evening)
My God, as this day comes to a close, I thank you for the green pastures
that I have walked through today. Come, holy Comforter, come!

Dear God, you are my beloved Creator, my blessed Shepherd, and my watchful Protector. Reveal yourself to those who do not know you as they merely exist on the highest mountains and in the lowest valleys. On this day, O God, I thank you for allowing me to experience the greener pastures of life during the good times and the tranquillity of the still waters during the challenging times. You and you alone have the power to restore my soul so that I may experience the fullness of life.

(Morning)
This morning I pray for the restoration of . . .
[name the individuals and families you know who are in need].
(Prayers of Intercession)

(Evening)
This evening, I continue to lift up in my prayer . . .
(Prayers of Intercession)

With renewed hope I pray.
(Pray the Prayer of Our Savior.)

(Morning)
I begin this day seeking the restorative power of the Creator. In the name of Jesus. Amen.

(Evening)
I end this day acknowledging the restorative power of the Creator. In the name of Jesus. Amen.

THURSDAY, APRIL 22
(Read Psalm 23)

(Morning)
Gracious God, I rejoice and look forward to this day with excitement and joy!

(Evening)
Gracious God, I end this day acknowledging the hopes and fears of those who
have come from all walks of life.

Dear God, I thank you for allowing me to experience life another day. Where
there are signs of love in the world, please encourage them. Where there is
evil, prick their hearts so that they may realize there is a better way. Let me
remember on this day that you are a God of love and peace, not evil and
war. And wherever there is unrest, I pray for and patiently await a miracle.
When goodness and mercy follow me, let me acknowledge that they are
gifts from you, as I diligently strive not only to dwell but to thrive in your
house my whole life long.

(Morning)
On this day I will fear no evil, for you will be with me.
I will rely on your rod and your staff as sources of comfort.
(Prayers of Intercession)

(Evening)
As I rest at the table that you have prepared. I acknowledge the goodness
and mercy that you have bestowed upon me all the days of my life.
(Prayers of Intercession)

With renewed hope I pray.
(Pray the Prayer of Our Savior.)

(Morning)
Holy Spirit, bring comfort and peace
to the world today. In the name of
Jesus. Amen.

(Evening)
Let the world continue to experience
your comfort and peace. In the name of
Jesus. Amen.

FRIDAY, APRIL 23

(Read 1 Peter 2:19–25)

(Morning)
Dear God, make me aware of your presence.

(Evening)
Dear God, thank you for being with me today.

Gracious God, as I experience this day, let me feel your presence. Allow my body, mind, and spirit to endure all that this world has to offer. When my endurance appears low, remind me of Jesus, the One who endured the pain and suffering of the world, hanging on that old rugged cross. When I forget the suffering of Jesus, please order my steps, that I may again become an example of the One who came before, suffered, and triumphed over two thousand years ago. Deliver me from complacency, so that I may seek righteousness and healing instead of sin and woundedness.

(Morning)
I rejoice as I remain focused on the task of
absorbing your presence all the day long.
(Prayers of Intercession)

(Evening)
I end this day in the presence of the Shepherd and Guardian of my soul.
(Prayers of Intercession)

I live by your righteousness, Sovereign Jesus.
(Pray the Prayer of Our Savior.)

(Morning)
I entrust this day into your hands,
O God. In the name of Jesus. Amen.

(Evening)
Free from sin, I strive for the
righteous life. In the name of Jesus.
Amen.

SATURDAY, APRIL 24
(Read John 10:1–10)

(Morning)
Loving God, may I usher in this day through the gates of righteousness.

(Evening)
Loving God, I end this day, calling upon you,
our heavenly Gatekeeper, to protect me through the night.

Magnificent God, Creator of heaven and earth, I thank you for this day. I trust in you to protect me from the evils of the world. May you keep your hedge of protection wrapped around me at all times, especially in those moments when you must move me beyond my comfort zone. Wherever you lead me, I will follow you as a sheep follows its shepherd. Wherever you tell me to go, I will press on with confidence, knowing that yours is a voice of truth. My trust, my hope, and my life are in your capable hands. And I submit myself totally to you.

(Morning)
Holy Spirit, empower me to hear and to yield to the voice of God.
(Prayers of Intercession)

(Evening)
Dear God, I pause in silence. Let me hear your still, quiet voice.
Help me to be able to differentiate between your voice
and the voices of the false prophets who dwell among us.
(Prayers of Intercession)

Out of the depths of silence comes a new revelation.
(Pray the Prayer of Our Savior.)

(Morning)
Be aware of the voice of the stranger.
In the name of Jesus. Amen.

(Evening)
The voice of God shall always remain
in the heart. In the name of Jesus.
Amen.

SUNDAY, APRIL 25
(Read John 10:1–10)

(Morning)
Loving God, I thank you for Jesus, the Christ.
Because of Jesus I will receive the gift of abundant life.

(Evening)
Loving God, I retire this day humbly accepting
the experiences of an abundant life.

Dear God, I thank you, the Gatekeeper, for being eternally present at the gate that leads to abundant life. With your saving power, I look forward to the day when I will experience your bounty in the greener pastures of the eternal life. But until that day, O God, I humbly seek your protection. Protect me from the violence that exists in the streets, shield me from lies and misinformation. When I have a doubting spirit, cleanse me. When I am anxious, calm me. When I am careless, guide me. When I am fearful, still my heart. For in you, O God, there is always a better way—the righteous way. And from this day forward, I extend my very being to you and to you alone, my Protector and Provider.

(Morning)
Help me to learn from my enemies today.
Convert the anxieties of my heart into experiences of love and joy.
(Prayers of Intercession)

(Evening)
I end this day with the blessed assurance that life is a sacred gift,
and I pray that I do not take it for granted.
(Prayers of Intercession)

The gates of hell will never prevail!
(Pray the Prayer of Our Savior.)

(Morning)
Jesus said, "Very truly, I tell you, I am the gate for the sheep." As a sheep in the pasture, I assuredly wait at Jesus' feet. In Jesus' name. Amen.

(Evening)
"Whoever enters by me will be saved, and will come in and go out and find pasture." Thank you, God! In the name of Jesus. Amen.

MONDAY, APRIL 26
(Read John 14:1–4)

(Morning)
O God, I am in between sleep and the activities of this day.
Into this quiet space, come show me your way, your truth, and your life.

(Evening)
O God, the gift of this day has been received. May we unwrap this present
together and marvel over the miracles we see.

What does it mean that you are the way? How are you the truth of my life?
Of all life? Is the life I make the same as the life you create? Inspire my
mind with your knowledge. Encourage my heart to live into your presence
and possibility. May I see with the eyes of spirit what you desire.

(Morning)
Equip me with what I need to live this day
as your servant and agent of holy love.
(Prayers of Intercession)

(Evening)
I am tired, God. Not only my body, but my heart and mind.
Remind me, again, in the depths of my spirit,
that it is you who fill everything with life and light and love.
And that my job is to bear witness to your presence in all that I see and do.
(Prayers of Intercession)

"I am the way, and the truth, and the life."

(Morning)
If I fall away from your presence
today, call me back. Guide me on
your way. Teach me your truth. Fill
me with your life. In our Savior's
name. Amen.

(Evening)
I bind around me the comfort of your
care. I wrap myself in the warmth of
your presence. I lay myself down upon
the foundation of your love. In our
Savior's name. Amen.

TUESDAY, APRIL 27
(Read John 14:1–14)

(Morning)
O faithful Companion God, show me your way, that I might follow faithfully.
Walk with me and be my guide through this day.

(Evening)
O faithful Companion God, we have come to the end of this day's journey.
Prepare me now to find my rest and my fulfillment in your mercy and peace.

You are the journey and the way. You are the beginning and the end. You are the hand that guides and the feet that walk; open my mind and heart to you. Where I am reluctant to venture forth, give me courage. Where I have fallen over obstacles on the path, gather me up and set me safely on the way. Where I am confused and lonely, guide and companion me, for I can only walk your way if you are with me.

(Morning)
Stepping out of bed this morning, O God, is an act of trust that you will guide
my feet. Lead me to know and to walk in your way.
(Prayers of Intercession)

(Evening)
This day has run its course. Look with merciful eyes upon the adventures and
challenges that we have met.
(Prayers of Intercession)

"I am the Way."

(Morning)
Now, we set forth. Don't let me wander off. May we walk this way and this day together. In Jesus' name. Amen.

(Evening)
I take off my shoes as in this moment I enter the holy ground of your presence. I lay down my cares and my burdens as to approach your heart. I offer myself and this day for your blessing and the gift of your peace. In Jesus' name. Amen.

WEDNESDAY, APRIL 28
(Read John 14:1–14)

(Morning)
Spirit of the living God, rise anew in me. May your truth shine
like a bright beacon leading me through this day.

(Evening)
Spirit of the living God, I gather the moments of this day
and lay them before you. Lay the moments, the thoughts, the desires
of your Spirit upon my heart and mind in this time of meditation.

"You will know the truth, and the truth will make you free." I am ready,
Eternal One, to know your truth. Let it break forth upon me as dawn breaks
forth over the darkness of night. May it shine into those lonely and frightened places within me, bringing its warmth and invitation. May it brighten
the faces of all those I see today. May it illuminate your presence throughout your creation, making the way clear for me to respond.

(Morning)
Help me to know you, to embrace you, and to trust you.
Open my eyes to this day and its opportunities.
(Prayers of Intercession)

(Evening)
I was blessed when I saw you today.
I cherish those moments of being with you and in you.
In this moment of recollection before sleep,
I thank you for this day and offer you my needs and my hopes.
(Prayers of Intercession)

"I am the Truth."

(Morning)	(Evening)
Send me into your world equipped with the sight to see your light and truth breaking forth all around. In Jesus' name. Amen.	At the close of this day, I offer you my deepest truth. I love you, trust you, and seek to abide in you in all ways. In Jesus' name. Amen.

THURSDAY, APRIL 29
(Read John 14:1–14)

(Morning)
O God, brighten my spirit with the abundance of your life.
Awaken me to the joy and glory of your presence in all that is this day.

(Evening)
O God, your life is rich and full. As I offer this day to you,
may I know the blessings that abound.

Your life is: secure, unwavering, rock-bottom dependable; passionate, responsive, filled with colors, sounds, and smells; gently caressing and constantly loving; seeking, finding, creating; being justice, mercy, peace. Open me to your life. Fill me to overflowing so that all that I am and all that I do bears witness to you.

(Morning)
Prepare me, O God, by giving me the thoughts, the words,
and the energy I need for the living of this day.
(Prayers of Intercession)

(Evening)
Enfold me in your infinite space and your limitless time,
Eternal One. Prepare a place in your heart that welcomes my heart this night.
(Prayers of Intercession)

"I am the Life."

(Morning)
Bless all life today. Bless the problems, turning them into possibilities. Bless the joys, widening the rings of their touch. Bless the love given and received. In Jesus' name. Amen.

(Evening)
Though it is dark outside, in you I always find light. Though the day has been busy, in you I always find rest. Though questions are on my mind, in you I always find a peace that enables me to live into the questions, knowing that you will provide the answers in your time. In Jesus' name. Amen.

120

FRIDAY, APRIL 30
(Read Psalm 31:1–5, 15–16)

(Morning)
Holy One, be my refuge today, Fortress of my life.
Do not let me stray from the surety of your presence.
I commit my spirit to you, trusting that you are
the breath I breathe moment by moment.

(Evening)
Holy One, may your face shine upon the life of this day.
Warm what was cold and unforgiving.
Channel what was unfocused and out of control.
May we look through your eyes at this day.

To know you as refuge and fortress means that I recognize my frailty and failures. To ask for your deliverance and salvation comes at the expense of my pride and success. The choice is my illusion or your truth. I commit my life to you, faithful God, and may I know that you have redeemed me.

(Morning)
May you see through my blind spots.
May you hear past my deafness.
May you speak across my faltering.
Be present in everything today.
(Prayers of Intercession)

(Evening)
Sift through this day with me, gentle Guide.
May I let go of the chaff and celebrate your goodness and love.
(Prayers of Intercession)

"You have redeemed me, faithful God."

(Morning)
Place your hand upon this day. Place your hand upon all I meet. In Jesus' name. Amen.

(Evening)
It is the assurance of your steadfast love that puts me to bed this evening. It is your kind hand that tucks me in. It is your sweet face that hovers over me as I close my eyes. It is your voice that sings me tenderly to my rest. In Jesus' name. Amen.

SATURDAY, MAY 1
(Read Acts 7:55–60)

(Morning)
Holy Spirit, come. Fill me. Teach me. Guide me. Protect me.

(Evening)
Holy Spirit, in gratitude I come to this quiet moment at the end of today.
Your Spirit has been my companion. We look together at what has been.

I am frightened, God. The difficulties, issues, and limits I face have a dangerous edge. Open your heavens, so that I might see you. Pour your illuminating power upon this world, so that we all might know you. Comfort and empower me with your presence, so that I might be part of your agency of love. Walk through the valley of the shadows with me and bring me safely through to the other side.

(Morning)
Sometimes the world is like a tidal wave. It overwhelms me,
and I am swept away. Be my compass as I navigate through this day.
(Prayers of Intercession)

(Evening)
I return to you at this quiet hour. You are my anchor and safe harbor.
With confidence in your secure keeping, I lay this day to rest.
(Prayers of Intercession)

"Look, I see."

(Morning)	(Evening)
Come walk with me, Blessed One. Through this day and together may we make your dreams come true. In the name of Christ I pray. Amen.	The voyage of this day is over. The sails are furled, and the crew is asleep. You are the captain of my life, and into your sure hands I place all that has happened. Comfort me with rest and gentle dreams. In the name of Christ I pray. Amen.

SUNDAY, MAY 2
(Read 1 Peter 2:2–10)

(Morning)
O God, this day comes newborn into my life.
May I receive it with the openness and trust of an infant
seeking to be fed with spiritual food.

(Evening)
O God, as a rock you have upheld my life.
Now may I lay myself upon your comforting breast
and with a sigh of completion render this day
into your hands and your keeping.

You are the living foundation stone upon which I seek to build. You are the precious cornerstone that connects and bridges all the elements of life. May I rejoice in such a strong base. You have worked your way among these people and with me, fashioning us into your own. May I be faithful to your desire and lead by example and word. Call me out of the shadows, that I may stand in awe and marvel at your abundant light.

(Morning)
Feed me, Creator God, for I am hungry for the sustenance that never fails.
(Prayers of Intercession)

(Evening)
Loving One, perhaps I have stumbled today, made mistakes,
distorted your will. Knowing your greatest desire
is for me to know myself as you know me,
I place this day in your heart and ask for your peace.
(Prayers of Intercession)

"A royal priesthood, God's own people."

(Morning)
Precious One, who knows me as
precious also, may all that I think and
do and say this day reflect the value
you hold for me and all your creation.
In Jesus' name. Amen.

(Evening)
My restless soul finds its rest in you.
In Jesus' name. Amen.

MONDAY, MAY 3
(Read Acts 17:22–25)

(Morning)
God, I thank you for giving me life, breath, and all the things that are necessary for me to live and enjoy life. (Do a simple breathing exercise as you offer this prayer. Be conscious of your breathing. Enjoy the gift of life!)

(Evening)
God, guide my thoughts as I sort out the experiences of this day.
Let me focus on those that nurture my faith and nourish my soul.
Open my mind to your greater truth about yourself.

As I go about the journeys of this day, I will resolve, like Paul, to look around me, attentive to the possibility that I will discover you, loving God, in the faith of others. I want to be open to the idea that you, the God I know in the Bible and in Jesus Christ, are the God of people of other faiths. I will note the different religious architecture in my community and say to myself, "Even their God is known and worshiped!"

(Morning)
I will pray for unity in the Christian church. I will also pray for . . . (Pick a religious faith or a people or community unlike your own, and pray for it.)
(Prayers of Intercession)

(Evening)
I thank you, O God, because I know you in Jesus Christ and in the Scriptures.
More important, however, you know me as your child!
(Prayers of Intercession)

**Today, whatever I do and wherever I go,
I will repeat this phrase as my personal statement of faith:
"In you, O God, I live and move and have my being."**

(Morning)
Help me to boldly love those who are different from me. In the name of Jesus I pray. Amen.

(Evening)
I claim the rest that the night offers me, knowing that in you I live and move and have my being. In the name of Jesus I pray. Amen.

TUESDAY, MAY 4
(Read Acts 17:26–31)
(Today repeat as your personal statement of faith:
"In you, O God, I live and move and have my being.")

(Morning)
Revealing God, today, starting this very moment, I seek you
in the fervent hope that I might feel you and find you!
Make yourself known to me and be alive in me!

(Evening)
Revealing God, I praise and thank you for this day,
for informing my mind with your truth, and for ways in which
you have made yourself known to me.

God, I will continue to have an open mind about your vastness—thinking outside the box, making my mind roam where it wills, yet praying that the Spirit will lead me into a new understanding of your truth. I will endeavor this day to free myself from closed-mindedness and to pursue new ideas.

(Morning)
I will repent of my own inability to celebrate diversity of ideas
and remember those with whom I disagree often.
(Prayers of Intercession)

(Evening)
Merciful God, let me now, in your loving presence, inquire into
the secrets of my heart: Was I honest in my pursuit for truth?
Did I try to find a basis of agreement with those with whom I disagreed?
Thank you for the gift of the mind.
(Prayers of Intercession)

Even as I seek to know and appreciate others' faith and understanding of God, I will resolve to deepen my own relationship with the risen Christ.
(Pray the Prayer of Our Savior.)

(Morning)	(Evening)
I will go forth into this day with a lively mind, open to new and different thoughts! In Christ's name. Amen.	Bless me this night, O God, with a restful and peaceful sleep. In Christ's name. Amen.

WEDNESDAY, MAY 5
(Read Psalm 66:8–20)

(Morning)
Blessed God, I will live this day with the thought and conviction
that in each step I take, I am accompanied by your blessing.

(Evening)
Blessed God, in your solemn presence I thank you,
and I thank all who blessed me this day.

Today's challenge for me is to bless and praise you, God. God, you put us through tough and difficult situations or allow them to happen to us. In our lives, there are times when we have to go through fire and water, to bear burdens, and have people walk all over us! But God, you are always there for me, caring, listening, blessing, answering my prayers, and steadfastly loving me!

(Morning)
Go with me, caring God, through the sunlit hours or shadowy moments of this day. Sustain me if I have to carry a heavy burden or walk on lonely and treacherous pathways. I especially remember those who are going through some difficult times in their lives these days.
(Prayers of Intercession)

(Evening)
At the close of this day, give me a thankful heart for what you have done for me. While I am in a thankful mood, hear my prayer of thanks for those who did something nice for me today.
(Prayers of Intercession)

You, who listen to my prayer, teach me to listen to your still, small voice.

(Morning)
I will be attentive to God's voice in the words I read or hear this day. In the matchless name of Jesus. Amen.

(Evening)
If I cherished sin in my heart today, forgive me, God, and remove not your steadfast love from me. In the matchless name of Jesus. Amen.

THURSDAY, MAY 6
(Read 1 Peter 3:13–16)
(Today repeat as your personal statement of faith:
"Even if you do suffer for doing what is right, you are blessed.")

(Morning)
Giver of abundant life, deliver me from suffering this day.
Yet, if I must suffer, may it be for the cause and in the name of the Christ.

(Evening)
(Softly sing or pray this verse from Henry F. Lyte's hymn:)
"Abide with me; fast falls the eventide; the shadows deepen,
Lord, with me abide; when other helpers fail, and comforts flee,
Help of the helpless, O abide with me."

Giving God, how can suffering be a blessing? The historical context here
is the persecution of the first-century Christians. The early church discouraged "this will-to-martyrdom" fanaticism, as there is no virtue in seeking
pain or hardship for its own sake. Nevertheless, O God, if one's faith is
tried and tested, one must be prepared to defend it clearly and courageously
but also with gentleness and respect.

(Morning)
(Use the following petition in Psalm 13 to offer a prayer of lament for
yourself or someone else:) "How long, O God? Will you forget me
forever? How long will you hide your face from me? How long must
I bear pain in my soul, and have sorrow in my heart all day long?"
(Prayers of Intercession)

(Evening)
(Pray for those who are abused, for yourself, and for others with the words of
Christ): "Peace I leave with you, my peace I give to you."
(Prayers of Intercession)

Humbly I pray.
(Pray the Prayer of Our Savior.)

(Morning)	(Evening)
I will advocate for my cause with gentleness and reverence. Thanks be to Christ. Amen.	Abide with me . . . O abide with me. Thanks be to Christ. Amen.

FRIDAY, MAY 7
(Read 1 Peter 3:17–22)
(Today repeat as your personal statement of faith:
"For it is better to suffer for doing good, if suffering should be God's will.")

(Morning)
My God, I realize that I cannot flee from human suffering,
nor can I be indefinitely free from pain. I will resolve to walk
with the Christ, who experienced human agony and triumphed!

(Evening)
My God, to your care I commend my life and my soul
as well as those whom I love and who love me.

"One lives long, suffers much" is a proverb that reflects realism about human life and existence. God, the debate whether you determine suffering or allow it will never be resolved. However, the fact of human pain or hardship is indisputable; it happens to everyone. Jesus suffered, and, as the gospel hymn puts it, he had to walk the lonesome valley all by himself. Pain is personal. Let Christ walk with those who must suffer.

(Morning)
(Touching your forehead with the tips of your hand in symbolic affirmation
of baptism, repeat the words:) "I am God's child, baptized in the Name
of the Father, the Son, and the Holy Ghost."
(Prayers of Intercession)

(Evening)
(Sing or say softly to yourself this verse from Henry F. Lyte's hymn:) "Swift to
its close ebbs out life's little day; earth's joys grow dim, its glories pass away;
change and decay in all around I see. O thou, who changest not, abide with me."
(Prayers of Intercession)

I am God's child; I am God's; I am.

(Morning)
Jesus said, "Blessed are you when people revile you and utter all kinds of evil against you falsely . . . your reward is great in heaven."
Thanks be to Christ. Amen.

(Evening)
O Christ, who changes not, abide with me. Thanks be to Christ. Amen.

SATURDAY, MAY 8
(Read John 14:15–17)

(Morning)
Spirit of the living God, abide with me today
and be in me as Christ has promised.

(Evening)
Spirit of the living God, true to your promise,
you were with me every moment of the day. Thank you.

Truth is a very rare commodity these days. Who's telling the truth? Whom should we believe? Loving God, society seems to value the "art" of disinformation. Do I tell the truth? Is the Spirit of truth in me? I wonder.

(Morning)
"Breathe on me, Breath of God, fill me with truth anew, that I may live
the life of Christ, and do that which is true" (Edwin Hatch).
(Prayers of Intercession)

(Evening)
"Breathe on me, Breath of God, until my heart is pure,
until with you I will one will, to do and to endure" (Edwin Hatch).
(Prayers of Intercession)

The Spirit of truth is in me, therefore, I will advocate for truth today!
(Pray the Prayer of Our Savior.)

(Morning)
The truth will make me free! In the name of Christ I pray. Amen.

(Evening)
(Sing to yourself or pray this hymn verse:) "Breathe on me, Breath of God, so shall I never die, but live with you the perfect life of your eternity" (Edwin Hatch). In the name of Christ I pray. Amen.

SUNDAY, MAY 9
(Read John 14:18–21)

(Morning)
Companion God, as the Christ loved being with you as a parent,
let my thoughts today be of my parents. For what will I thank my parents?
What is it that makes me think of them, long for them?

(Evening)
Companion God, it must be terrible to be orphaned,
to be without someone who cares for you. But thanks be to Christ
for promising presence and companionship; I'm never alone!

Companion God, no matter the circumstance, no matter the loss, I have life abundant: because my Christ lives, I, too, will live. I will reflect on those who gave me human life and nurtured me. I take this occasion to offer my gratitude to them and pray for them. Am I myself a nurturer of life for someone, for others?

(Morning)
Into the care of a loving parent, God, I place my life, my all, this day.
I am your child, loved and cared for.
(Prayers of Intercession)

(Evening)
Receive, my God, my thanksgiving for bringing me to the close of this day.
(Prayers of Intercession)

What a glorious assurance from Christ: I in Christ and Christ in me.

(Morning)
I will resolve to keep your commandment of love every moment of the day, O God, with your help. Thanks be to Christ. Amen.

(Evening)
If I failed to keep your commandment, grant me your peace anyway, forgiving God! Thanks be to God. Amen.

MONDAY, MAY 10
(Read Psalm 68:1–10)

(Morning)
God, you are here in my home and have comforted me while I slept.
Be with me now as I begin my day, and help me to be jubilant
as I thank and praise you all this day.

(Evening)
God, I am home again, here and in you.
Thank you for welcoming me home and helping me to feel at home in you.

God, in you we find a dwelling place, a home you have provided for all in need and in desolation. But what of our enemies and yours? Do you, as the psalmist says, drive them away to parch and perish? How would you have us relate to those wicked and rebellious, to those who hate you, O God? Are we ourselves ever among these rejected? We know you care for orphans, widows, and prisoners. Who are we in your sight? Rain your abundance on us all, caring God, and help us all be jubilant with joy.

(Morning)
Open my heart, O God, to friends and enemies alike.
Help me to admit my own sin and rebellion against you.
Fill me with compassion for all your people.
(Prayers of Intercession)

(Evening)
In your goodness, O God, I have found a dwelling.
Help me welcome all your people home.
(Prayers of Intercession)

"God gives the desolate a home to live in."
(Pray the Prayer of Our Savior.)

(Morning)
Help me to sing your praises, O God, all this day long. In the name of the Christ. Amen

(Evening)
Restore in me your heritage, O God, and bless me as I rest in you. In the name of the Christ. Amen.

TUESDAY, MAY 11
(Read John 17:1–5)

(Morning)
Dear God, this is an hour of glory, as is every hour, to praise and honor you.

(Evening)
Dear God, I have finished today's work as one way of glorifying you.

Glory, glory hallelujah! Glory be to you, God! This day and every day, I will try to give you the glory. We hear Jesus praying to you that he has given you glory, and that he needs your glory. Like Jesus, I try to give to you all the glory, literally "praise and weight," by doing the work you give me. Thank you for showing me your glory, as you did for Jesus, in light that streams from heaven afar, in angelic songs from realms of glory, in your glorious love and truth. Change me, God, from glory into glory.

(Morning)
Ever-loving God, let my light so shine today
that all may see you in my work and give you glory.
(Prayers of Intercession)

(Evening)
May I continue to grow in your light and truth, Savior God,
and to share those gifts with others.
(Prayers of Intercession)

"And this is eternal life, that they may know you, the only true God."
(Pray the Prayer of Our Savior.)

(Morning)
May I know you, the only true God, and Jesus Christ whom you have sent. In the name of the Christ. Amen.

(Evening)
May I know your eternal life, given through the Christ to all who are Christ's. In the name of the Christ. Amen.

WEDNESDAY, MAY 12
(Read John 17:6–11)

(Morning)
God, I begin this day believing Jesus' prayer that I am yours
and that I was given by you to Jesus, to keep your Word.

(Evening)
God, I have felt today your promise and protection, one with you and one with
all. For these and all your gifts, I give you humble thanks.

God of all, God of many, God of one; in you there is no me or my, or yours
or mine, or we or they. Rather, as we read today, "all mine are yours and
yours are mine," "we are one," "may they be one." With Jesus, I pray that
we all may be one; with you, with Jesus, with one another, with the world,
with the universe, with your Word, with your name, with your truth—all
one! May it be so and "yours are mine," "we are one."

(Morning)
God of one and God of all, help me truly to be one with you
and with all your people.
(Prayers of Intercession)

(Evening)
God of one and God of all, may I know you and make your name known.
(Prayers of Intercession)

"So that they may be one, as we are one."
(Pray for unity.)

(Morning)
Dear God, yours is the glory. May I
know and do your will and so be
changed from glory into glory. In the
name of the Christ. Amen.

(Evening)
As I enter into your peaceful night,
may I rest, at one with you. In the
name of the Christ. Amen.

THURSDAY, MAY 13
(Read Acts 1:6–14)

(Morning)
God of time and timeless God, I call this the beginning of my day,
but I know that you set your own time and periods of authority.
Help me follow your timing today.

(Evening)
God of time and timeless God, help me look back over my day and see
you in it. Help me to remember the surprises, the delightful times
when life triumphed over death, the great variety of disciples I met.
Thank you for this day filled with your "Acts."

God, you keep surprising us. We want to know what's next—dates, places, plans. But you give us a surprising Savior who defies death, rises from the grave, and now ascends into heaven. We want explanations, but you keep giving us mysterious messengers. Help us to be like those first disciples. Help us to watch and wait, to stay together, to devote ourselves to prayer. Help us to be as in one room with the great diversity of your many disciples. Help us to be ready for the power of the Holy Spirit. And keep surprising us.

(Morning)
Help me this day to look out for strangers, O God, to listen to them,
to help them, to believe them, to welcome them.
(Prayers of Intercession)

(Evening)
May I spend these last minutes of this day like your apostles
and women, constantly devoted to prayer.
(Prayers of Intercession)

**"You will receive power when the Holy Spirit has come upon you;
and you will be my witnesses to the ends of the earth."**
(Pray for empowerment.)

(Morning)
Holy Spirit, empower me to witness to you, in all times and places. Allow your Spirit to ascend in and through me, to the ends of the earth. In the name of the Christ. Amen.

(Evening)
God, our world is like that small upstairs room in Jerusalem, filled with a great variety of men and women, waiting in expectation for you. I am thankful to be part of this band. Help me and all my "roommates" to know your presence and your will. In the name of the Christ. Amen.

FRIDAY, MAY 14
(Read 1 Peter 4:12–14)

(Morning)
Dear God, this day seems so new and hopeful. I do not want to hear about fiery ordeals and suffering. But I know you will be with me all the day, perhaps even especially in the hard times. Open me to all of it and to you.

(Evening)
Dear God, bless me with the spirit of glory,
which is your Spirit. I can feel it resting on me.

God, I'd rather have joy without any suffering. I'd prefer to be blessed without being reviled. Couldn't I skip the fiery ordeals and go right to your spirit of glory? Shouldn't my faith make my life easier? No, I know that faith is not a prize but a way of life. You have been present to me in the midst of my own fiery ordeals, in many valleys of the shadow of death, deep suffering, and shame. Help me with strength and patience in the midst of these times of trial, so that I can experience again that yours are the power and the glory and the blessing, forever and ever.

(Morning)
To share in Christ's sufferings helps me shout for joy
in Christ's glory. May I share in the sufferings of all people,
so that Christ's glory may be revealed.
(Prayers of Intercession)

(Evening)
Thank you, God, for calling me "beloved."
(Prayers of Intercession)

I now pray the prayer that Jesus taught us.
(Pray the Prayer of Our Savior.)

(Morning)
Even in my suffering, I know I am never alone. Thank you, God, for that comfort and company. In the name of the Christ. Amen.

(Evening)
May God bless me and keep me. May God's face shine upon me and be gracious unto me. May God lift the divine countenance upon me and give me peace, this night and every night. In the name of the Christ. Amen.

SATURDAY, MAY 15
(Read 1 Peter 5:6–14)

(Morning)
O God, as I begin this day, I can already feel the anxieties building.
Help me cast them on you, because you care for me.

(Evening)
O God, turn my thoughts this night to my brothers and sisters
in all the world, many of whom are suffering as I am suffering.
Help me to know that you, God of all grace, support us all.

This is hard advice, O God, for this modern American; to humble myself under your mighty hand, to cast all my anxiety on you, to discipline myself, to resist the devil. Am I supposed to accept suffering just because many of my brothers and sisters in all the world are suffering? Help me, caring God, to embrace these words of faith, to embrace this style of faith, to embrace this huge suffering family of faith of which I am a part. I pray that you will restore me, support me, strengthen and establish me and all your people, to your eternal glory.

(Morning)
May I this day be disciplined and alert.
(Prayers of Intercession)

(Evening)
Even as I prepare for sleep, help me resist evil and remain steadfast in my faith.
(Prayers of Intercession)

"The God of all grace will restore, support, strengthen, and establish you."
(Pray for grace.)

(Morning)
God, you have called me to your eternal glory in Christ. Help me answer your call, this day and every day. In the name of the Christ. Amen.

(Evening)
God, to you be the power, forever and ever. In the name of the Christ. Amen.

SUNDAY, MAY 16
(Read Psalm 68:32–35)

(Morning)
Creator God, I begin this day with a song, a psalm.
And with that poet of old, I sing to you, raising my voice in praise.

(Evening)
Creator God, as I began this day with a song,
so I end it by listening—listening for your mighty voice and blessing you.

Like the psalmist of old, O God, I stand in awe of your power and might.
Even as I feel your gentleness and comfort, so also you are to me the mightiest force of all. You are majesty. You are power. You are strength. You are
an awesome presence with a mighty voice. You do not stand still but ride,
strong and fast, over all the ancient heavens! Help me to honor and bless
your fierceness, awesome God, to sing aloud your praises with all the realms.
Help me not to fear your power but to respect it, remembering that you
share it with us, your people. Blessed be God.

(Morning)
You are God of earth and sky. Help me today to honor all of your creation.
(Prayers of Intercession)

(Evening)
Many are your sanctuaries, O God, in all your creation—those built by your
hands and those of human hands. Today was a special day for sanctuaries.
Thanks for being in so many holy places.
(Prayers of Intercession)

"Awesome is God."
(Pray the Prayer of Our Savior.)

(Morning)
Sing to God, sing praises to the God
of Israel! In the name of the Christ.
Amen.

(Evening)
God gives power and strength to the
people; blessed be God! In the name of
the Christ. Amen.

MONDAY, MAY 17
(Read 1 Corinthians 12:12–13)

(Morning)
Eternal God of creation, I thank you for this day, which you alone have made.
Open my mind and my heart, that I may be receptive and responsive to the
guidance and power you provide through your Holy Spirit.

(Evening)
Eternal God of creation, I give you thanks and praise for your presence as I
journeyed through this day. Thank you for teaching me the universal language
of love, which you teach through the Holy Spirit.

Loving God, because you chose to be among us and to experience what it
is to be human, you know the many challenges we face. Most often it is
difficult to demonstrate the love of Christ in a world that judges me by the
color of my skin. The diversity of the human family you created is a reality, yet we have allowed it to be a stumbling block to the fulfillment of
your domain. Sometimes I want to withdraw and associate only with those
who look like me. Help me never to lose the hope of knowing that one day
all of your people will hear and speak the common language of love and
unity. May your will be done on earth as it is in heaven.

(Morning)
God, you are the Giver and Sustainer of my life.
Help me to be an instrument of your love and justice. Anoint my speaking
and my hearing, that I might be a blessing to someone today.
(Prayers of Intercession)

(Evening)
Eternal God, help me to realize that while I am a unique creation,
I am also one with all you have created. Give me the courage
to act justly and responsibly toward your creation.
(Prayers of Intercession)

**Most gracious God, help me to realize that when I look
into the eyes of another, I will see a reflection of myself.**

(Morning)
God who is Creator and Sustainer of
life, help me never to underestimate
the power of the Holy Spirit. Help me
to sustain the conviction of things not
yet seen. In Jesus' name I pray. Amen.

(Evening)
I give you thanks and praise for all I
have done that has pleased you, O
God; for I can do nothing for you
without you. In Jesus' name I pray.
Amen.

TUESDAY, MAY 18
(Read 1 Corinthians 12:3b–12)

(Morning)
God of liberation, truly this is a day that you have made.
Help me to realize today that all things work for the good
of those who love you and are called according to your purpose.

(Evening)
God of liberation, I never cease to be amazed at the many ways
you speak your liberating Word to your children.
Thank you for looking beyond our pettiness and jealousy to meet our needs.

God, I'm always puzzled when members of a congregation belonging to a given denomination do not celebrate with joy and thanksgiving when a person joins the church. Didn't this person become a part of the body of Christ in response to the preached Word, ministering community, or prophetic witness? Should we have the attitude that "we lost one" because someone did not join "our church"? Or should we have an attitude of joy because yet another has come to Christ? Do we really believe it when we read, "For just as the body is one and has many members, and all the members of the body, though many, are one body, so it is with Christ"?

(Morning)
Loving God, thank you for the many ways your Spirit manifests itself through persons from every walk of life. Help me to celebrate and not to condemn the creative and grace-filled ways you draw your children unto you.
(Prayers of Intercession)

(Evening)
God, I give you the praise, honor, and glory because in
and through you all things are possible.
(Prayers of Intercession)

When someone else in our family of faith does a good thing, we should give God the glory and remember the message, "It's all good."

(Morning)
God of grace, whenever and wherever I see evidence of the fruit of your Spirit, help me to give you the praise. In Jesus' name I pray. Amen.

(Evening)
God of love, throughout the day you spoke to me, through persons and events. In spite of me, you continue to reach out and draw me near. Thank you! In Jesus' name I pray. Amen.

WEDNESDAY, MAY 19
(Read Psalm 104:27–34, 35b)

(Morning)
Creator God, this is the day that you have made, and I rejoice
and am glad in it. Truly you are the one and only God,
and above you there is no other. Only you are worthy of my praise.

(Evening)
Creator God, you are the Potter, and I am the clay. Mold me,
God of creation, so that I might be a vessel of your light.
Shape and use me so that I might live harmoniously with your creation.

God, help me to learn from your children, the indigenous peoples of Africa, Asia, and the Americas, what many of us who claim to follow Christ have yet to learn. These people traditionally understood themselves as not having dominion over the earth. They, however, saw themselves as intimately and inextricably related to the earth and all creation. Theirs was (and, in many cases, continues to be) a commitment to provide reverence, respect, and responsible maintenance for the earth and all creation.

(Morning)
God of liberation, help me to embody those values of my ancestors who tried to live in harmony with your creation. Help me to love the neighbor who has not come to understand the responsibility of maintaining the gifts of your creation.
(Prayers of Intercession)

(Evening)
Merciful God, before time was measured, you set into motion
the rhythm of the universe as perfect love.
Order our steps that we might walk in sync with the rhythm of your love.
(Prayers of Intercession)

Holy Spirit, help me to pray the prayer of my greatest Ancestor.
(Pray the Prayer of Our Savior.)

(Morning)
Today, loving God, help me to express
my love for you by loving your
creation. In Jesus' name I pray. Amen.

(Evening)
God of love and justice, all praise,
honor, and glory belong to you. You
and you alone are worthy of such
praise. In Jesus' name I pray. Amen.

THURSDAY, MAY 20
(Read John 20:19–23)

(Morning)
Merciful and gracious God, when I let you down, I often try to run from you.
Thank you for not allowing a place to exist where I can hide from you.

(Evening)
Merciful and gracious God, thank you for the gift of the Holy Spirit which
convicts, comforts, challenges, counsels, changes, and cleanses.

God, you are a radical lover. You create and re-create me, rear me, nurture
me, feed me, teach me, suffer for me, and even die for me. In return, I have
bowed down to other gods, squandered your gifts, done things I had no
business doing, and failed to do things I should have done. I even dis-
owned you in your direst hour. Yet, when I was trying to hide from you,
you found me and said, "Peace be with you." You love me more than I love
myself. Your love has no end. Nothing can separate me from your love.
You love me unconditionally. God, you are my radical Lover.

(Morning)
Eternal and gracious God, I don't have to love you or serve you. But because of
your radical love for me, I do love you and seek only to serve you this day.
(Prayers of Intercession)

(Evening)
Bless me, God of love, to love others as you have loved and promise to love me.
(Prayers of Intercession)

**I am not what I ought to be, but I thank the living God
that I am not what I used to be.**

(Morning)
Spirit of the living God, fall afresh on
me; melt, mold, fill, and use me.
Spirit of the living God, fall fresh on
me. In Jesus' name I pray. Amen.

(Evening)
Merciful God, you continue to look
beyond my faults and see my needs.
Help me to walk in a love such as this.
In Jesus' name I pray. Amen.

FRIDAY, MAY 21
(Read Acts 2:1–21)

(Morning)
Eternal God and perfect Giver, I give you praise,
for you are a faithful God, a God whose promises are never broken.
On this day, you are the solid rock upon which I will stand.

(Evening)
Eternal God and perfect Giver, thank you for the perfect gift.
I praise you for whatever good thing I thought, said, or did this day.

Indeed, God, you are the Giver of every good and perfect gift. The greatest gift you have bestowed upon me is yourself, in Christ Jesus and through your Holy Spirit. The giving of this perfect gift is what you promised, and you offer it continually every second of every day. No matter what I do, say, or think, you extend the perfect gift in perfect love, and you give it unconditionally. Over the years, some have tried to frighten me into believing in you. But it is not fear that continues to transform my heart; it is your perfect love, as given to me in and through Jesus the Christ and the Holy Spirit.

(Morning)
God, you are perfect Love. Bless me today to be a vessel through which the light of your love will shine. Bless me to be a blessing.
(Prayers of Intercession)

(Evening)
O Spirit of the living God, fall fresh upon those who have been known to drift away. Fall anew upon those who have not known you or your perfect love.
(Prayers of Intercession)

Whom have I loved unconditionally today?

(Morning)
Merciful God, you have saved me, and now you send me. Help me to love the least of these, my sisters and brothers, in the way you have loved and continue to love me. In Jesus' name I pray. Amen.

(Evening)
God of liberation, you died for me. Help me be clear about what I am asking of you when I ask for help in loving my neighbor as you have loved me. Let your Holy Spirit continually fall fresh upon me. In Jesus' name I pray. Amen.

SATURDAY, MAY 22
(Read Psalm 104:24–26, 35b)

(Morning)
O God of creation, how great you are!
You are the Creator of the universe and all therein.
You are the Giver and Sustainer of all life,
and only you are worthy to be praised!

(Evening)
O God of creation, thank you for all that you provide for me
in and through your creation—much more than I am aware of.
Help me to increase my knowledge of the healing gifts within your creation.

God, so often I get caught up in the busyness of day-to-day living in the city. Days come and go without my taking time to behold the beauty of your creation. A ride in the country, a picnic in the park, a long walk on the beach, sitting on the shore of a lake and watching a sunset, gazing upon a starlit sky from the lights of the city—these are but a few of the simple and free joys of life of which I often deprive myself. Your creation is so full of the songs of nature, which sing your praises. Open my eyes to the beauty of your creation. Help me to pause and take the time to receive and enjoy your free gifts.

(Morning)
God of creation, help me to be mindful that many live in conditions
that make it difficult, if not nearly impossible, to enjoy the beauty of your
creation. Help me to be sensitive and responsive to their needs.
(Prayers of Intercession)

(Evening)
Eternal God, help me to be increasingly aware of my interrelatedness
with your creation. Help me to interact with it in ways
that are pleasing and acceptable in your sight.
(Prayers of Intercession)

**Melody Maker, order my steps in your Word,
so that I may walk in harmony with the rhythm of your creation.**

(Morning)
Have your way with me, most high God. Today, help me to experience your creation in new and profound ways. In Christ's name. Amen.

(Evening)
Gracious God, thank you for the gift of this day. Help me always to take time to behold the wonder and beauty of your creation. In Christ's name. Amen.

SUNDAY, MAY 23
(Read Acts 2:14–21)

(Morning)
Eternal God, thank you for last night's lying down and this morning's rising.
I give you the praise! Surely this is the day you have made.
I am rejoicing, and I am glad in it!

(Evening)
Eternal God, thank you for miracles seen and unseen. On this day, I give you praise. Help me to receive and be empowered by the Holy Spirit, so I may be an instrument in the building of your domain on earth.

God, you work in mysterious ways and have wonders to perform. You never fail to amaze me in the way you move in and through the Holy Spirit: the prophetic word spoken through a friend or stranger; wisdom spoken through a child who seems to transcend his/her years; the friend, family member, or guest who unexpectedly walks down the aisle during worship to profess her/his belief in your child, Jesus; the empowerment of a disempowered person or group; the healing of an ostensibly terminally ill relative that defies scientific explanation. These are just some of the ways you move, often unexpectedly, in and through your Holy Spirit. Indeed, all things are possible through Christ, who strengthens me.

(Morning)
God of love, help me to be open to the limitless possibilities of your power.
Bless me to be an instrument of love, meaning, and hope to your people.
(Prayers of Intercession)

(Evening)
Merciful and liberating God, the numbers of the hopeless seem to be increasing.
Pour out your Holy Spirit on those who are forced to the margins of our society.
(Prayers of Intercession)

The appreciation of a gift is measured by how it is used.

(Morning)
God of power, help me to walk today by faith and not by sight. Help me to demonstrate in my life my belief that all things are possible through you. In Jesus' name I pray. Amen.

(Evening)
God, again today you gave me the gift of the Holy Spirit. You did so yesterday, and you will tomorrow. I thank you for today and stand on your promise of eternal life, which is forever my tomorrow. In Jesus' name I pray. Amen.

144

MONDAY, MAY 24
(Read Psalm 8:1–2)

(Morning)
This morning I rise, anticipating new beginnings.

(Evening)
I sleep in the rich darkness of night, created by our Creator.

Creator God, you who gave form to nothingness, help me to form my prayers today. Help me to concentrate on your purpose for me in the midst of this creation. Help me to understand the sense you make from confusion.

(Morning)
As God swept winds of change over the face of the waters,
may God's presence sweep over me as I pray.
(Prayers of Intercession)

(Evening)
As God separated light from dark,
may God separate my inner discord from discernment.
(Prayers of Intercession)

"And God saw that it was good."

(Morning)
Thank you, God, for creating a place for me in the boundless universe of your love. In Jesus' name. Amen.

(Evening)
Thank you, God, as you gave form to my day and rest to my night. In Jesus' name. Amen.

TUESDAY, MAY 25
(Read Psalm 8:3–4)

(Morning)
How great is God! How great is God, who gives me the gift of this morning!

(Evening)
How great is God! How great is God, who gives me the gift of this evening!

God, my mind reels as I meditate on your power and planning. I am humbled when I realize the same God who creates all that I eat, drink, or see is able to hear my prayers. I thank you, God, for numbering all the seeds on earth yet acknowledging the seeds of my heart and inner longings.

(Morning)
May my meditations be as pleasing in your sight
as were those first fruits of creation.
(Prayers of Intercession)

(Evening)
May my prayers find your Holy Spirit,
as those first-created birds found their wings.
(Prayers of Intercession)

In awe of your creation I pray.

(Morning)
O God, may you be pleased with me today as you were first pleased with creation. In Jesus' name. Amen.

(Evening)
O God, I hope you found in me all that was pleasing in your sight. In Jesus' name. Amen.

WEDNESDAY, MAY 26
(Read Genesis 1:1–2:4a)

(Morning)
God, may you bless my day this morning as you blessed the seventh day.

(Evening)
God, I prepare for my rest, cradled in your care.

Creator God, in your image I exist on this earth. In your image I establish my relationships with all of your creation. In your image I realize my potential to be as you would have me be.

(Morning)
Create in me the desire to do your will, gracious God.
Hold me as I kneel in the dawn of another day,
seeking your grace and love.
(Prayers of Intercession)

(Evening)
You held me in your compassion today, God, and I praise you! Give voice to my prayers; give voice to the kindness I seek for others.
(Prayers of Intercession)

"So God created humankind in God's image, in the image of God, God created them; male and female God created them."

(Morning)
O God, remind me that I am wonderfully, lovingly, and powerfully made. In Jesus' name. Amen.

(Evening)
O God, assure me that I am wonderfully, lovingly, and gracefully made. In Jesus' name. Amen.

THURSDAY, MAY 27
(Read Psalm 8:5–6)

(Morning)
Sovereign God, holy God, my soul sings your praises as I rise!

(Evening)
Sovereign God, holy God, I contemplate your love this evening.

Gratitude to you, O God, floods within me! Gratitude and wonder at the benevolence of you gives me pause. You, the same God who established the stars and the moon, take time to hear my prayer. You, the same God who breathes the first breath in the mouths of babes, consider me and all I bear each day. Glorious God! Wonderful God! Infinite God!

(Morning)
Sovereign God, touch me with generosity this morning.
Prepare my heart, my soul, and my mind for prayer.
(Prayers of Intercession)

(Evening)
Sovereign God, touch me with compassion this evening.
Prepare my heart, my soul, and my mind for prayer.
(Prayers of Intercession)

"O God, our Sovereign, how majestic is your name in all the earth!"

(Morning)
Thank you, God, for preparing me for this day in ways unknown. In Jesus' name. Amen.

(Evening)
Thank you, God, for preparing my rest at the end of another day. In Jesus' name. Amen.

FRIDAY, MAY 28
(Read Psalm 8:7–9)

(Morning)
God, of the many miracles you have made,
I thank you for the miracle of today.

(Evening)
God, as dusk approaches, I approach you.

Questions overwhelm me, God—questions about your aims and deeds with humanity. How is it possible that you created humanity and, even with our imperfections, allow us to claim salvation through Jesus Christ? How is it possible that even with our destruction of parts of your creation—the seas, the lands, the air—you still love us? I trust that love now, O God. I trust your love right now.

(Morning)
Gracious God, center me in your foundation with prayer.
(Prayers of Intercession)

(Evening)
Gracious God, center me in your foundation with prayer.
(Prayers of Intercession)

"O God, our Sovereign, how majestic is your name in all the earth!"

(Morning)
Thank you, God, for providing answers to all my questions and worries, even questions I have yet to utter in my heart. In Jesus' name. Amen.

(Evening)
Whisper in my ears words of comfort, God. Whisper in my soul that I am loved by you. In Jesus' name. Amen.

SATURDAY, MAY 29
(Read 2 Corinthians 13:11–13)

(Morning)
Caring God, the love of Jesus Christ is mine today!

(Evening)
Caring God, the grace of God is mine this night!

God, just as the apostle Paul cautioned the early church members to live in peace, I remind myself to follow the teachings of your child, the Christ. Would not the world be a better place if we did indeed treat one another with respect? Would not the world be a better place if we could respect ourselves as your creations?

(Morning)
Respecting all that is holy, I seek the communion of the Holy Spirit in prayer.
(Prayers of Intercession)

(Evening)
Direct me, God, in all I may say to you in prayer.
(Prayers of Intercession)

"Live in peace."

(Morning)
O God, let me strive to live in peace this morning, afternoon, and evening. In Jesus' name. Amen.

(Evening)
Dearest, gracious God, thank you for allowing me the attempt to live in peace today. In Jesus' name. Amen.

SUNDAY, MAY 30
(Read Matthew 28:16–20)

(Morning)
Loving and understanding God, remove all doubt from my heart today.

(Evening)
Loving and understanding God, refresh my spirit at close of day.

How do we get ready for special events? Do we make lists, check the calendar, or engage in conferences with friends, neighbors, and coworkers? In all our hustle and bustle, did we stop to converse with you, God? Or are we like the remaining eleven disciples before the great commission: we know Jesus is standing there, but still we doubt.

(Morning)
Allow me, dear God, to set my doubts and fears before you, trusting that through the Holy Spirit you may work a miracle with me today.
(Prayers of Intercession)

(Evening)
My inner doubts fade like the setting sun;
I rejoice in your presence, O God, again.
(Prayers of Intercession)

"And remember, I am with you always, to the end of the age."

(Morning)
Thank you, God, for replacing doubt with certainty and conviction. In Jesus' name. Amen.

(Evening)
What a blessing you have been to me today, God. I call out your name with gratitude. In Jesus' name. Amen.

MONDAY, MAY 31
(Read Genesis 12:1–9)

(Morning)
God of all blessings, I set out this day led by your Spirit
and open to all your blessings. Make me a blessing, too.

(Evening)
God of all blessings, you make and keep promises;
so I place my life in your loving care.

Wonderful, surprising, faithful God, you call me from the familiar and the
comfortable to journey into the unknown. Sometimes fear immobilizes me.
Sometimes the complacency of the comfortable keeps me from answering.
Yet, when Abram and Sarai heeded your call, they were blessed and were a
blessing to others. Just so, lead me. Help me to trust you, so I may follow
where you would lead.

(Morning)
Faithful God, you set before me a path that will lead to blessings—
not only for me but for others. Give me strength for the journey.
(Prayers of Intercession)

(Evening)
Faithful God, you have laid claim on my life, given me a journey
and a promise. May I journey on—moment by moment,
day by day, stage by stage, ever faithful.
(Prayers of Intercession)

"I will make of you a great nation, and I will bless you."
*(Sing or read aloud "God Made from One Blood"
or another familiar hymn.)*

(Morning)
The journey today may be into the
unknown intimacy of those among my
own family members, friends, and
colleagues. May all I do honor you. In
Jesus' name I pray. Amen.

(Evening)
Let me rest in you tonight, O God, so
my strength is renewed. This day has
moved me one stage closer to doing
your will. In Jesus' name I pray.
Amen.

TUESDAY, JUNE 1
(Read Psalm 33:1–12)

(Morning)
Creator God, I awaken to a new day full of possibilities
to experience your steadfast love.

(Evening)
Creator God, throughout this day I have praised you—
not just for what you give me but
because of who you are and what you have done.

Powerful, just, and upright God, you have called worlds into being by your glorious Word. Everywhere I look, I see your work. Everywhere I go, I am in the midst of your stupendous creation. Everything around me reminds me of you. Bring into being new worlds of possibility for me to serve you and your people. Just for now, let me stand before you in awe.

(Morning)
Speak, and the world will know justice and mercy.
May I be, with you, a cocreator of a world of peace and justice.
(Prayers of Intercession)

(Evening)
Speak, and the whole earth is full of your steadfast love.
Give me strength always to know and share your love.
(Prayers of Intercession)

"God loves righteousness and justice."
(Sing or read aloud "Sing Praise to God" or another familiar hymn.)

(Morning)	(Evening)
Sometimes our human plans are frustrated by your wisdom. Guide me so that all I say or do will be based on your Word, which is upright and faithful. In Christ's name. Amen.	Grant to me and to all your people the happiness that comes by knowing and accepting who you are, O Sovereign One. You alone are God. In Christ's name. Amen.

WEDNESDAY, JUNE 2
(Read Psalm 33:1–12)

(Morning)
O God, Creator of harmony and rhythm, I awaken to a day
that you have made. I will rejoice and sing a new song of praise to you.

(Evening)
O God, Creator of melody and rhyme, I have enjoyed this day that you have
made. I sing soft hallelujahs as I thank you and place my trust in you.

Mighty Sovereign, Ruler of the universe, when I come before you, I am
overwhelmed by your majesty, judged by your holiness, challenged by your
justice, and humbled by your love. When your mighty deeds of creation
and deliverance are recited, I feel like singing. Let the instruments play,
the voices sing, the hands clap, and the feet dance in celebration of who
you are. Yet there are times when I do not feel like singing. Still, grant me
the strength and the will to continue steadfastly in my love song to you.

(Morning)
Keep me in tune and in harmony throughout this day.
(Prayers of Intercession)

(Evening)
Having sung this measure, let me rest appropriately, so I can sing again.
(Prayers of Intercession)

"Sing to God a new song."
(Sing or read aloud "Glory, Glory, Hallelujah" or another familiar hymn.)
(Prayers of Intercession)

(Morning)
Grant me the skill to sing in harmony
with your will, the courage to sing in
counterpoint to injustice, and the
alertness to follow you, my Leader.
Thanks be to Christ. Amen.

(Evening)
The new songs bring me excitement
and challenge. The old songs bring
comfort and strength. Keep me
singing songs of love, peace, and joy.
Thanks be to Christ. Amen.

THURSDAY, JUNE 3
(Read Romans 4:13–25)

(Morning)
O God of glory and grace, you have promised to be my God
even before I opened my eyes. Now that I am awake, let me trust you.

(Evening)
O God of glory and grace, you have called into being many opportunities to
serve you. I offer them in honor and glory to you.

Creative, amazing, and promise-keeping God, you made guarantees to
Abram and Sarai that they would be the parents of many people of faith.
Yet the circumstances in which they lived seemed hopeless. How can it be?
Help me, O God, to believe that you "call into existence the things that do
not exist." Let my faith never waver, my hope never falter, my love never
fail, my life never end. If they do, be there for me.

(Morning)
O God of hope, help me choose to be hopeful.
(Prayers of Intercession)

(Evening)
O God of hope, help me know that hope is a given
when I believe that you raised Jesus from the dead.
(Prayers of Intercession)

**"Faith will be reckoned to us who believe in the One
who raised Jesus from the dead."**
*(Sing or read aloud "Let Us Hope When Hope Seems Hopeless"
or another familiar hymn.)*

(Morning)
Grace-filled God, I am so thankful
that my relationship with you depends
not on my goodness but on your
mercy. Thank you for loving me,
accepting me, calling me, and using
me. In Christ's name. Amen.

(Evening)
Grace-giving God, when the barrenness and frailty of my life stare me in
the face, I am so thankful that you are
a God who can do what you promise.
In Christ's name. Amen.

FRIDAY, JUNE 4
(Read Romans 4:13–25)

(Morning)
O life-giving God, create in me new vigor and vitality for the day that lies
ahead. I seek to bring affirmation and blessings to all whom I meet.

(Evening)
O life-giving God, through joy and sorrow, you have been a God of grace and
mercy. Grant me now the peace of resting in you.

Awesome, compassionate, merciful God, I struggle with all the *should*s,
*ought*s, and *must*s of life. I struggle with my faith and my ability to trust. I
struggle with my concern and compassion for others. You have given promises, yet I am slow to trust. You have given examples of unwavering faith,
yet I forget so soon. Help me to know that it is not my keeping your law
which creates your love, but your love which prompts my life of faith.

(Morning)
O faithful God, help me spend this day in the consciousness of your presence.
(Prayers of Intercession)

(Evening)
O faithful God, help me know the promises of your faithfulness were not for
Abram and Sarai only. They are also for me, right now, here in this place.
(Prayers of Intercession)

"No distrust made him waiver concerning the promise of God."
*(Sing or read aloud "If You But Trust in God to Guide You" or another
familiar hymn.)*

(Morning)
Through Christ, my offenses are
removed, my sin forgiven, my life
made new. Now, grant me grace to
accept your gifts. In the name of Jesus.
Amen.

(Evening)
It is hard to enumerate all I have
inherited, O God. Make me a faithful
steward of all your goodness. In the
name of Jesus. Amen.

SATURDAY, JUNE 5
(Read Matthew 9:9–13, 18–26)

(Morning)
O seeking God, through Jesus you call me to follow you.
In the midst of my every day you seek me to be your disciple.

(Evening)
O seeking God, in the marketplace, at the dinner table,
in the midst of conflict and dispute, you call me to be merciful.

Astonishing, seeking, forgiving God, you care about the lost and lonely.
You love the detestable, welcome the outcast. In your incredible compassion, you have scandalized the holy people by even calling me. You give mercy, and you desire mercy. Free me from prejudice and hate. Tear down walls that separate. Make me well—not to be better than others, but because I need to be touched by the seeking Savior.

(Morning)
O welcoming God, let me be at home in your presence.
May I be open and welcoming to all your people.
(Prayers of Intercession)

(Evening)
O welcoming God, let me understand that I am not saved
until I become a savior to others.
(Prayers of Intercession)

**"I desire mercy, not sacrifice.
For I have come to call not the righteous but sinners."**
*(Sing or read aloud "Your Ways Are Not Our Own"
or another familiar hymn.)*

(Morning)
If it is mercy you desire, then it is mercy I want to give. Do not allow me to think too highly of myself or too lowly of someone else. With your love, may I build a bridge and not a wall. In Jesus' name. Amen.

(Evening)
Well, God, you did it again! You led me through a day in which I discovered my need to love and be loved. In Jesus' name. Amen.

SUNDAY, JUNE 6
(Read Matthew 9:9–13, 18–26)

(Morning)
O healing God, I need the touch of Christ the healer to make me whole.
Let me touch the hem of Christ's garment and I shall be healed.

(Evening)
O healing God, in the face of human agony, brokenness,
and sorrow, touch my soul and make me whole.

Holy, healing, hopeful God, everywhere I look—both inside myself and around me—I see pain, sickness, sorrow, and death. There seems to be an epidemic of grief in our world. Sometimes it has happened because of my insensitivity, sometimes because I am a part of a society that is broken; sometimes life is just plain hurtful and difficult. But today you showed me that you want me well, whole, and alive. Help me believe, act, pray, and speak so as to allow your healing power to work. Even if the symptoms of my dis-ease cannot be removed, grant me at-oneness with you, which is the healing I most need.

(Morning)
O healing Christ, may my life be a source more of healing than of pain.
(Prayers of Intercession)

(Evening)
O healing Christ, let me be a caregiver while you are the One who cures.
(Prayers of Intercession)

"Take heart, daughter, your faith has made you well."
*(Sing or read aloud "If I Have Been the Source of Pain, O God"
or another familiar hymn.)*

(Morning)
O God, you are the Creator of life. Touch my soul with Christ's life-giving Spirit. In Jesus' name I pray. Amen.

(Evening)
O God, you are the Source of life. Heal me in body, mind, spirit, and in all my relationships. In Jesus' name I pray. Amen.

MONDAY, JUNE 7
(Read Genesis 18:1–15)

(Morning)
Gracious and loving God, this is the day that you have made.
I resolve to rejoice and be glad in it. May my joy be contagious,
uplifting and encouraging to others I encounter.

(Evening)
Gracious and loving God, I commit my life to you,
asking that you cause me both to be blessed and to be a blessing,
as I ever strive to follow your Spirit's leading.

I thank you, O God, for your many promises to bless us with well-being in every aspect of our lives. For as we delight ourselves in you, we often find that you not only meet our needs but also grant us the desires of our hearts. You promised Abram and Sarai a longed-for child in their old age, assuring them that nothing is too hard for you. Help us to internalize the spiritual truth that with you nothing is impossible and with you all things are possible.

(Morning)
Creator God, inspire me with strategies for balancing the many demands of my day in a manner that brings glory to you.
(Prayers of Intercession)

(Evening)
You who are a shelter from the stormy blast, help me to look beyond the needs of "us four and no more," and to open my heart and my home to someone who might need refuge from life's raging winds.
(Prayers of Intercession)

"Do not neglect to show hospitality to strangers, for by doing that some have entertained angels without knowing it."
(Pray the Prayer of Our Savior.)

(Morning)
O God, sharpen my spiritual senses so that I might perceive you doing extraordinary and unusual things in the midst of the ordinary and usual responsibilities of my day. In the matchless and marvelous name of Jesus I pray. Amen.

(Evening)
Gracious God, I retire with the assurance that your divine protection surrounds everyone and everything that concerns me. Let my rest be sweet, for only you can make me dwell in safety. In Jesus' name. Amen.

TUESDAY, JUNE 8
(Read Genesis 21:1–7)

(Morning)
Holy, holy, holy, Sovereign God almighty! Early in the morning my song will rise to you. Keep a song of praise in my heart throughout the day as I work to show my love for you and my sisters and brothers in creation.

(Evening)
Holy, holy, holy, Sovereign God almighty! I settle in after a productive day, grateful for all you helped me to accomplish, for myself and others.

I praise you, O God, for making our dreams reality, even when we have the lost hope of realizing them because they have been deferred for such a long time. The birth of Isaac to the hundred-year-old Abram and the ninety-year-old Sarai lets us know that a promise you make to us is a promise kept. Give us the patience to wait with joyful expectation for the fulfillment of your promises and the grace to accept that these will be fulfilled on your timetable and not ours.

(Morning)
Thank you, all-wise God, for teaching me that necessary delay in the answer to my prayer does not mean you have denied my request.
(Prayers of Intercession)

(Evening)
Gracious God, I often know not what to pray for as I ought. Let your Spirit make intercession for me with groanings that cannot be uttered.
(Prayers of Intercession)

"God is not a human being, that God should lie, or a mortal, that God should change God's mind."
(Pray the Prayer of Our Savior.)

(Morning)	(Evening)
I have renewed hope, O God, that today I will come ever closer to long-held dreams and desires which you have planted in my heart. Grant me the necessary vigor and vitality to tackle all you intend in the pursuit of my goals. In Jesus' name. Amen.	With the night's rest, loving God, bring renewed energy to mount up on eagle's wings, to run and not grow weary, to walk and not faint in the work you have assigned me, to benefit my family and my neighbors near and far. In the name of Jesus Christ. Amen.

WEDNESDAY, JUNE 9
(Read Psalm 116:1–2, 12–19)

(Morning)
O God, I arise with my own plans for the day. May I receive your Spirit's direction and submit my will to yours, so that your agenda becomes mine.

(Evening)
O God, whose gentleness has made me great, I come to the end
of the day with an incredible sense of peace and well-being.
Thank you for the gentle ways you have guided and corrected me today.

What can I render, dear God, for all your many blessings to me? I so often take for granted my five senses, my ease of mobility, your provision of food and comfortable shelter. Most people around the world would be happy to have half of what I possess. In the midst of life's vicissitudes, when tests and trials seem many, teach me to offer the sacrifices of praise and thanksgiving. For when I stop to count my blessings, I realize that they far outnumber the challenges I face.

(Morning)
Help me to pay my vows to you today, loving God,
through faithful stewardship of my time, talent, and treasure,
to help spread your Word and work in the world.
(Prayers of Intercession)

(Evening)
All-wise Creator, when I learn of the death of one of your servants
at ungodly hands, I am comforted by the knowledge that their passing
is precious in your sight. Avenge your martyrs speedily.

**"Because God has inclined an ear unto me,
therefore will I call upon God as long as I live."**
(Pray the Prayer of Our Savior.)

(Morning)
It is so easy in life to reside at the corner of Grumble Boulevard and Complaint Avenue. Help me to look around, O God, to see the more pressing needs of others, so that I might change my address to Thanksgiving Drive and Praise Parkway. In Jesus' wonderful name. Amen.

(Evening)
Thank you, merciful God, that before I call, you have already answered, and while I yet speak, you are hearing. Grant me the confidence that answers to my prayers are on the way. In the blessed name of Christ. Amen.

THURSDAY, JUNE 10
(Read Psalm 100)

(Morning)
O three-in-one God, I will be joyful in you today because there is nothing
I will encounter that you and I together cannot handle.
Help me to reach out to others this day.

(Evening)
O three-in-one God, my sufficiency has been in you today.
Through me, help others to see that you are all they truly need and desire.

You have made us, Creator God, and not we ourselves. Show us the error
of our ways when we think we are self-sufficient and successful through
our own efforts alone. For without you, we are nothing and can do nothing.
Without you, we have no strength, health, power, or opportunity to create
wealth, to render public service, or to do justice. As we walk humbly with
you, teach us that in the absence of true spiritual riches we are rich in
things but poor in spirit. We have eyes but cannot see, ears but cannot hear.
Give us a sense of our true neediness, so that we may have compassion
rather than be judgmental and help others in need.

(Morning)
Merciful God, let your sufficiency be manifest today, especially
in the lives of the most vulnerable among us. May small children,
the elderly, the poor, the battered, and others who are marginalized
in society experience and recognize your loving care.
(Prayers of Intercession)

(Evening)
Renew a right spirit within me, O God, that I might be an instrument of your
love, joy, and peace, within the church gates as well as in the world beyond.
(Prayers of Intercession)

"Fools say in their hearts, 'There is no God.' "
(Pray the Prayer of Our Savior.)

(Morning)
As a sheep in your pasture, I ask that
you lead me, O God, so that I stray not
from your flock or your ways. Help me
to perceive the cunning distortions of
your truth in conventional and societal
wisdom. In Jesus' name. Amen.

(Evening)
Our God, our help in ages past, our
hope for years to come, let me awake
from sleep tomorrow with a
newfound sense of purpose and
hopefulness, assured of your goodness toward me. In the wonderful
name of the Savior. Amen.

FRIDAY, JUNE 11
(Read Romans 5:1–8)

(Morning)
Dear and gracious God, as this new day dawns,
your Spirit reminds me once again of the unmerited favor
you have shown us by Jesus' death and resurrection.
Thank you for forgiveness of sins for all.

(Evening)
Dear and gracious God, make me steadfast and immovable,
always abounding in your love and work.

Teach me, O God, not to despise your chastening. For our tribulations and tests come not to break us but to make us. These experiences build our character and conform us more nearly to the image of Christ—making us more patient, loving, and compassionate. During those periods of our lives when we feel imprisoned, when we are serving time in isolation due to illness or hard times, let us recognize that you intend for the time out of the fray to serve us spiritually rather than for us to serve it.

(Morning)
Even as Christ died for the ungodly and not just for "good" men and women,
cause me to be a blessing today to someone considered untouchable in society.
(Prayers of Intercession)

(Evening)
Merciful God, I encountered some today who wound others intentionally
and continually. Jesus died for us all while we were yet sinners.
Forgive them, for they know not what they do.
(Prayers of Intercession)

**"My brothers and sisters, whenever you face
trials of any kind, consider it nothing but joy."**
(Pray the Prayer of Our Savior.)

(Morning)	(Evening)
Lest I be tempted today to replace attention to the good news of the gospel with carrying out good works in your name, remind me that I am justified by faith. I cannot work my way into heaven, only believe my way in. Through Christ I pray. Amen.	I close my eyes to rest, sorry for my mistakes but grateful for your continued patience with me, O God. You are not through with me! Heavenly Potter, continue to mold my clay as you choose to fashion it. For Jesus' sake. Amen.

SATURDAY, JUNE 12
(Read Matthew 9:35–10:8)

(Morning)
O great Physician, your tender mercies are new every morning.
Thank you for imbuing my life with your compassion for the multitudes.

(Evening)
O great Physician, our world is in need of the healing
that only you can give to individuals, tribes, and nations.
Use me as a source of cure for those who are ailing.

Even as you sent the twelve disciples first to the lost sheep of Israel, their own kind, open my eyes to the mission fields nearby, O God. For those close at hand as well as those abroad often need to feel your touch through my hands. Forgive our tendency to throw a check at a charity or a problem and feel that we have done what you require. You sometimes call us to get our hands dirty through hands-on involvement as we work to heal the hurts and meet the needs of others.

(Morning)
God of abundant provision, freely I have received from you.
Help me to give freely to those in need.
(Prayers of Intercession)

(Evening)
I felt overwhelmed and inadequate today,
dear God, when confronted with all the needs I could not meet.
Send more laborers into your vineyard to minister to a lost and dying world.
(Prayers of Intercession)

"The harvest is plentiful, but the laborers are few."
(Pray the Prayer of Our Savior.)

(Morning)
I go into the world today, gracious God, clear that my spiritual mission is to heal and not hurt, to help and not hinder, to lift the downtrodden rather than to further demoralize them by unfairly blaming them for their situation. Grant me the spiritual power of the twelve to make a difference in the lives of people. In Jesus' name. Amen.

(Evening)
I welcome sleep tonight, O God, as a respite from the cares and demands of the day. Yet I ask that rest would fortify me with new strength and a fresh vision to resume my work on your mission field of souls tomorrow. Through Christ I pray. Amen.

SUNDAY, JUNE 13
(Read Matthew 10:9–23)

(Morning)
O Creator, like David, I was glad when they said unto me,
"Let us go into the house of God." Let me both find and bring joy
in your house of worship this Sabbath day.

(Evening)
O Creator, my life is in your hands. By your Spirit, order my steps,
that I might accomplish what pleases you.

Mighty God, cure me of my fear and timidity in speaking out in your name against the highly placed who use their power and authority to mete out injustice. When I am tried in the courts or councils of the dishonest and corrupt, you have promised to give me words to say on your behalf that will be a witness against them. Help me not to count the cost of fighting your causes, for no sacrifice of mine could ever be as great as Jesus' on the cross of Calvary.

(Morning)
Gracious God, as I prepare to enjoy worship with other members
of the congregation, my prayers are with the sick, the homebound,
and other members of the congregation scattered for your richest of blessings.
(Prayers of Intercession)

(Evening)
God of justice, I lift up prayers of remembrance and thanksgiving for martyrs,
human-rights activists, prisoners of conscience, and others who have paid or
continue to pay the high price of challenging the status quo at your direction.
(Prayers of Intercession)

**"If anyone will not welcome you or listen to your words,
shake off the dust from your feet as you leave that house or town."**
(Pray the Prayer of Our Savior.)

(Morning)
As I hear a fresh word from heaven this day, grant me new resolve, O God, and the necessary holy boldness to do the right thing in the tests I face, despite the criticisms and consequences that might come. In Christ's name. Amen.

(Evening)
In the beauty and richness of worship today, I have been reminded, loving God, of who I am and whose I am. This has created in me a sense of excited anticipation for the week ahead. As I slumber, increase my ebullience of spirit. In Christ's name. Amen.

MONDAY, JUNE 14
(Read Genesis 21:8–14)

(Morning)
Good morning, God! Thank you for keeping me through the night.
Awaken me to your Word as I begin my day.

(Evening)
Good evening, God! Help me step away from the day's cares and toward you
during this special time. Remind me of how my life can be centered in you.

God of grace, my unspoken yearnings and fervently uttered prayers often
focus on seeing your decisive action in my own life or in the affairs of the
world. My innocent hope is that if you act in some dynamic way, the mess
I have helped to create or the disastrous condition of human affairs will be
fixed, once and for all. Yet Abraham and Sarah experienced extraordinary
attention by you, including a pregnancy that ended Sarah's shame and vin-
dicated Abraham's faith. But the birth of Isaac does not fix everything; life
still presents difficult choices. By your grace, O God, may I see my choices
clearly and the way you invited me to follow.

(Morning)
Attune my heart to your bidding, O God, and help me to trust in your way.
(Prayers of Intercession)

(Evening)
Bring to mind, O loving God, those who have walked with me this day.
Hear my prayers for their safety and well-being.
(Prayers of Intercession)

"I give thanks to you, O God, my Sovereign God, with my whole heart"
(repeat silently throughout the day).
(Pray the Prayer of Our Savior.)

(Morning)	(Evening)
Where will you send me this day, O God? Whose voices will call out to me, and which will I answer? Help me to discern your voice and to answer your call. In the name of the Christ I pray. Amen.	Have I heeded your voice this day, my calling and inviting God? Let me rest now, trusting in your love and grace to see me through the night. In the name of the Christ I pray. Amen.

TUESDAY, JUNE 15
(Read Genesis 21:15–21 and Psalm 86:1–10)

(Morning)
O God and Spirit of Life, I hope the morning brings warmth and light,
but I fear that my hopes will not be realized.
Preserve me from desperate circumstances, I pray.

(Evening)
O God and Spirit of Life, as I prepare to close my eyes
and breathe a deep cleansing breath, help me to release
this day's anxieties and be engaged by your calming Spirit.

God, it is not fair! Hagar has only been a dutiful servant. No doubt she
hopes that her son will be blessed by Abraham. But no! Instead, she is cast
out and watches her son waste away, close to death. But what Abraham
will not do, God, you do. Ishmael, too, will become a great nation.

(Morning)
Ever-watchful God, watch over those in desperate circumstances.
Save us and keep us from harm.
(Prayers of Intercession)

(Evening)
Many have cried out to you this day, O God.
All of humanity turns to you, the Source of hope and life.
(Prayers of Intercession)

**"Gladden the soul of your servant, for to you, O my Sovereign,
I lift up my soul" (repeat silently throughout the day).**
(Pray the Prayer of Our Savior.)

(Morning)
O God, open my eyes to what you will provide me, so that I might give to others for their well-being this day. In the name of the Christ. Amen.

(Evening)
You have shown me the well of your provisioning, bringing me through this day. Now watch over me as I find my night's rest in you. In the name of the Christ. Amen.

WEDNESDAY, JUNE 16
(Read Psalm 86:1–10, 16–17)

(Morning)
Ever-faithful God, I turn to you this morning
to open me to your Word and way.

(Evening)
Ever-faithful God, hear my praise
and thanks for your strength and love.

Loving God, comfortable in our pretensions, we may not want to admit that we are needful in any way. It is better to be self-sufficient, we think. But God, your grace is made perfect in our weakness. Can we know the power of your grace if we make no room for you to exercise in our lives?

(Morning)
Listen to my prayers for this day, O God; hear my cry of supplication.
(Prayers of Intercession)

(Evening)
O God of constant grace, you continually turn to me with your forgiving and empowering love. I especially thank you for such times during this day.
(Prayers of Intercession)

"Teach me your way, O God, that I may walk in your truth"
(repeat silently throughout the day).
(Pray the Prayer of Our Savior.)

(Morning)
Ever-faithful God, may the details and demands of my day not distract me from your outpouring of steadfast love. In the name of the Christ I pray. Amen.

(Evening)
Quiet my cares and ease my anxieties. Grant me a restful night. In the name of the Christ I pray. Amen.

THURSDAY, JUNE 17
(Read Romans 6:1b–11)

(Morning)
My ever-present God, awaken my heart this day,
so that I may follow only you.

(Evening)
My ever-present God, dwell gracefully with me at the closing of this day.
Speak gently to me through your Word.

Loving God, as Christians, alone and with others, we continue the life of Christ. We live as Christ would live; we die to the world as Christ did. We are called to set ourselves apart obediently from those things that would divert us from this Christ-centered life: a life of sacrificial love, redemptive suffering, and praise for you, the One who makes all things possible.

(Morning)
As I seek to walk with Jesus, O God,
I must contend with competing voices and claims.
Help me to put each one in its place this day.
(Prayers of Intercession)

(Evening)
You have brought me safely through another day.
I give you thanks for your special graces.
(Prayers of Intercession)

**"If you, O God, should mark iniquities, who could stand?
But there is forgiveness with you, that you may be revered."**
(Pray the Prayer of Our Savior.)

(Morning)
Help me to be clear about to whom I belong, this day, O God. I pray that today someone will recognize that I live for Christ. In Jesus' name I pray. Amen.

(Evening)
I entrust my soul to you, O God, as I give way to sleep and the dreams you will send. In Jesus' name I pray. Amen.

FRIDAY, JUNE 18
(Read Romans 6:1b–11)

(Morning)
Creator God, with my eyes open and my body rested,
I welcome your Spirit into every moment given to me
by your creative will.

(Evening)
Creator God, with gratitude for your grace, I turn to your loving presence for a
time with your Word, knowing that you are turning to me. Greet me in this time.

Ever-faithful God, the proof of Paul's words may not be readily apparent
to the new or young Christian. As Christ's life continues within us, over
years and years, our conscious sins are brought to graceful light so that we
can confess them and be free of them. Our less-conscious sins, arising from
our anxieties, compulsions, and obsessions, are revealed over time as well.
Reveal to me, loving God, so that I might be healed by the Christ within.

(Morning)
Allow me to trust that I am no longer living alone
but that my life is grounded in the life of Christ, especially
with regard to the persons and challenges I face this day.
(Prayers of Intercession)

(Evening)
O living Christ, your life is growing within me.
I give you thanks for renewing my life
as I lived through these moments during this day.
(Prayers of Intercession)

**"But as for me, my prayer is for you, O God.
At an acceptable time, in the abundance of your steadfast love,
answer me" (repeat silently throughout the day).**
(Pray the Prayer of Our Savior.)

(Morning)	(Evening)
The day's busyness no doubt will distract me from you, O God, diluting my sense of your presence. May the interruptions of my routine remind me to open my heart to you. In the name of our Savior. Amen.	I may close my books, my door, and my eyes, but I will not close my heart to you, even as I sleep. In the name of our Savior. Amen.

SATURDAY, JUNE 19
(Read Matthew 10:24–39 and Psalm 69:1–10, 16–18)

(Morning)
Spirit God, you awakened me to another day of life with you.
Speak your Word to me this day through my questions,
my insights, my imagination, and my dreams.

(Evening)
Spirit God, with gratitude for the life you have given me to live,
I turn to you at the close of this day to be sustained
by your Word and quieted by your Spirit.

Jesus did not give us a way that was supposed to work in this kind of world. Jesus' way is not one that helps us keep everything balanced. Jesus wants to upset the balance. It is not "be true to yourself," but "be true to your Sovereign and Teacher." It is not "keep matters of faith personal," but "announce the way from the very rooftops!" It is not "family above all else," but "keep Christ at the head of all things." In the new order, all things find their proper place in light of the Christ event: God among us.

(Morning)
Move me out of my comfort zone, O calling God. May I not be ashamed to
speak and act as one of your children and as a follower of the way of Jesus.
Hear me, especially regarding the following persons and circumstances.
(Prayers of Intercession)

(Evening)
Thank you, dear God, for the witness of others in my life;
for those who have made your love and way clear to me and others.
I remember them in the closing moments of this day.
(Prayers of Intercession)

**"Answer me, O God, for your steadfast love is good; according to your
abundant mercy, turn to me" (repeat silently throughout the day).**
(Pray the Prayer of Our Savior.)

(Morning)
May I go nowhere this day where
"whose I am" is not evident by what I
say and do. In the name of our Savior.
Amen.

(Evening)
By your grace, I have walked the way
of Jesus this day. By your grace, I have
been included among your children.
Grant me now a restful sleep. In the
name of our Savior. Amen.

SUNDAY, JUNE 20
(Read Matthew 10:24–39)

(Morning)
O day of the Risen One! May this day, of all my days this week,
be a blessing to my growing faith.

(Evening)
O night of the Risen One! One week ends; another begins.
I open myself in the closing moments of this day to your stirrings and call.

God, you hold a deep and passionate love for us that is both pervasive and inclusive of all of humanity. Out of this love comes this invitation: to know our true worth not by what we hold but by what we are willing to release. Compassionate God, to suffer for others and to be willing to give it all away reveals that our humanity can be transformed into divinity.

(Morning)
O Spirit of God, help me to discern what I give freely
and what I hold onto. Help me to recognize
what stands between me and grant me a deeper trust in the way of Jesus.
(Prayers of Intercession)

(Evening)
O God, when fear makes me hesitant to acknowledge you,
forgive my silence and encourage me to give a clear witness,
especially in the following areas of my life.
(Prayers of Intercession)

**Have no fear; do not be afraid. You are of highest value
to the Creator and Lover of the Universe.**
(Pray the Prayer of Our Savior.)

(Morning)
Open me to the gifts of my faith community. May I give my whole self to you in worship and praise you for all that you are, O God, and for all that you are making of me. Thanks be to Christ. Amen.

(Evening)
Hold me close to your heart, O God, as I ease out of this day, through the coming night, and into the morrow that awaits me. Thanks be to Christ. Amen.

MONDAY, JUNE 21
(Read Psalm 13)
(Reading from Genesis 22:1–14)

(Morning)
O God, you call us into difficult places;
help us to trust your Word and to obey.

(Evening)
O God, your Word is true, and your promises have provided us strength
and peace to enter into the challenges before us.

Like Abram, O God, you send us out into the wilderness experiences of life. Yet you are a faithful and loving God who provides us with courage and strength to be all you have created us to be in Christ Jesus. You send forth upon us a fresh spirit of anointing each day, which gives us power to endure. Let us walk each day with steadfast assurance and immovable strength as your instruments and abound in the work before us in our God. Grant us, O God, your holy spirit of obedience.

(Morning)
Keep me focused, O God, that you are the lamp unto my feet
and your love is everlasting.
(Prayers of Intercession)

(Evening)
O God, your blessings are before me as sure as the rest and peace of this day.
(Prayers of Intercession)

I bow in your presence, O God, with a thankful heart.
(Pray the Prayer of Our Savior.)

(Morning)
As I face my challenges, allow me your grace and strength to trust and love you, O God. In your Child's name. Amen.

(Evening)
I lift up my eyes to you and give you praise for every blessing of the day. In your Child's name. Amen.

TUESDAY, JUNE 22

(Read Jeremiah 28:5–9)
(Sing "I Am on the Battlefield" or another familiar hymn)

(Morning)
Thank you, God, for the promises of restoration this day.

(Evening)
Thank you, God. I rejoice and bow down in humble prayer
that you are a God of covenant.

God, you are a healing to the nations in the midst of chaos of wars, starvation, despair, devastation, and separation. Keep us faithful to your words of promise. Help us to be thankful that your love is wider and deeper than what we see with our eyes or hear with our ears. For as Christ calls us into boldness as children of the most high God, likewise you will provide a way out of no way for us. We thank you, O God, for just being our God—a God of empowerment, love, and abundant grace. I pray that you will continue to anoint us with your Spirit in unity and love. Keep us focused, God!

(Morning)
We awaken to a new day of your possibilities of being our God.
Send us forth with rejoicing.
(Prayers of Intercession)

(Evening)
As we have come to the close of this day,
O God, we lift up our voices in praise.
(Prayers of Intercession)

Our God will light our paths in ways that we cannot envision.
(Pray the Prayer of our Savior.)

(Morning)
Thank you for loving us. Thank you for providing ways that nobody but you, O God, could provide. In your Child's name. Amen.

(Evening)
Thank you for keeping us, O God, in the midst of our storms in courage and faith. In your Child's name. Amen.

WEDNESDAY, JUNE 23
(Read Psalm 89:1–4, 15–18)

(Morning)
Good morning, God. I thank you for last night's rest and this day of grace.

(Evening)
Good night, God. I thank you for your faithfulness all day
and your promises, which are constant.

God, I sing your praises, for your love and promises go before me, leading and guiding my way. As you promised your servant David, you have preserved my life each day. I thank you that you look beyond my faults and continue to bless and meet my needs. You are truly a great God, a precious Savior. I live in the light of your kindness and rejoice each day in your love. You are my joy in a weary land that springs forth new, holy waters of blessings. Truly you are my God!

(Morning)
I am mindful that you are my Protector. You are my Light in a weary land.
(Prayer of Intercession)

(Evening)
As I come to the close of my day, O God,
I rejoice in my accomplishment through your anointing Spirit.
(Prayer of Intercession)

God will direct your paths and guide you with an all-encompassing eye.
(Pray the Prayer of Our Savior.)

(Morning)	(Evening)
Help me to live in the acknowledgment of your love, grace, and promise. In your Child's name. Amen.	I turn this day over to you and look forward to a new day of giving you praise. In your Child's name. Amen.

THURSDAY, JUNE 24
(Read Romans 6:12–14)

(Morning)
God of mercy, I awaken to new freedom because you live anew in me.

(Evening)
God of mercy, I live as a new creation from the worries of the world
which surround me. Let me rest in your peace.

O Holy One, I can rejoice that I'm a new creature in Christ Jesus. I can
rejoice that while I am *in* the world, I can be not *of* this world. I praise you,
O God, that your Holy Spirit keeps anointing and empowering me to go
beyond my flesh to a place of your will. As such, I can be pleasing in your
sight. Continue to bless me as I hold to your unchanging grace.

(Morning)
As I start this day, give me strength to move according to your will.
(Prayers of Intercession)

(Evening)
As I end this day, thank you for every moment.
(Prayers of Intercession)

In celebration of your sovereignty, O God, I bow.
(Pray the Prayer of Our Savior.)

(Morning)
Let Christ abound in me, so that I may
live justified in your love and grace. In
your Child's name. Amen.

(Evening)
Tonight I sing all praises and release
myself to your care. Let me rest in
your peace. In your Child's name.
Amen.

FRIDAY, JUNE 25

(Read Romans 6:15–23)
(Sing "Amazing Grace")

(Morning)
Potter God, create in me a clean and right spirit as I start this day.

(Evening)
Potter God, keep molding me in your ways.

I am reminded, O God, that you are the Creator and I am the human clay by which you re-create in me a justified body through your grace in Christ Jesus. I embrace your Holy Spirit as it moves from within my heart, soul, mind, and body to be what you would have me be—free and holy.

(Morning)
Let my spirit, which is yours, be empowered today, O God.
(Prayer of Intercession)

(Evening)
Amazing grace which leads me from day into evening,
continue to bless and renew me in peace.
(Prayer of Intercession)

Spirit of the living God, fall anew upon me.
(Pray the Prayer of Our Savior.)

(Morning)
God, continue to keep your anointing fresh in my life. In your Child's name. Amen.

(Evening)
Blessed are those who love and thank you, O God. In your Child's name. Amen.

SATURDAY, JUNE 26
(Read Matthew 10:40–42)

(Morning)
O God, let your love of others radiate in me.

(Evening)
O God, let your love continue to be a part of my evening.

God, I am reminded that you are abundant with all of us, and as an instrument of your grace, I must push toward loving all of your people. O God, keep this reminder foremost in my mind when I come upon the challenges of this day and those that push me in ways to love you more and myself less. Let me walk in your words to Matthew.

(Morning)
Keep me unselfish in service to others.
(Prayers of Intercession)

(Evening)
Only you know what is in my heart. Give me rest in my innermost parts.
(Prayers of Intercession)

Let your love of God be a beam of light to others.
(Pray the Prayer of Our Savior.)

(Morning)
I take my cross within me each minute of the day. In your Child's name. Amen.

(Evening)
Thank you for giving me boldness of spirit to be more like you, O God. In your Child's name. Amen.

SUNDAY, JUNE 27
(Read Psalm 13)

(Morning)
God, my prayers are always before you.

(Evening)
God, keep me thankful, and help me to wait with patience.

At times it seems that you don't hear my prayers, O God. Then I am reminded that your clock is not my own. Help me to stay steadfast in my trust and love of you in my waiting. Give me strength to remember all of your blessings and to be grateful. Teach me in these times of crisis that you are truly an "on-time God" in all that you do.

(Morning)
Keep my heart fixed on your goodness,
O God, in the midst of the storms of life.
(Prayers of Intercession)

(Evening)
Truly, you are a Comforter in my time of needs. Thank you, God!
(Prayers of Intercession)

You are a God who never fails in our times of need.
(Pray the Prayer of Our Savior.)

(Morning)
This day was forged with hard and difficult decisions, but thank you for helping me. In your Child's name. Amen.

(Evening)
Praises be to you for seeing me through this day, O God. In your Child's name. Amen.

MONDAY, JUNE 28
(Read Matthew 11:16–19, 25–30)

(Morning)
Gracious God, from whom all blessings flow, I thank you for this day.
As I seek your face, may a new image of you be revealed to me today.

(Evening)
Gracious God, I thank you for every task and activity that I performed during
this day. May today's learnings be instilled in my heart forever.

I thank you, Creator, Guardian of heaven and earth. You have hidden yourself from the clever and the intelligent and have revealed your wisdom to
the ordinary. As you choose what is foolish in the world to shame the wise
and choose what is weak in the world to shame the strong, may your wisdom and strength be revealed to those who never have known of your glory
and righteousness. As you choose Christ, choose us, and instill in us a faith
that surpasses all human understanding.

(Morning)
On this day, I accept your yoke as a symbol of your teaching power.
(Prayers of Intercession)

(Evening)
Dear God, as I end this day with a spirit of peace and joy, may I continue to
acknowledge the many signs and wonders that you reveal to me.
(Prayers of Intercession)

As you increase the numbers of those who are saved,
may I always hold sacred the Prayer of Our Savior.
(Pray the Prayer of Our Savior.)

(Morning)
With a sense of joy, I wait upon Jesus
today. In Jesus' name. Amen.

(Evening)
Jesus Christ, anoint me with the
things that you have taught me today.
In Jesus' name. Amen.

TUESDAY, JUNE 29
(Read Matthew 11:16–19, 25–30)

(Morning)
Blessed Creator, Maker of all things that are good,
I give you praise and honor today.

(Evening)
Blessed Creator, this day and all that is in it are gifts from you.
As I end this day, I commit to you all of the good things that I have done.

Generations have come, and generations have passed away. Yet how does this generation compare to those now gone? Dear God, I pray for all generations today. For my ancestors, I praise you. For my forebears, I praise you. For those who gave me life, I praise you. For those who raised and nurtured me, I praise you. I accept the positive attributes of all those who have come before me, while casting away the negative. Instill in me a clean heart, so that generations yet conceived may know of your glory.

(Morning)
God, I commit this day to doing things
that contribute positively to the next generation.
(Prayers of Intercession)

(Evening)
Magnificent God, I acknowledge that you are my God
and that I am one of your people.
(Prayers of Intercession)

**Generations come and generations go,
but the Spirit of God lives on forever.**
(Pray the Prayer of Our Savior.)

(Morning)
With a sense of joy, I celebrate life!
In Jesus' name. Amen.

(Evening)
Jesus Christ, anoint me with the things
that you have taught me today. In your
name. Amen.

WEDNESDAY, JUNE 30
(Read Song of Solomon 2:8–13)

(Morning)
Dear God, anoint my ears, that I may clearly hear you today.

(Evening)
Dear God, as this day comes to a close,
I thank you for all things that exist in creation.

O Beloved, Creator of mountains, hillsides, and plains; Maker of gazelles, turtledoves, and foxes; Molder of the true vine, the fragrant flowers, and fruit trees. I pause this day just to observe the bounty of your earth. Where there is barrenness, I pray for life. Where there is sterility, I pray for vitality. Where there is silence, I pray for singing. May those who dwell upon the earth recognize your glory!

(Morning)
This morning, I pray for the restoration of . . .
(Prayers of Intercession)

(Evening)
This evening, I continue to lift up in prayer . . .
(Prayers of Intercession)

With renewed hope I pray.
(Pray the Prayer of Our Savior.)

(Morning)
I begin this day seeking the voice of the Creator. In the name of the Christ. Amen.

(Evening)
I end this day acknowledging the voice of the Creator. In the name of the Christ. Amen.

THURSDAY, JULY 1
(Read Zechariah 9:9–12)

(Morning)
Gracious God, I rejoice and look forward to this day with excitement and joy!

(Evening)
Gracious God, I end this day acknowledging the hopes
and fears of those who have come from all walks of life.

Rejoice in God always. Again, I say rejoice! For God is good, and God's grace and mercy endure forever. God, I shout aloud today as I remember the victories and triumphs that you have already shown me. As I seek inner peace, remind me each day that I have freedom to choose behaviors of peace or violence. Push me, challenge me, and prod me to choose peace in all occasions. Allow me to be a living example for someone who is contemplating the whys and why-nots of choosing you. May your dominion be made manifest from sea to sea, so that the whole earth will be filled with your glory on this day.

(Morning)
On this day, I will rejoice and be glad in God.
(Prayers of Intercession)

(Evening)
As I rest at the end of this day, I rejoice and claim
the triumphant victory that you have extended to humankind.
(Prayers of Intercession)

With renewed hope I pray.
(Pray the Prayer of Our Savior.)

(Morning)	(Evening)
Holy Spirit, bring comfort and peace to the world today. In Jesus' name. Amen.	Let the world continue to experience your comfort and peace. In Jesus' name. Amen.

FRIDAY, JULY 2
(Read Psalm 145:8–14)

(Morning)
Dear God, make me aware of your grace and mercy.

(Evening)
Dear God, thank you for being gracious and merciful with me today.

O gracious and merciful God, I thank you for your steadfast love. Throughout the millennia, you have been good to all, and your compassion has been unending. As I exist at the midpoint of this year, I continue to give you thanks and praise for all of your good works. With each new day, your realm draws nearer to me. And when I am called to pass over, I, too, will speak of you and tell of your power. But until that day, I will use the rest of my earthly existence to make known to all people your mighty deeds and glorious splendor.

(Morning)
I rejoice as I remain focused on the task of
absorbing your presence all the day long.
(Prayers of Intercession)

(Evening)
I end this day in the presence of the God of my ancestors.
(Prayers of Intercession)

I live by your righteousness, Jesus.
(Pray the Prayer of Our Savior.)

(Morning)
I entrust this day into your hands, O God. In the name of the Christ. Amen.

(Evening)
I entrust this night to you with a vision of your realm in my heart. In the name of the Christ. Amen.

SATURDAY, JULY 3
(Read Romans 7:15–25a)

(Morning)
Caring God, may I usher in this day seeking to understand
and believe in my own actions.

(Evening)
Caring God, I end this day calling on you to free me
from the sins that I have committed.

Magnificent God, today I seek to understand the meaning of truth. Save me, a sinner, from myself today. When I do not understand my own actions, give me a spirit of discernment, so that I do not commit the same sin over and over again. I confess that at times I do not do what I should. Instead, I do the very thing I hate. Fix me, God. I invite you to dwell within me all the day long, that I might exemplify the Christ rather than the sin that dwells in me. And in the end, may truth reign today, tomorrow, and forever more.

(Morning)
Holy Spirit, empower me to hear and to yield to the voice of God.
(Prayers of Intercession)

(Evening)
Dear God, I pause in silence. Let me hear your still, quiet voice.
Give me the wisdom to be able to differentiate between truth and sin.
(Prayers of Intercession)

Out of the depths of silence, let truth reign forever.
(Pray the Prayer of Our Savior.)

(Morning)	(Evening)
As I move through the day, may a spirit of truthfulness dwell in my heart. In the matchless name of Jesus I pray. Amen.	As I rest this evening, may I be cleansed and redeemed from the sins that I have consciously and unconsciously committed. In the matchless name of Jesus I pray. Amen.

SUNDAY, JULY 4
(Read Romans 7:15–25a)

(Morning)
Loving God, I thank you for Jesus, the Christ. Because of him,
I will be freed from sin.

(Evening)
Loving God, as this day closes, anoint me with your redeeming power.

Blessed Jesus, the Sinless One who sojourned upon the earth, I thank you for committing the sacrificial act on the cross. As this week comes to a close, I pause once again to seek your face. As an image of you dwells in my mind, I call upon your Spirit to help me strive toward the path of righteousness. Spirit of the living God, fall afresh on me.

(Morning)
Help me and others to do the right thing.
(Prayers of Intercession)

(Evening)
I end this day with the blessed assurance that redemption is a sacred gift,
and I pray that I do not take it for granted.
(Prayers of Intercession)

Anoint me with the desire to spread goodness in the land.
(Pray the Prayer of Our Savior.)

(Morning)
"I delight in the law of my inmost self through Jesus Christ." In Jesus' name I pray. Amen.

(Evening)
"Thanks be to God through Jesus Christ." In Jesus' name I pray. Amen.

MONDAY, JULY 5
(Read Isaiah 55:10–13 and Psalm 119:105–112)

(Morning)
God, I thank you for your Word and its creative power
to accomplish your purpose. May your Word be a lamp to my feet
and a light to my path as I move through this day.

(Evening)
God, I thank you for all you have accomplished in me
and through me this day. Your guiding presence is the joy of my life.

Can the rain fall upward? Does the snow return to the clouds? Neither does your Word fail to go where you send it, watering the earth. Like a seed that grows slowly, unseen, as seasons pass, so is your Word at work in me. In your time, the seed bears grain. Through the labors of many, the bread of life is offered through me.

(Morning)
Holy Sower, my life is the soil. I begin this day open to your Word,
trusting to you my concerns for myself and others.
(Prayers of Intercession)

(Evening)
In my mind's eye, I replay the events and encounters of this day,
pausing to pray for the needs of persons I met.
(Prayers of Intercession)

"Your word is a lamp to my feet."
(Sing "O Word of God Incarnate" or another familiar hymn.)

(Morning)
Speak your Word, O God. I am listening. Help me to embody your purpose. In the name of Jesus I pray. Amen.

(Evening)
The day is done, and evening has come. I trust to your hands all that I have done and left undone. To you be all glory, God! In the name of Jesus I pray. Amen.

TUESDAY, JULY 6
(Read Romans 8:1–11)

(Morning)
Holy One and eternal God, I want to live by your Spirit. Without the gift of your Spirit, my words fall flat, my love does not bear fruit in growing relationships, and my days fill with business but not with praise. Fill me this day.

(Evening)
Holy Spirit and eternal God, I thank you for whispers
I heard today of your living in me.

I affirm that through my baptism into Christ you work in me in ways beyond all I know and feel. I seek to live by your Spirit, who dwells within my body, your temple. When the cares and the values of this world seduce me away from Spirit-filled life, free me, righteous God! Guide me, that I may live and move in accord with your divine presence.

(Morning)
Fiery wind of God, blow through my life
and all the world, bringing life and peace.
(Prayers of Intercession)

(Evening)
Gentle dove of God, spread your wings over my life
and over the lives of those for whom I pray.
(Prayers of Intercession)

Spirit of God, breathe in me.
(Sing "Spirit, Spirit of Gentleness" or another familiar hymn.)

(Morning)
Spirit of God, breathe life into my mortal body—in life, in death, and in life beyond death. I ask this prayer in Christ's name. Amen.

(Evening)
Spirit of God, breathe in me, even as I trust myself to sleep. Breathe through my sleep and through my dreams, that all that has been frayed today may be mended. I ask this prayer in Christ's name. Amen.

WEDNESDAY, JULY 7
(Read Genesis 25:19–34)

(Morning)
Reconciling God, family conflict is as old as human history:
mothers and fathers favoring one child over another,
brothers and sisters arguing over food and inheritance rights. Today's
reading suggests that you are at work in families, even in the conflicts.
May your will be fulfilled in my primary relationships.

(Evening)
Reconciling God, sometimes, like Rachel, I wonder why
life is so hard and whether anything good will come
of my labor. Compassionate One, reassure me that my life matters.

Liberating God, I have understood the story of Jacob and Esau through the adage against "trading one's birthright for a pot of stew." I've never wondered if Esau was actually dying from hunger. I have thought him foolish, not noticing how Jacob exploited his brother's need. This is the world's way—cashing in on others' misfortune. May I live by your Spirit, moving past assumptions to empathy for all my sisters and brothers.

(Morning)
Today I pray that your will be done in those with whom I share my life—
parent, child, partner, or friend. Surround them with your love.
(Prayers of Intercession)

(Evening)
I pray now for the hungry of earth, that they may have
both food and their birthright of human dignity.
(Prayers of Intercession)

I pray to you, God my Father and Mother.
(Pray the Prayer of Our Savior.)

(Morning)
I thank you, God of wisdom, that you will be with me this day, even in moments of conflict. In Jesus' name. Amen.

(Evening)
I rest in you, God of wisdom, for you have accompanied me today. In Jesus' name. Amen.

THURSDAY, JULY 8
(Read Matthew 13:1–9, 18–23)

(Morning)
Holy Sower, what kind of soil am I?
Am I ready to receive your Word today?

(Evening)
Holy Sower, what kind of soil have I been today?
Have birds eaten the seed or weeds choked the new shoots?
Or have I been rich soil, producing much fruit?

I remember now how through the cares of the world, the lures of wealth, or opposition from other people, I have closed my heart to you. So soon I forget that true life comes from you; so often I hold back in fear. Calm my anxiety and free me for greater openness to your Spirit, through the grace of Jesus Christ. I want to cooperate with the unfolding of your purpose on earth.

(Morning)
Spirit of life and growth, I pray that in your mysterious working, you may bring forth fruit in the lives of those for whom I pray.
(Prayers of Intercession)

(Evening)
Wonder-working Power, I thank you for the signs
of your presence that I noticed today.
(Prayers of Intercession)

God works in mysterious ways.
(Sing "We Are Not Our Own" or another familiar song.)

(Morning)
I begin this day open to the small seeds you are planting in my life. May these seeds take root, that your will may be done in me. Thanks be to Christ. Amen.

(Evening)
I lie down in peace, releasing to you the cares of this day, ready to be renewed through your gift of sleep. Thanks be to Christ. Amen.

FRIDAY, JULY 9
(Read Matthew 13:1–9)

(Morning)
God, today help me devote myself less to completing everything
on my list than to noticing what you are doing in the world.

(Evening)
God, thank you for everything you accomplished
through me and in spite of me today.

What an outrageous parable Jesus told! He promised an abundant harvest, despite all threats to growth. Some seeds fall on rocky ground, sprouting quickly, only to wither with the sun. The finches may eat the seeds, weeds may crowd in, and rabbits may nibble the tender shoots. Just the same, you will bring a great harvest! How can this be? Could it be that you will bring about your promise, no matter how we fail and fall away? What grace!

(Morning)
Holy One, you work mysteriously in the world
to bring about your purpose. May your will be done on earth,
especially concerning those people and situations for which I now pray.
(Prayers of Intercession)

(Evening)
Teach me, abundant God, to look beyond my own failures
and the resistance to your will that I experience around me,
with hope in your promised harvest.
(Prayers of Intercession)

With hope in your promise I pray.
(Pray the Prayer of Our Savior.)

(Morning)
I am watching, surprising God, for your wonders today! Thanks be to Christ. Amen.

(Evening)
For all that has been fulfilled today, I give you thanks. Compassionate One, I remember what was frustrating or difficult, asking you to make a way where no way is clear. Thanks be to Christ. Amen.

SATURDAY, JULY 10
(Read Psalm 65)

(Morning)
Awesome God, do you really establish mountains and water furrows?
What does it mean to be a person of faith while considering
the constant changes in nature that scientists call evolution?

(Evening)
Awesome God, I thank you for the gifts of nature that I encountered today:
a bird's warble, a fragrant fir tree, the warm sun, and the refreshing rain.

May your praise overflow, O God, River of Life, for you answer prayer. You forgive human sin and bring freedom and hope to all people and to the earth itself. You send rain from your deep river to refresh the land. You quench the thirst of flocks and water the fields. With hills and valleys, meadows and pastures, we sing for joy in your praise!

(Morning)
This morning, Creator, I pray with the earth and its creatures:
send your Spirit and renew the face of the earth. Teach me and my human
sisters and brothers to walk gently on this planet, our holy ground.
(Prayers of Intercession)

(Evening)
I thank you, God, for the gifts I received today from the earth
and from human labor: food to eat, clothes to wear,
beauty to delight me, strangeness to inspire me.
(Prayers of Intercession)

**"Nature with open volume stands to spread the Maker's praise abroad"
(Isaac Watts).**

(Morning)
All the earth is filled with your glory, O God! May I ever sing your praise. In Christ I pray. Amen.

(Evening)
When I consider the universe your hands have created, I am amazed that you care for me, O God. In Christ I pray. Amen.

SUNDAY, JULY 11
(Read Isaiah 55:10–13, Psalm 65:9–13, and Romans 8:18–25)

(Morning)
Loving Maker, all nature sings your praise, for by your Word you create
and renew the earth! The mountains and the hills burst into song before me.

(Evening)
Loving Maker, I thank you for the promise that evergreen trees shall grow up
instead of thorns, and flowers instead of briers. Give me patience in pulling
weeds today, in hopes that new life will blossom.

Some theologians say that it is dangerous to love nature too much lest the
creation lead away from the Creator. Yet psalmist and prophet alike proclaim that mountains and valleys worship you with song. I watched a thrush
sing, and it seemed to be wholehearted praise, without consciousness of
self, purer than any human hymn. Tune my ears to hear nature's unending
song of praise, that I may go out in joy and be led back in peace.

(Morning)
With your Spirit I yearn for the renewal of creation
and the revealing of your children, O God.
(Prayers of Intercession)

(Evening)
With all creation, I long for the glorious freedom of your children.
(Prayers of Intercession)

"All nature sings your praise!"
*(Sing "I Sing the Mighty Power of God" or "Cantemos al Creador
[Señor]" or another familiar song.)*

(Morning)
Your Word, your Spirit, your creation, all lead my heart to you, Holy One. I thank you for the promise of this new day. Thanks be to Christ. Amen.

(Evening)
Your Word and Spirit give life, Holy One. I thank you for your presence in the world you have made. Thanks be to Christ. Amen.

MONDAY, JULY 12
(Read Genesis 28:10–19a)

(Morning)
Blessing and loving God, as we awake, your voice lingers in our minds.
The memory of heaven's gate awes our minds. The promise of your touch
encourages us to face the dawn with courage and faith.

(Evening)
Blessing and loving God, receive these pillars glazed with the oil
of living faith as a testimony of our encounter with you in this holy place.

Let us dream of ways to search for you, of ways to reach you, O God. Let us hear in our memories the promises of blessing you have shared with us and our families. Remind us again that we are kin to all of creation, so that the highway to you is open to all the peoples of the earth. We thank you for your assurance that you are with us until you have done all that you have promised us. May we be brave to live our faith today.

(Morning)
As we welcome the new day of our life, may we burst out in joy
and thanksgiving saying, "Surely God is in this place!"
(Prayers of Intercession)

(Evening)
As you have given us land and future, may we provide resources
and space for those who have no stones to lay their heads upon at night.
(Prayers of Intercession)

"I did not know it!" But now we do.
Share the good news with your family and neighbors.
(Pray the Prayer of Our Savior.)

(Morning)
Wake in us the awesome power of awareness, knowing that we are at home with you, O God. In Christ's name. Amen.

(Evening)
May we rest ever on the stone pillow that brings to us dreams, visions, and promises. In Christ's name. Amen.

TUESDAY, JULY 13
(Read Psalm 139:1–12)

(Morning)
O God, even in my dreams I sometimes flee from you. Yet even as I wake,
I discover joyfully that you are still with me. Trembling and thankful,
I know I cannot escape from you. Help me to live with ambivalence.

(Evening)
O God, what a day! Striving to live without you! Scrambling throughout the
avenues of life I have struggled to forget you. And as I lay my head on the
pillow, I find that you are with me, filling me with new life and new courage.
I know that you will find me in the stillness of the dark.

God, your incredible stubbornness compels us to faith. The ubiquitous
searching for you opens our souls, hearts, and minds. In the often contra-
dictory spaces of our lives, O God, you are present, urging us to wholeness. While at times our hearts and minds are full of hatred, judgment,
separation, and isolation, you are there calling us to return to love and
grace. As we utter the thoughts of escape, our hearts reach out for you,
thankful that you are always with us, thankful that you know us, and thankful that "you are acquainted with all of our ways."

(Morning)
Thank you, loving God, for being so diligent in your search of our thoughts,
our place, and our flights. Help us make our soaring searches for your will,
love, and grace, and not journeys of escape.
(Prayers of Intercession)

(Evening)
For the faithful presence of your Spirit and for leading us
in the everlasting way, we thank you.
(Prayers of Intercession)

**As you hem us in from behind and before,
we feel the touch of your hand upon us and discover freedom.**
(Pray the Prayer of Our Savior.)

(Morning)	(Evening)
What hope I have as I rise knowing you will be with me, my God, as I struggle to act justly. In Christ's name. Amen.	The evening comes to a close; my hectic heart calms, knowing that you will find me in the darkness of the night. In Christ's name. Amen.

WEDNESDAY, JULY 14
(Read Romans 8:12–17)

(Morning)
O God, we welcome the morning, confident that you
have the concerns of all the world in your hand.
We know there is no one but you to judge the just and unjust.

(Evening)
O God, with thanksgiving for your justice
and your forgiveness we seek repentance as the road to you.

God, the paradox of the premise for your justice, mercy, forbearance, for-giveness, overwhelming power, and strength speaks to the most powerful of nations and persons today. I am awed by the understanding that you are strongest when confronted by humankind's doubts of your perfect power. At that point, you reveal yourself by demonstrating mercy and forgiveness. God, not only do you insist that humanity be just but also that it be kind-hearted and forgiving. Oh, that the powerful nations would act in such ways, or that the rulers show their strength through kindness, justice, and mercy! The continuing violence of nations and people would not prevail.

(Morning)
O God, you are so powerful yet so merciful.
Help us to be loving in our strength.
(Prayers of Intercession)

(Evening)
May the hope of forgiveness give us the courage to repent our sins.
May the power of our faith lend love and justice
to our churches and communities.
(Prayers of Intercession)

For in strength you were forgiven, so in strength forgive others.
(Pray the Prayer of Our Savior.)

(Morning)
Your love for the world is clear, your justice for all people is shown. Invite us all to repent so that we can also be just and kind. In Christ's name. Amen.

(Evening)
We trust in your powerful strength. God, help us to invite the strong to become just, merciful, and forgiving. In Christ's name. Amen.

THURSDAY, JULY 15
(Read Isaiah 44:6–8)

(Morning)
Loving God, the one and only God, we proclaim our awe of you
as we ponder your promises anew. With thankful hearts and bodies,
we testify to you, our Redeemer and our Hope.

(Evening)
Loving God, the coming evening manifests our faith, for you have told us
not to be afraid because you are our God, our Rock, and our Salvation.

The reminder of your uniqueness, O God, is appropriate for our times. We labor under illusions of our powers and abilities, and therefore we stray from the path of righteousness. All who have attempted to usurp your place have shattered under their self-delusion. The tragic events of Jonestown, Waco, and Oklahoma City demonstrate the futility of acting without faith, without love, without foundation. It is only as we remember your proclamation that you are our God, our Sovereign, and our Rock that we begin to manifest our witness of your faithfulness. We thank you for our redemption and for your love.

(Morning)
Let us leap faithfully from the foundation of our Rock
to do justice in our world, O God.
(Prayers of Intercession)

(Evening)
We rest now, assured of your announcement that redemption is ours.
(Prayers of Intercession)

Just as Christ taught his disciples I pray.
(Pray the Prayer of Our Savior.)

(Morning)
We thank you, God, for the assurance that there are no others but you, that you alone reign in all of creation, and that you have sent those to declare your goodness through the blessings of sacred history. In Christ's name. Amen.

(Evening)
We do not fear, we are not afraid, for you have consistently shared with us the good news of your loving will. So we welcome the night, knowing that tomorrow we will be witnesses of your saving acts of grace. In Christ's name. Amen.

FRIDAY, JULY 16
(Read Psalm 86:11–17)

(Morning)
Savior God, the morning brings the teachings of your way.
We glorify your name, for we seek to walk in your way.

(Evening)
Savior God, you have shown us signs of your favor,
so that any one of us who may see it repents of our shame.

Creator God, we seek to know truth. As we receive evidences of your great love for us, we pray, as the psalmist did, for you to deliver us from our enemies. Even as we proclaim the glory of your name, we look vengefully at those whom we have declared our enemies. God, if you have touched our minds with the truth of your way, then we, too, will reflect the qualities that you have bestowed upon us; we will look at those "insolent ruffians" who assail us not with fear but with love and forgiveness. Immigrants seeking work, gays and lesbians seeking justice, poor people seeking fairness, and those seeking racial justice will become not enemies but people with whom we can share your grace and love.

(Morning)
As you turn to us this morning in love and mercy,
help us to turn to our enemies with love and mercy.
(Prayers of Intercession)

(Evening)
With peace and confidence we rest now,
knowing that you are comforting us and helping us.
(Prayers of Intercession)

**Even as you save the child of your serving girl,
save all children abandoned, abused, and rejected.**
(Pray the Prayer of Our Savior.)

(Morning)
We give thanks to you, beloved God, for teaching us your truth, for showing us the qualities of character you would have us share with your beloved creation. In Christ's name. Amen.

(Evening)
We have learned your way, our God, and we thank you and glorify your name for the sign of favor you have shared with us. Give us your strength so that we may have the courage to show all people our mercy, love, and justice. In Christ's name. Amen.

SATURDAY, JULY 17
(Read Romans 8:18–25)

(Morning)
God of love and grace, we thank you for sending your Spirit,
so that it may guide our feet upon the path.

(Evening)
God of love and grace, we rest serene knowing our hope
has redeemed us. Thank you for calling us to be your children,
to be the heirs of the One you sent to set us free.

I live in a state that is considered to be one of the least churchgoing communities in the country. Journeying through the state, I have found a great hunger for love, peace, justice, and community. I have seen young people desperate to receive the love and acceptance that can only come from people who have discerned your Spirit, O God. I have seen people of all colors demand the justice and fairness of the love of Christ. I have seen our churches respond with generosity and affection to the despair of others. Truly it can be said that the whole creation groans for your love. We are all eagerly longing for "the freedom of the glory of God." Many people wait patiently for your child's love. And many people wait for us to demonstrate Jesus' love. May we seek the many ministries that will share justice, peace, mercy, love, and community with the people around us.

(Morning)
Your waking touch makes me recall that we are your children, adopted to be
coheirs with Jesus Christ. This sustains and energizes our entire being.
(Prayers of Intercession)

(Evening)
We rest with the assurance that our hope in the unseen
has saved us from the power of our sin.
(Prayers of Intercession)

The cries of all creation call for redemption.
Listen to the groans of the green forests, the seas and oceans,
the ice fields, the skies, and the rivers that cry out for wholeness.
(Pray the Prayer of Our Savior.)

(Morning)	(Evening)
We live because we are led by the Spirit. In Christ's name. Amen.	We are free through God's adoption of us. In Christ's name. Amen.

SUNDAY, JULY 18
(Read Matthew 13:24–30, 36–43)

(Morning)
God, your child, Jesus Christ, has scattered the seeds of goodness through the land. May we grow in the spirit of loving bounty, alert to the dangers of the day.

(Evening)
God, may we shine as doers of the gospel, even as we lie in the fields of life.

The parable reminds us of the difficulty of determining who is faithful. Loving God, in your fields we find ourselves in a mix of different people. Some will be kind and caring, others will be hateful and dangerous, while others will be indifferent. Side by side we will live and labor. What an opportunity for us to share the love of Christ. Can the weeds be saved? God, only you will determine who is weed and who is wheat. What folly lies in attempting to name the evil among us! Might not our love, compassion, and mercy transform even the thorniest of weeds into the wheat of life?

(Morning)
God, help us to act and serve as children of your reign.
(Prayers of Intercession)

(Evening)
God, as darkness approaches, may we shine like the sun, thanking you that the love of Christ can transform choking weeds into embracing shafts of wheat.
(Prayers of Intercession)

Jesus Christ sows the seed; the seed reflects the sower.
May the field be radiant with flora of the Creator,
remembering that all creation is of God, even the weeds!
(Pray the Prayer of Our Savior.)

(Morning)
You love all of creation. Help us to transform into gardens the unkempt fields of injustice and oppression. In Christ's name. Amen.

(Evening)
We pray that through the love of Christ and the power of the Holy Spirit, there be no weeds and no more evil in the meadows of our God. In Christ's name. Amen.

MONDAY, JULY 19
(Read Genesis 29:15–28)

(Morning)
Creator, Sustainer, Redeemer, as I open my eyes to the sunlight coming through my window, keep me ever mindful that I must do only those things that are pleasing in your sight. I will seek to obey your will at all times.

(Evening)
Creator, Sustainer, Redeemer, as I close my eyes, I ask for forgiveness for anything I did today that was not pleasing in your sight. I ask for the peace that comes from knowing that you always listen to my prayers.

God, you have taught us that patience is a virtue, and each day we feel your patient love. As Jacob sought Rachel as his love, he remained patient for seven years, only to learn that as his love for Rachel was great, greater must be his patience. There are times in our lives when we must exercise great patience. God, only the blessed knowledge and memory which you have bestowed on us through your patient love can sustain us and bring us to the prayerful conclusion that without you, we would be nowhere. Gracious God, all praises be to you!

(Morning)
Loving God, as I bow my head and lift my heart to you, I implore you to give me the sustenance so necessary to carry the burdens of those I love.
(Prayers of Intercession)

(Evening)
God, as I kneel before you, help me to be humbled by your healing grace, which I saw in the individuals who crossed my path today.
With renewed patience I pray.
(Prayers of Intercession)

May your mercy and your grace always be present.
(Pray the Pray of Our Savior.)

(Morning)
Loving others and celebrating the joy that they bring will keep me smiling, for I am assured that your Spirit will be present. In Jesus' name I pray. Amen.

(Evening)
Yes, here I am again, God, knocking at your door of love, believing as I do that you will beckon me to enter. Thank you. In Jesus' name I pray. Amen.

TUESDAY, JULY 20
(Read Psalm 105:1–11)

(Morning)
Holy One, Maker of heaven and earth, I count it a blessing to awaken with
sound mind and body, eager to do your will. Help me to do so with exuberance.

(Evening)
Holy One, my sound mind and body were tested today,
so I called on your strength and you granted it to me. Thank you.

Dear God, every day we should say, "Thank you for your wondrous works
in our lives!" As we look back through the ages on the story of your eternal
faithfulness, we see how when Abraham and Isaac and Jacob sought you,
you were always there. We thank you, Savior God, for surrounding our
ancestors, thereby enabling us to stand tall today. Our gratitude is unending, and so we continually give thanks for your endless giving. We are
truly blessed, and we should give your name the praise.

(Morning)
On this day, help me to appreciate the sights and sounds
which you have placed in this world to remind me of your presence.
(Prayers of Intercession)

(Evening)
Dear God, my cup runs over. Grant me the wisdom
to see how I can help fill the cups of others.
(Prayers of Intercession)

Make me a blessing as I pray.
(Pray the Prayer of Our Savior.)

(Morning)
Yes, God, here I am again, seeking
your strength to buttress me as I
attempt to conquer yet another day by
doing your will. I ask this prayer in
Jesus' name. Amen.

(Evening)
Now, dear God, quiet my mind and
still my body as I lie down to sleep
with your faithfulness as my cover. I
ask this prayer in Jesus' name. Amen.

WEDNESDAY, JULY 21
(Read 1 Kings 3:5–12)

(Morning)
All-wise God, I awaken this morning wishing to be bathed in your wisdom
as I embark upon another day.

(Evening)
All-wise God, as the night darkens, I am reminded of how I have been blessed
to have my spirit lightened by your presence with me today. Thank you.

God, Solomon had the nerve to ask, and you graciously granted his request
and bestowed wisdom upon him. What a bold request; what an awesome
challenge you afforded to Solomon and to us! Loving God, as we grow in
your grace and receive more wisdom, we should also pray for more guidance to use that wisdom justly. We should follow Solomon's example and
then boldly step out, ever praying that your will be done.

(Morning)
Grant us wisdom for our journey, so that we can witness as worthy servants.
(Prayers of Intercession)

(Evening)
Grant us courage to stand reminding others of how great you are and how
overjoyed we are to be servants, called to do your bidding.
(Prayers of Intercession)

Lead us as we pray.
(Pray the Prayer of Our Savior.)

(Morning)	(Evening)
Giver of all good and gracious gifts, I eagerly await your presence and a new word in which to step out today. In my Savior's name I pray. Amen.	My, what a blessing to call your name and to be known personally by a great and just God. In my Savior's name I pray. Amen.

THURSDAY, JULY 22
(Read Psalm 119:129–136)

(Morning)
Worthy One, Giver of all good and perfect gifts, joy fills my heart this morning
as I ponder the gifts with which I have awakened—
touch, taste, smell, sound, and sight. I celebrate anew your goodness.

(Evening)
Worthy One, today I jumped over many a hurdle,
buttressed by your everlasting and enduring strength.

When we look up in wonder at how just and fair you are, Creator God, we
become as little children, grateful for so loving a parent. Let us look to you
to feed us, mold us, guide us, use us, and order our steps, for we are out
here on your Word. We know that you will rescue us from the evils that
beset the world and anchor us in your truth. God, in that way we will become a beacon for others, as your light shines through us. As we cry out for
you to shoulder our burdens, God, please shield us from harm and look
down on us in love.

(Morning)
I beseech you, O God, to rain down blessings on needy families everywhere
today. Give them continual hope in their hunger for you.
(Prayers of Intercession)

(Evening)
I beseech you, O God, to rain down blessings on my family
as they retire from a troubled day.
(Prayers of Intercession)

We must pause now to pray.
(Pray the Prayer of Our Savior.)

(Morning)
It is time now to begin anew with
energy and expectancy, dear God. Go
with me as I approach another day.
Thanks be to Christ. Amen.

(Evening)
With energy low and enthusiasm
waning, help me to be silent and to
hear your still, small voice. Thanks
be to Christ. Amen.

FRIDAY, JULY 23
(Read Romans 8:26–39)

(Morning)
Gracious and loving God, thank you for awakening me and for knowing my
needs as I stretch to meet another day. I don't know what is ahead of me,
but I do know that you are in charge, so I have no fear.

(Evening)
Gracious and loving God, keep me leaning on your everlasting arms as
I surrender the night to you, faithfully praying for rest
after a blessed yet busy day.

God, your living Spirit falls afresh on us as we come before your throne
once again. May your Holy Spirit anoint our hearts as we trust that all
things that happen to us are for our good. We trust you know that nothing
can separate us from your love. Even when we are unsure, we merit your
love; we are comforted that your love for us never fails. God, we pray that
you will help us to show our love to those whom you love and for whom
you sent your child, Jesus.

(Morning)
As I move through this day, I shall praise your holy name for loving me.
I pray that your goodness and mercy will continue to surround me.
Grant me understanding.
(Prayers of Intercession)

(Evening)
As the evening draws to a close, let me feel your love
and grant me the peace of your closeness.
(Prayers of Intercession)

And now I give my heart to you,
believing ever more in the prayer you taught your disciples.
(Pray the Prayer of Our Savior.)

(Morning)
I ask for a closer walk with you today,
to draw me nearer to your Holy Spirit
as I meet my fellow travelers on this
journey of life. In Jesus' name. Amen.

(Evening)
May my heart rest satisfied with how
wonderfully you have blessed me. I
pray that my night's sleep may be
rejuvenating. In Jesus' name. Amen.

SATURDAY, JULY 24
(Read Matthew 13:31–33)

(Morning)
Just and righteous God, I come as an eager learner to understand your way.
Teach me, O blessed Savior, teach me.

(Evening)
Just and righteous God, I come, having learned enough today
to fill only a mustard seed. Yet I know how blessed I am,
and I shall rest in comfort with that thought.

Joy, joy, joy envelops our souls as we contemplate your Word. We know that the lessons you teach us are designed to create in us an understanding which we must share with the world. Holy God, you pave the way for us out of the wilderness of darkness. Renewing God, you teach us that we can start with a tiny mustard seed and begin on the road to building a realm, so others who see us bursting with your brightness will be inspired to join us on the road. The majesty of the thought of a tiny mustard seed becoming a magnificent tree inspires our imagination as we visualize those who will stand together for Jesus Christ. As we learn your Word, then we can lead the way.

(Morning)
Ever-present God, help my unbelief and fortify me with your Word.
(Prayers of Intercession)

(Evening)
I needed to be and I felt fortified today. For this, I gratefully say thank you.
(Prayers of Intercession)

"Just as I am without one plea" I pray.
(Pray the Prayer of Our Savior.)

(Morning)
No, God, I cannot walk alone; nor do I want to—today or any day. Walk with me. I ask this prayer in Jesus' name. Amen.

(Evening)
Well, well! It's me, O God, standing in the need of prayer tonight. I ask this prayer in Jesus' name. Amen.

SUNDAY, JULY 25
(Read Matthew 13:44–52)

(Morning)
Precious One, as I stare in awe of your magnificence as shown
in the colors of the flowers and in the songs of the birds,
I am eager to discover what today will bring. Be with me.

(Evening)
Precious One, I pray that today I brought some sunshine into the lives I touched.

God, your precious Spirit permeates our beings and sometimes leaves us
speechless. Yet we know that your realm will come. Our prayer should be
that we will be found worthy, not only because we are faithful to you but
also because we tried to teach others to follow you. God, use us to share
your goodness, so that others will see your good works in us and through
us and will give your name all the glory. Yes, "your kingdom come." Lead
us, "O thou great Jehovah."

(Morning)
Grant to me the reward of the satisfying love of my God.
(Prayers of Intercession)

(Evening)
In my eagerness to serve, I pray that even as I falter,
I always will remember to give your name the praise.
(Prayers of Intercession)

Now we request your indulgence in the life of this humble servant.
(Pray the Prayer of Our Savior.)

(Morning)
Yet another Sabbath in which to rest
and declare your infinite goodness. I
pray in Jesus' name. Amen.

(Evening)
My eyes are heavy, yet my heart is
light, for I know that my Redeemer
lives. I pray in Jesus' name. Amen.

MONDAY, JULY 26
(Read Genesis 32:22–31)

(Morning)
Loving God, on this day I arise in anticipation of serving you.

(Evening)
Loving God, this day has been set aside for you and your glory.
This evening I call to mind the ways in which my life
has given praise to you today.

O God, Jacob wrestled all night with your messenger until he received his blessing. Help me to struggle with your Word until it blesses me anew. Give me the tenacity to strive to live out your precepts, even though it may be difficult for me. Abide with me through the day, that I, too, may receive a blessing from your hand.

(Morning)
For all those who wrestle with life, I offer prayers this day.
(Prayers of Intercession)

(Evening)
Because of your great mercy, I remember all those who are in need.
(Prayers of Intercession)

Now by your grace I pray.
(Pray the Prayer of Our Savior.)

(Morning)
Walk with me, God, as I go forward with your blessing upon my life. In the name of the Christ I pray. Amen.

(Evening)
May I rest knowing that I am blessed in you and enhanced by your Spirit. In the name of the Christ I pray. Amen.

TUESDAY, JULY 27
(Read Psalm 17:1–7, 15)

(Morning)
O vindicating God, this morning I rest
in your protective care as I face persecution.

(Evening)
O vindicating God, I am comforted in knowing
that you are my sure defense in the face of hard trials.

Mighty God, though I strive to live for you, it seems that I still have enemies who persecute me unjustly. I do not fear, O God, for you are a God of justice, vindicating the righteous and protecting those who walk in your ways. Help me, God, to be an advocate for those weaker than I, that I, too, may be a vindicator of those who are falsely accused. Empower me so that through me, the captives may be set free and the oppressed liberated.

(Morning)
Righteous God, I offer prayers for all those who need you this day.
(Prayers of Intercession)

(Evening)
I lift up to you, God, those who I know have need of you.
(Prayers of Intercession)

And now, O God, trusting in your power, I pray.
(Pray the Prayer of Our Savior.)

(Morning)
Walk with me, O God, as I face this day with courage and faith. In the name of Jesus. Amen.

(Evening)
This night I rest in your loving arms of protection, knowing that you care for me. In the name of Jesus. Amen.

WEDNESDAY, JULY 28
(Read Isaiah 55:1–5)

(Morning)
Providing and wonderful God, I come to you hungering
and thirsting for the bread of heaven today.

(Evening)
Providing and wonderful God, I thank you for feeding me with the bread of life.

Eternal God, your prophet Isaiah called those of us who are hungry and thirsty to come to you so that you would feed us. I come to you this day hungering for hope and thirsty for a fresh drink of your refreshing Spirit. Today, help me to come to you, because you alone can supply my every need. Remind me that I always come away empty when I waste my time striving to satisfy my hungers with the things of this world. Fill me now, transforming God, with the good gifts that come from your hand, so that I may share these gifts with others.

(Morning)
Now I pray for those who also are hungry.
(Prayers of Intercession)

(Evening)
I call to mind this evening those with whom
I have shared the bread of life today.
(Prayers of Intercession)

And now with thankfulness I pray.
(Pray the Prayer of Our Savior.)

(Morning)	(Evening)
I want to drink deep from the fountain of life and eat the manna of God. In Jesus' name. Amen.	You have fed me, O God, now give me peace and rest. In Jesus' name. Amen.

THURSDAY, JULY 29
(Read Psalm 145:8–9)

(Morning)
God, today is a new day that presents ever new possibilities for serving you.

(Evening)
God, this day has shown me again how wonderful
your love is to all of your creation.

Marvelous God, compassion is one of your attributes that I try so hard to emulate. However, it seems that my humanness gets in the way. Unlike you, I too quickly become angry over little things. I fail to see each encounter as an opportunity to show your love to all people. Help me, O Loving One, to always remember how you have shown compassion and mercy to me as I relate to others. Fill me with your love until it overflows to everyone I meet.

(Morning)
With your heart of compassion, I pray for the needs and concerns of others.
(Prayers of Intercession)

(Evening)
Trusting in your mercy, I recall the encounters
of this day when I have failed to show love.
(Prayers of Intercession)

With deep compassion I pray.
(Pray the Prayer of Our Savior.)

(Morning)
Send me into your world ready to
love unconditionally. In the matchless
name of Jesus I pray. Amen.

(Evening)
Hold me in your arms of compassion
as I sleep this night, O God. In the
matchless name of Jesus I pray. Amen.

FRIDAY, JULY 30
(Read Psalm 145:14–21)

(Morning)
Loving God, there is power in your name.

(Evening)
Loving God, this evening I come to you for comfort
and solace after this day's journey.

O God, you are the Provider of every need and the Giver of life. You provide for all who look to you and who trust in your name. Today, I place all my trust in you, for there is nowhere I will go this day where you will not be. You provide good gifts to all who call on your name. Help me this day not to look to my own abilities to provide for my needs but to rely on you to satisfy the desires of my heart. Allow me to be the instrument of your peace.

(Morning)
Use me in your service as I pray for the needs of others.
(Prayers of Intercession)

(Evening)
Guide my feet while I run this race, O God.
(Prayers of Intercession)

And now I pray as our Savior, Christ, has taught.
(Pray the Prayer of Our Savior.)

(Morning)
O God, walk with me this day on my journey of faith. Through Christ I pray. Amen.

(Evening)
Bless me this night to find rest and renewal in you. Through Christ I pray. Amen.

SATURDAY, JULY 31
(Read Romans 9:1–5)

(Morning)
God, I praise you for having come to earth
in human flesh to share my infirmities.

(Evening)
God, you have been with me all this day,
and your love has made a difference in my life.

Gracious and loving God, you send us prophets and teachers, like Paul, who tell us of your goodness, your mercy, and your grace. You graft us into your family by the blood of your child, Jesus. You show us each day how we must live our lives toward you and others. Today I need a special dispensation of your Spirit so that I may be able to live out your precepts. Walk with me every step of the way and every hour of this day, that despite my humanness, I may be a witness to the world of your redeeming love.

(Morning)
I lift to you the needs and concerns of others.
(Prayers of Intercession)

(Evening)
Nothing has come between us this day, God.
(Prayers of Intercession)

In fervent love and hope I pray.
(Pray the Prayer of Our Savior.)

(Morning)
I go out to serve you filled with your Spirit. In Christ's name. Amen.

(Evening)
Because of your truth and grace, this day has been a blessing to me. In Christ's name. Amen.

SUNDAY, AUGUST 1
(Read Matthew 14:13–21)

(Morning)
O God, who provides for even our smallest needs,
bless us this day to be guided by your love.

(Evening)
O God, today your love has given me everything that I needed to serve you.

Merciful God, when your child, Jesus, shared with his disciples, he never sent them away hungry. Why then, O God, do we go to church Sunday after Sunday and come home still hungry for sustenance from heaven? Today as I go to worship, let me go with an attitude of sharing what I already have been given. In giving, I may receive a fresh portion of your Holy Spirit and a good helping of your divine word.

(Morning)
Bless me this day to be a blessing to the world.
(Prayers of Intercession)

(Evening)
Guide me as I lift up those whose lives I have embraced this day.
(Prayers of Intercession)

And now with gratitude I pray.
(Pray the Prayer of Our Savior.)

(Morning)
Blessed God, guide me today in both worship and works. Through Christ our Savior. Amen.

(Evening)
Wonderful God, hold me in your arms of love and care as I rest this night. Through Christ our Savior. Amen.

MONDAY, AUGUST 2
(Read 1 Kings 19:9–10)

(Morning)
God who is always there, I arise to do your will.

(Evening)
God who is always there, I thank you for your peace.

This day I heard you speaking through voices that I had not credited to you before. I heard your voice in the whisper of two people in love. I heard your voice in the whisper of two parents as they watched their baby sleep. I heard your voice in the laughter of the elderly. I heard your voice through the directions of those who have authority over me. I heard your voice, and I moved from my cave to the secret place of the most high God. How pleasant it is to dwell with you, Savior God!

(Morning)
God who is always there, I give you thanks for the many voices through which I heard you speak. I pray for those who have yet to hear your voice.
(Prayers of Intercession)

(Evening)
Thank you, God, for preserving those who are called by your name.
(Prayers of Intercession)

God, speak to my heart.
(Recite Psalm 23.)

(Morning)
God who is always there, speak to my heart. In the Savior's name I pray. Amen.

(Evening)
Thank you, God, for one more day. In the Savior's name I pray. Amen.

TUESDAY, AUGUST 3
(Read 1 Kings 19:11–13)

(Morning)
Dear God, I feel so powerless. Infuse me with your power.

(Evening)
Dear God, thank you for protecting me from all hurt and harm today.

God, you called Elijah out of his cave. As we go about our day, I can reflect on all the caves in which you have found me hiding. You—the same God who gave courage to Elijah, rescued Daniel from the lion's den, elevated Joseph to high office, protected and provided for Naomi and Ruth, and opened Sarah's and Elizabeth's barren wombs—still have the power over evil, death, and the grave. God, give me the power you gave Elijah to seek where you can be found.

(Morning)
Dear God, help me to see you where you are and not where I want you to be.
(Prayers of Intercession)

(Evening)
God, I give you the highest praise.
(Prayers of Intercession)

Be still and know that God is God.
(Recite Psalm 23.)

(Morning)	(Evening)
Keep me close to you today. In the Savior's name I pray. Amen.	Thank you, God, for keeping your loving arms around me. In the Savior's name I pray. Amen.

WEDNESDAY, AUGUST 4
(Read 1 Kings 19:18)
(Reading from Genesis 37:1–4, 12–28)

(Morning)
God, help me to be loyal to you today.

(Evening)
God, thank you for guiding my feet this day.

Creator God, the Israelites ascribed names to you according to your many attributes. El Shaddai is one of those names. El Shaddai occurs forty-eight times in the Old Testament and means "God Almighty" or "God who is more than enough." God, you who are more than enough, promised Abram and Sarai children, blessed Jacob with wealth, brought Naomi's grandchildren out of a dead situation, and gave Elijah victory over those who sought to take his life. God, you who are more than enough, have more than enough blessings for those who are called by your name.

(Morning)
God who is more than enough, please bless me today
and make me a blessing to others.
(Prayers of Intercession)

(Evening)
God who is more than enough, for your loyalty
and steadfast goodness I praise your holy name.
(Prayers of Intercession)

Our God is more than enough for what we need.
(Pray the Prayer of Our Savior.)

(Morning)
God, use me in your service today! In our Savior's name I pray. Amen.

(Evening)
Thank you, God. In our Savior's name I pray. Amen.

THURSDAY, AUGUST 5
(Read Psalm 85:8–13)
(Reading from Psalm 105:1–6, 16–22, 45b)

(Morning)
God, thank you for waking me with your love this morning.

(Evening)
God, thank you for granting me peace this day.

Everlasting God, the psalmist was asking you to revive your people by bringing them back to a spiritual life. O God, you are able to do far more, and more abundantly, than we think you can. Our challenge is always to surrender our will to you, to place our trust in you alone, and to listen to what you have to say. If we listen and follow your Word, we have the assurance that righteousness will go before us and prepare the way.

(Morning)
Speak, God, for your child stands ready to hear and obey.
(Prayers of Intercession)

(Evening)
Thank you, God, for Jesus, who is our righteousness.
(Prayers of Intercession)

God grant us your peace which surpasses all our understanding.
(Pray the Prayer of Our Savior.)

(Morning)
God, make me a blessing to someone today. In the Savior's name I pray. Amen.

(Evening)
God, please look upon today's works with favor and grant me your peace. In the Savior's name I pray. Amen.

FRIDAY, AUGUST 6
(Read Romans 10:5–15)

(Morning)
Magnificent God, I begin this day trusting in your promises.

(Evening)
Magnificent God, for the many ways by which
I received your saving grace today, I say amen.

God, you have placed your Word in our mouths and in our hearts, that we may not sin against you. How liberating to know that we have your Word within us! When we stumble and fall short of your glory, all we have to do is turn to your Word, which is within us, and allow it to direct us back to the path of righteousness. God, you placed your Word within us so that we might not sin against you. I need to spend more time reading your Word and listening to your voice in prayer.

(Morning)
Hear me, God, when I call.
(Prayers of Intercession)

(Evening)
Thank you, God, for your saving grace.
(Prayers of Intercession)

As Christ taught his disciples I pray.
(Pray the Prayer of Our Savior.)

(Morning)
God, help me to show someone the way to Christ today. In the Savior's name I pray. Amen.

(Evening)
Thank you, God, for making me a blessing today. Now grant me your peace. In the Savior's name I pray. Amen.

SATURDAY, AUGUST 7
(Read Matthew 14:22–23)

(Morning)
God, I am anxious and afraid. Please replace my anxiety
and fear with your perfect peace.

(Evening)
Thank you, Jesus, for walking the waters with me today.

Blessed God, your child, Jesus, came to save us from our sins. Jesus came to deliver us from our fears and to give us your peace. In the midst of our fears, worries, and doubt, I can hear Jesus say, "My peace I leave to you, my peace I give to you." Whatever the day may bring, I know that Jesus is always there to offer me your peace and say to the waves that buffet me, "Peace! Be still!"

(Morning)
God, give me courage today.
(Prayers of Intercession)

(Evening)
God, for all those who need you to calm their sea right now,
we pray in Jesus' name. Let it be done.
(Prayers of Intercession)

"Take courage! It is I."
(Pray the Prayer of Our Savior.)

(Morning)
Jesus, in your name, give me the
strength to walk out on faith today. In
the Savior's name I pray. Amen.

(Evening)
Thank you for calming the raging sea
for me today. In the Savior's name I
pray. Amen.

SUNDAY, AUGUST 8
(Read Matthew 14:23)

(Morning)
Dear Jesus, because of all that I have to do,
and all that lies before me today, I kneel to you in prayer.

(Evening)
Dear Jesus, meet me. I am alone with you at last.

Redeeming God, seeking solitude was an important priority for Jesus. In solitude, the silence, we find you. Jesus always made room in his busy schedule to be alone with you in prayer. The time I spend alone with you in prayer is valuable. It is sacred time. It will help me grow spiritually in your grace as I become more and more like Christ.

(Morning)
Help me to be patient with others as you are with me.
When out of frustration I lose patience with another, remind me
of the times when, like Peter, I have needed your patience.
(Prayers of Intercession)

(Evening)
Dear Jesus, thank you for your patience with me today.
(Prayers of Intercession)

As Jesus taught his disciples I pray.
(Pray the Prayer of Our Savior.)

(Morning)
Dear Jesus, as I begin this day, I kneel to praise your name. Hallelujah! In your name I pray. Amen.

(Evening)
At the end of this day I kneel to you in thanks. In the Savior's name I pray. Amen.

MONDAY, AUGUST 9
(Read Psalm 133)

(Morning)
Eternal and loving God, as I rise this day,
may I be mindful of the need for unity among your people.

(Evening)
Eternal and loving God, allow me to reflect on the ways
in which I failed to promote unity this day.

O God, whose Spirit makes us one, this day I want to be a vessel to bring unity among your people. We are a diverse people with differing cultures and perspectives on how best to serve you. Help me to be a channel through which your unifying spirit may flow. Help us all to find our common ground in you.

(Morning)
I lift to you now my petitions for your world.
(Prayers of Intercession)

(Evening)
This evening I offer concerns for others and for myself.
(Prayers of Intercession)

And now with renewed joy I pray.
(Pray the Prayer of Our Savior.)

(Morning)
By the power of your Spirit, may we all be one. Through Jesus Christ I pray. Amen.

(Evening)
As I prepare for this evening's rest, may I find assurance in the knowledge of your love and power. In Jesus' name I pray. Amen.

TUESDAY, AUGUST 10
(Read Genesis 45:1–15)

(Morning)
O God, awaken in me this day a spirit of reconciliation and forgiveness.

(Evening)
O God, this day has surrounded me with many
opportunities to be reconciled and to forgive.

Gracious God, sometimes, like Joseph, we feel abandoned by our friends
and loved ones. In fact, God, it is often those with whom we are closest
whose betrayal is most painful. Help us, like Joseph, to forgive and to be
reconciled one with another, and help us to see your divine hand above our
selfish desires.

(Morning)
Help me now to pray for those who have hurt me and for others.
(Prayers of Intercession)

(Evening)
Let me be mindful of the ways in which this day's trials have strengthened me.
(Prayers of Intercession)

And now I humbly pray.
(Pray the Prayer of Our Savior.)

(Morning)
Help me, O God, to be a reconciling
presence in my family and community. In Jesus' name. Amen.

(Evening)
I thank you for rest and renewal after
this day's journey. Bless me to be a
blessing. In Christ's name. Amen.

WEDNESDAY, AUGUST 11
(Read Isaiah 56:1, 6–8)

(Morning)
Loving God, your welcoming spirit invites me to communion
with you and with all people.

(Evening)
Loving God, today you have shown me that all
are welcome at the table of grace.

O God, you teach us through your prophet that you welcome all who become one with you. Enable us to welcome others who may be outside our circle of concern and to receive all who love you as part of our family.

(Morning)
I pray now for all whose needs are known to me.
(Prayers of Intercession)

(Evening)
I offer to you all those whose lives I have touched today.
(Prayers of Intercession)

And now with faith I pray.
(Pray the Prayer of Our Savior.)

(Morning)
Creator God, your inclusive love
enfolds all who call on your name.
Through Christ I pray. Amen.

(Evening)
Merciful God, your love has been a
source of comfort and strength
throughout this day. Allow me to rest
in this assurance as I take my rest. In
Jesus' name I pray. Amen.

THURSDAY, AUGUST 12
(Read Psalm 67)

(Morning)
Gracious God, allow me to see the light of your
countenance as I begin this new day.

(Evening)
Gracious God, your light has shown round about me throughout this day.

Giving God, your blessings are beyond my imagining. You have made a way for me when I thought that a way could not be made. Remind me this day that you are a God who is more than worthy of my praise. Help me to praise you in the midst of your people and when I am alone, that in all times and in all places, I will remember to give thanks and praise to your holy name.

(Morning)
With my whole heart, I magnify your name as I offer these prayers for others.
(Prayers of Intercession)

(Evening)
How wondrous your love has been to me this day.
I thank you for those through whom that love has come.
(Prayers of Intercession)

**All glory, honor, and praise belong to you as I pray
the words of our Savior, Christ.**
(Pray the Prayer of Our Savior.)

(Morning)
Miraculous God, I see your majesty
and marvel at your mercy as I go
forth into this day. In the name of
Jesus. Amen.

(Evening)
As I find rest this evening, may I sleep
in the comfort of your amazing
faithfulness. In the name of Jesus.
Amen.

FRIDAY, AUGUST 13
(Read Romans 11:1–2a, 29–32)

(Morning)
God of great mercy, I thank you for giving me the opportunity
of living another day in your service.

(Evening)
God of great mercy, today you have shown me afresh the depth of your mercy.

O God of grace and mercy, so often I find myself feeling undeserving of your abundant blessings and unworthy of being called your servant. In these times, I allow my humanness to cause me to want to hide my face from your presence and to seek refuge from your Spirit. But then your servant Paul reminds me that you, O God, have shaped us in disobedience so that you might have opportunity to show us your mercy. Great is your faithfulness!

(Morning)
Help me to be the instrument of your mercy
and love as I lift up to you the concerns of those in need.
(Prayers of Intercession)

(Evening)
Today you have not failed to show me your mercy.
Help me to show that same mercy to others as I offer them to you in prayer.
(Prayers of Intercession)

What a mighty and merciful God we serve. In deepest humility I pray.
(Pray the Prayer of Our Savior.)

(Morning)
Let me embark on this new day,
confident of your never-ending mercy.
For Christ's sake. Amen.

(Evening)
May I rest in the expectation of new
mercies when I awake. In Jesus'
name. Amen.

SATURDAY, AUGUST 14
(Read Matthew 15:10–20)

(Morning)
Blessed God, I arise with a song of praise on my lips and your joy in my heart.

(Evening)
Blessed God, your presence today has been a source of comfort and strength.

Liberator God, you challenged the powers that be with your divine wisdom and insight. You showed them and us that our earthly traditions are meaningless unless they are based upon your divine decrees. Help us, O God, to be freed from our desire to follow form and fashion. And instill in us a hunger and thirst for your way.

(Morning)
Today, dear God, help me to remember
that you are all-knowing and all-sufficient.
(Prayers of Intercession)

(Evening)
Today has offered me many challenges and manifold blessings.
Help me to reflect upon them.
(Prayers of Intercession)

Mindful of your wondrous love, I pray as our Savior, Christ, has taught us.
(Pray the Prayer of Our Savior.)

(Morning)
Guide me as I go out into your world
to make a difference. In Jesus' name.
Amen.

(Evening)
As I rest this evening, grant me the
assurance of your providential care.
Through Christ, our Savior. Amen.

SUNDAY, AUGUST 15
(Read Matthew 15:21–28)

(Morning)
Mighty God, I thank you for this day and the ever-new possibilities that it holds.

(Evening)
Mighty God, today's journey has been a maze of turns and curves.
Tonight help me to center on your grace.

O God, your child, Jesus, challenges my understanding of grace through his encounter with the Canaanite woman. I am encouraged by the woman's relentless faith and perseverance on behalf of her child. Help me to see her as an example of how I must come to you with my needs and my petitions. Teach me that every response from you that seems negative does not always mean no; often, it is a simple test of my faith. Grant me the strength to persevere until I get my blessing.

(Morning)
Holy One, with a sincere heart, I come seeking answers to the questions in the depth of my soul. Speak to me now as I pray for those who need you.
(Prayers of Intercession)

(Evening)
Ever-living God, guide me into paths of peace
and safety this night as I seek solace and repose.
(Prayers of Intercession)

Now in reverence I pray.
(Pray the Prayer of Our Savior.)

(Morning)
God, I look to you for new miracles as
I go forward into this day! In Jesus'
name. Amen.

(Evening)
Unfailing God, I reflect on your
blessings this evening, knowing that
in you I find perfect peace. In Jesus'
name. Amen.

MONDAY, AUGUST 16
(Read Exodus 1:8–2:10)

(Morning)
Creator God, thank you for the gift of this day.
Help me to make the most of the opportunities and challenges.

(Evening)
Creator God, for the energy you have provided for the living of this day,
I now give you my thanks. Thank you for courage
to meet the challenges and the grace to face the obstacles.

God, you always find a way. The midwives had the courage to outwit Pharaoh with the wisdom of their trade. They knew what was right and what was wrong. You can almost hear them saying, "You know, Pharaoh, those Hebrew women are just too quick for us. They are not like the Egyptian women; for they are vigorous and give birth before the midwife comes to them." God, you blessed the midwives and gave them families. Their "fear" of you strengthened them to do the extraordinary—to stand against the political system that destroyed life. These women were ordinary people who risked their own lives to save others.

(Morning)
O God of compassion, your care for us is more than we can imagine.
(Prayers of Intercession)

(Evening)
Tomorrow is a new day. Thank you, God, for your care through this long day.
(Prayers of Intercession)

**God, help us be creative and bold in our response
to the injustices in our world.**

(Morning)
Each new day, I know you are with me, O God. I am grateful! In the name of the Christ. Amen.

(Evening)
God, my Companion, be present with me even in my rest. In the name of the Christ. Amen.

TUESDAY, AUGUST 17
(Read Psalm 124)

(Morning)
O God, Guardian of lives, help me be aware today that you are in charge,
not me. You are on my side even when life may seem against me.
My help is in you, who made heaven and earth.

(Evening)
O God, Guardian of lives, I have felt your presence with me this day.
Help me put to rest all the worries and concerns of the day,
so that my spirit will be refreshed by dawn.

How often we try to do things on our own! How often we want to be in control! We would do well to be reminded to relinquish control and trust in you, loving God! Like the psalmist, we sing out, "Blessed be God, who has not given us as prey to our enemies. We have escaped like a bird from the snare of the fowlers; the snare is broken, and we have escaped." Indeed, our help is in you, who made heaven and earth.

(Morning)
O God who has faithfully created the dawn,
may the light of this day give fullness and strength to my life.
(Prayers of Intercession)

(Evening)
God, you are a refuge for those who trust in you!
At the close of this day, be my refuge and strength.
(Prayers of Intercession)

With God on our side, all things are possible.

(Morning)
God is good and gracious, our help when the storms of life rage. May I be reminded of this as I live out the day. In the name of the Christ. Amen.

(Evening)
Thank you, God, for your constancy in a very busy day! In the name of the Christ. Amen.

WEDNESDAY, AUGUST 18
(Read Isaiah 51:1–6)

(Morning)
O God of light, this day has the possibilities of joy and gladness.
Help me find the joy and sift away the bad.

(Evening)
O God of light, I have tried to listen to you in all the voices
I have heard today. Now in this evening time,
I listen again for your comfort, so that my rest may be peaceful.

God, you promise joy and gladness if we but listen. "Listen to me, my people, and give heed to me, my nation; for a teaching will go out from me, and my justice for a light to the peoples." Yes, God, how we yearn for the waste places in our world to be comforted and the desert of our lives to be turned into a garden. Your words are our joy, our light, and our hope!

(Morning)
O God, bring me comfort today as I seek to discern your will for my activities.
Help me listen to your voice and your teaching in all that I do.
(Prayers of Intercession)

(Evening)
Thank you, God, for the light you bring to all.
(Prayers of Intercession)

"Listen to me, my people, and give heed to me, my nation; for a teaching will go out from me, and my justice for a light to the peoples."

(Morning)
O God, I give you thanks today for the gift of the dawn. In the name of the Christ. Amen.

(Evening)
O God of light, the sun is fading, and so is my energy. You have been present in all the moments of this day, giving comfort and courage. May this night of rest restore me. In the name of the Christ. Amen.

THURSDAY, AUGUST 19
(Read Psalm 138)

(Morning)
I give you thanks with my whole heart, O God. I sing your praise and give thanks to your name for your steadfast love and faithfulness.

(Evening)
I give you thanks with my whole heart, O God. I sing your praise and give thanks to your name for your steadfast love and faithfulness.

"Though I walk in the midst of trouble, you God preserve me against the wrath of my enemies; you stretch out your hand and your right hand delivers me." So what do I fear? What holds me back from speaking the truth in love? What holds me back from being courageous and bold when wrong clashes with right? "God will fulfill God's purpose for me," the psalmist proclaims! God will fulfill God's purpose through ordinary persons. God, you are an awesome God!

(Morning)
O God of steadfast love, I give you thanks with my whole heart.
Use me for your purpose this day.
(Prayers of Intercession)

(Evening)
I sing God's praises with my whole heart
and give thanks for God's steadfast love and faithfulness.
(Prayers of Intercession)

God's purposes may be fulfilled through us!

(Morning)
Let me be filled with thanksgiving this day. In the name of the Christ. Amen.

(Evening)
I have called upon you this day, O God, and you have increased my strength of soul. In the name of the Christ. Amen.

FRIDAY, AUGUST 20
(Read Romans 12:1–8)

(Morning)
Merciful God, I approach this new day
hoping to do what is good and acceptable in your sight.

(Evening)
Merciful God, this day has been filled with challenges.
I pray that my actions have been in keeping with your will.

The world is so demanding! How easy it is to be conformed to the world, rather than transformed by God's will.

(Morning)
Renew me today, O God, to do your work.
(Prayers of Intercession)

(Evening)
Transforming God, you have blessed me with the gift of your presence throughout this day. Hear my prayers for . . .
(Prayers of Intercession)

God's love is transforming.

(Morning)
God of wonders, you have given me the gift of another day. Help me do your work graciously. In the name of the Christ. Amen.

(Evening)
God of holy love, thank you for this day. Renew me with this evening of rest. In the name of the Christ. Amen.

SATURDAY, AUGUST 21
(Read Romans 12:1–8)

(Morning)
O inexhaustible God, as I face this new day, be present with me
as I try to use those gifts with which you have blessed me.

(Evening)
O inexhaustible God, thank you for the many gifts you have given me.
Thank you, God, for the gifts of so many people
which have been used to enrich this day.

Thank God that we have many gifts. Wouldn't it be a dull world if only one gift were present? As a community, how rich we are because of one another. "We have gifts that differ according to the grace given to us." Honoring the gifts of one another enriches us all.

(Morning)
O God, I consecrate the living of this day to you.
(Prayers of Intercession)

(Evening)
Be with me now, O God, as I reflect upon the ways in which
I have used the gifts with which you have blessed me.
(Prayers of Intercession)

**I am aware that I don't always use God's gifts and that I don't always
celebrate the gifts of others. I hope I will be more aware.**

(Morning)
Thank you, God, for the dawn. I know
you are with me as I face the new day.
In the name of the Christ. Amen.

(Evening)
O inexhaustible God, I am exhausted.
Thank you for being with me always.
In the name of the Christ. Amen.

SUNDAY, AUGUST 22
(Read Matthew 16:13–20)

(Morning)
Faithful God, I am awakened to new possibilities that this day holds.
Help me make the most of my time today.

(Evening)
Faithful God, you have been with me each step of the way today. Thanks.

When asked the tough questions, it is always easier to defer to others. But Jesus did not let the disciples get away with that! "Who do you say that I am?" And impetuous Peter proclaimed, "You are the Christ!" And Jesus said to Peter, "Blessed are you. . . . You are Peter and upon this rock I will build my church." God, when confronted with naming the Christ in my daily activities, I pray that I, too, can proclaim, "You are the Christ!"

(Morning)
O God, our Rock, and our Guide, hear the prayers for the church and for others.
(Prayers of Intercession)

(Evening)
You have been present today in so many ways, O God.
I have been challenged and comforted by your presence
in all I have said and done. Be with me now in my resting, that I may be
renewed for the new day. Hear my prayers of intercession now.
(Prayers of Intercession)

On the solid rock of Christ I stand; all other ground is sinking sand.

(Morning)
The sunrise ushers in the new day!
May God's peace and presence
surround me today. In the name of the
Christ. Amen.

(Evening)
The sunset marks the ending of the
day. As evening falls, be present, God,
in my resting. In the name of the
Christ. Amen.

MONDAY, AUGUST 23
(Read Exodus 3:1–15)

(Morning)
Voice from the burning bush, dawn has barely broken, and I find myself standing on holy ground when all the while I thought I was at home.

(Evening)
Voice from the burning bush, through this day, I have
encountered you again and again, telling me to take off my shoes.

What kind of God are you that the mere sound of your voice transforms desert shrubs into sacred visions? If your passion will turn a weed into an instrument of holy encounter, what might it do to me? If you plant godly barriers in my path to draw me aside from the day's labor and enlist me in consecrated toil, what will become of my schedule? If you commission a wandering, tongue-tied sheepherder to go striding up to the seat of government, demanding justice, what might you ask of me for heaven's sake? It is this, O Voice of flaming mystery, that I fear most. Like Moses, I would be really grateful if you would send someone else. But then I remember: Moses went. And I recall something else, too: he did not go alone; you went with him, your resounding "I Am" undergirding his irresolute "I can."

(Morning)
Undergird me, too, so that this day's demons feel the heat of my courage.
I begin by entreating your mercy for those I am to serve.
(Prayers of Intercession)

(Evening)
Thank you for the times today that your mystery surprised me,
refreshing my awareness of your love.
(Prayers of Intercession)

In the name of Jesus, whose words live again on my lips.
(Pray the Prayer of Our Savior.)

(Morning)
I have to go now. Alert me, through this day, to your mercy burning around me. In Christ's name. Amen.

(Evening)
As I go to my rest, let the vision of your flame renew my courage, for I mean to serve you tomorrow. In Christ's name. Amen.

TUESDAY, AUGUST 24
(Read Psalm 105:1–6, 23–26, 45c)

(Morning)
At the rising of the sun, great Source of all blessing,
creation's glory opens my eyes, and words of praise, my lips.

(Evening)
At the setting of the sun, great Source of all blessing,
my eyes close with thanksgiving and my mouth with words of thanks.

Of all the people of earth, Sovereign of history, we have most for which to praise you. All about us spreads a world too sublime for realization—this blue-green jewel floating in the ebony of space, frame for inert things and spirited creaturehood arrayed in splendid complexity, each owning its own glory and testifying to yours. From it, we are privileged to derive not just our livelihood but comfort—not just recreation but aesthetic enjoyment. Through its history, we discern your participation in the affairs of the human family, to which we testify in the recital of our sacred story. Your glorious acts on your people's behalf, rehearsed in details of formation and frustration, captivity and liberation, redeem our struggles also, encouraging us the more entirely to strive to become your people. We will, indeed, "Praise God!"

(Morning)
This day, Creator God, I want to praise you even more with action than with
thought, more with deed than word, beginning with these petitions.
(Prayers of Intercession)

(Evening)
Before I let this day go, Creator God, I pause once again
to thank you for these special blessings, which I receive
from your unbounded mercy and covet for others.
(Prayers of Intercession)

One more time I reclaim the words of Jesus.
(Pray the Prayer of Our Savior.)

(Morning)	(Evening)
I go to my day's work remembering more than ever "the wonderful works you have done." In Christ's name. Amen.	Now I am content to lay this day to rest, knowing that your love sustains this world, even while I sleep. In Christ's name. Amen.

WEDNESDAY, AUGUST 25
(Read Jeremiah 15:15–21)

(Morning)
O God, I who am called by your name, begin my day by turning
anew to you, who are the source of my being and my salvation.

(Evening)
O God, I, who am called by your name, conclude my day by turning again to
you, who are my defense against all that intend my undoing.

How will I live, O Ground of my being, unless you continually remember
me and visit me? I seek to conform my life to your precepts because your
Word, a delight and joy to my heart, lives in my flesh and compels my
devotion. But hear my confession; sometimes it is so hard. I am all flesh
and blood, a creature preoccupied with place and reputation. In spite of my
best intentions, your way evades me; not always, but often enough to sap
my confidence and paint my days the color of gloom. Hardest of all to bear
is not the ravaging of enemies but the betrayal of false friends. I am not
able to walk your way alone. If one whom the generations have lauded as
your true servant cries in fear, why should my own moments of dread as-
tonish or discourage?

(Morning)
With Jeremiah, I plead; your hand can heal what seem to me
wounds incurable. Grant me this restoration, merciful God;
and hear, too, my prayer for those others in need.
(Prayers of Intercession)

(Evening)
By the power of your Word within me, merciful God, make me, too,
a wall of bronze against which none who seek to diminish
my servanthood may prevail; for whom, even now, I pray.
(Prayers of Intercession)

By the mercy of Jesus, who framed for us these redeeming words.
(Pray the Prayer of Our Savior.)

(Morning)
I go now to face my day, not as one
who does not know fear, but as one in
whom dread no longer is the control-
ling authority. Please, valiant God,
walk with me. In Christ's name. Amen.

(Evening)
I return the day you gave me, O God,
conceding that your faithfulness, not
my fear, defined its labors and
redeemed its hours. In humility I
reaffirm it. I am so proud to be called
by your name! In Christ's name.
Amen.

THURSDAY, AUGUST 26
(Read Psalm 26:1–8)

(Morning)
God of righteousness, hear the morning prayer of one who
desires to live this day uprightly according to the teaching of my God.

(Evening)
God of righteousness, as at morning's first light,
now in the twilight of this day I ask your vindication of my labors.

I do not seek, Ground of all justice, to assert my own virtue, lest true virtue expose my words as illusion, the merchandise of self-deception. Where I sink into a gloat of self-congratulation, purge me, O God, and forgive me. Yet I know, as the psalmist knew, that virtue is both precious to you and essential for our welfare. Where hypocrisy and evil prevail, rectitude withers and integrity dies. How, then, will I live? Can I claim to be a servant of the God of righteousness if I am not myself clothed in righteousness? Will integrity find a home in the world if it cannot first find shelter among the people of God? So teach me to wear your steadfast love as my countenance and measure my stride by the rule of your fidelity; for I mean not to betray you but to serve you as one who loves the place where your glory abides.

(Morning)
I begin this day by remembering, before you, persons known to me
and circumstances of which I am aware that need your mercy.
(Prayers of Intercession)

(Evening)
I end this day by remembering before you persons and circumstances that I do
not know about, but which are known to you and are in need of your mercy.
(Prayers of Intercession)

On behalf of all of these, everywhere, I pray the dearest prayer of all.
(Pray the Prayer of Our Savior.)

(Morning)	(Evening)
Prove me this day, my God, and try me. Test my heart and mind and let me be counted among your righteous ones. In Christ's name. Amen.	I submit this night to your judgment, knowing that your mercy will perfect in me the virtue that returns faithfulness for faithfulness, seeking steadfastly to serve God. In Christ's name. Amen.

FRIDAY, AUGUST 27
(Read Romans 12:9–21)

(Morning)
God of creation and re-creation, another new day is mine,
this gift of opportunity, to become what you call me to be.

(Evening)
God of creation and re-creation, the coming embrace of night bids me pause to
take stock: where have I served you, where have I failed you, this day?

What a humiliation is this, O God, that the title "Christian" should be
freighted with shame as much as honor, not because the word of faith is
wrong but because what we do tarnishes what we say. Is it really such a
mystery—the matter of right conduct—or do we simply mean to excuse
ourselves? With heedless disregard, we transform the gospel's candor into
hardship and your church into a poster-child of hypocrisy. Now comes your
apostle Paul to rescue us, scribing with breathless eloquence the character
traits of the people of the way, a laundry list of the sublime. Studying it, the
realization dawns: the difficulty lies not in the list but in ourselves. To live
as Jesus' re-created people is a hard task only if we are so devoted to living
according to other criteria that we are not free to live by those of Jesus.

(Morning)
Shame me, patient God, who waits for our turning with even greater compassion
than you expect us to employ in our dealings with others, for whom I pray.
(Prayers of Intercession)

(Evening)
Free us, patient god, from all the hindrances that we strew in our own paths,
so that we can see more clearly the path of Christ and walk it.
(Prayers of Intercession)

Praying again Jesus' simply eloquent words, I say . . .
(Pray the Prayer of Our Savior.)

(Morning)	(Evening)
Now I embark on my new day of opportunity, unsure where it may lead but confident that so long as you lead, it will go where it ought. In Christ's name. Amen.	Remind me, as I wrap this day up and lay it away forever, that at my waking you will give me a new one, alive with your re-creative Spirit. In Christ's name. Amen.

SATURDAY, AUGUST 28
(Read Matthew 16:21–23)

(Morning)
My God, I just read again of Jesus' anger at the failure of his disciples in general—and Peter in particular—to comprehend the price of redemption.

(Evening)
My God, I am still trying to get straight how differently you
and I look at things: what is important and what trivial.

This is the real hard stumbling block, isn't it, God of surprising ways, that our minds seem always to focus on human things to the exclusion of things that are eternal? Poor Peter—the big-framed, well-intentioned bumbler— once again on the short end of Jesus' patience. How that caustic rebuke must have stung: "Get behind me, Satan!" The child in me knows Peter's shame. I am more familiar with it than I care to admit—the flushed face that comes from being well and publicly scolded. Chagrin gives way to petulant anger at the insult. Yet I know, down deep, that I am hurt most for having been singed by truth. And herein is truth, that I have it coming! The suffering of Christ speaks to eternal things, while my mind is preoccupied with the trivial, my life spent in pursuit of that which cannot save.

(Morning)
Dear God, I need your correction but also your forgiveness: the first, that I may live aright; the second, that I may live at all. So I pray for myself and others.
(Prayers of Intercession)

(Evening)
Dear God, thank you for your correction and your forgiveness: the first,
aligning my mind with yours; the second, freeing me to forgive others,
who I remember before you.
(Prayers of Intercession)

Finally, in the words of my Savior I pray.
(Pray the Prayer of Our Savior.)

(Morning)
Sovereign of history, align my heart and mind with divine intention, so that this day I am not a stumbling block to Christ, to myself, or to anyone else. In Christ's name. Amen.

(Evening)
Like Peter, I sometimes earn your rebuke. Like Peter, I also know your unconditional forgiveness. In the end, like Peter, tip the balance in me from the human to the divine, not for my sake but for the sake of Christ. Amen.

SUNDAY, AUGUST 29
(Read Matthew 16:24–28)

(Morning)
God of redemptive suffering, I am shaken awake this morning
by the exorbitant claim that Jesus makes on my loyalty.

(Evening)
God of redemptive suffering, it would be so much easier
to reject Jesus' invitation to embrace his sacrifice if only
he had not already done everything he now asks of me.

I thought I had it all straight when I sifted through Paul's list of the hallmarks of Christian living. I concluded, "I can do this. All I have to do is put my mind to it." Now, all of a sudden and before I have had time to absorb the shock, Jesus raises the stakes, instructing me that I must be prepared to take up my cross and haul it down life's road after him. I do not like crosses. They promise too much of pain and humiliation, too little of recognition and contentment. Nor does it help to learn that this is a condition of my adoption as a child of heaven—that to save my life, I must let it go. But then I am confronted by the holy punch line: if I am willing to accept Christ's death as a gift worthy to secure my redemption, can I deny my own life as the only gift sufficient to affirm my reconciliation?

(Morning)
Knowing how hard this equation is for me to absorb, Sovereign Majesty,
it must be equally so for others, for whose courage and endurance I now plead.
(Prayers of Intercession)

(Evening)
Knowing that you ask nothing of us that you have not already given,
Sovereign Majesty, I pray for your whole church—all who are redeemed by
Christ's sacrifice.
(Prayers of Intercession)

Christ's gift makes me bold again to pray.
(Pray the Prayer of Our Savior.)

(Morning)
The shadow of the cross marks my path today, O God, whether I wish it or not. Help me, I humbly pray, not to shrink from it, but to live and embrace it, for my Savior's sake. In Christ's name I pray. Amen.

(Evening)
The shadow of the cross rests on my bed tonight, O God, whether I wish it or not. Mark me with it, as one bought with a price, who will rise with Christ tomorrow and in the life to come. In Christ's name I pray. Amen.

MONDAY, AUGUST 30
(Read Romans 13:8–14)
(Sing "It Is Well with My Soul" or another familiar song)

(Morning)
God of love and peace, I give you thanks and praise this day.
This day, pour out your Holy Spirit upon me so that everything I do
will be pleasing and acceptable in your sight.

(Evening)
God of love and peace, clothe me with your armor
of protection as I slumber this night.

Gracious God, even after we've been baptized by water, blessed with the presence of the Holy Sprit, and heard it proclaimed in your Word, we are still blinded by unbelief. Savior God, help our unbelief this day. Help us to love you and our neighbors as we should. Make me an example to someone who may need to know of your love and your grace. Help me live by your Word. Let it abide in me, so that my mouth is forever uttering your praises.

(Morning)
You are a God of forgiveness, peace, and love.
Bless us, watch over us, and grant us your mercy and peace.
(Prayers of Intercession)

(Evening)
Most loving and merciful God, I pray for your holy presence
in our lives and for your ever-present peace to watch over us.
(Prayers of Intercession)

Hear my earnest and humble prayer.
(Pray the Prayer of Our Savior.)

(Morning)
Your Word teaches us to love our neighbors as ourselves. Yet we are judgmental and always at war with those around us. Grant us your peace. In Christ's name. Amen.

(Evening)
I give you thanks for this day, for the trials and for the joys. I ask forgiveness for all that was done that was not pleasing in your sight. I pray for you to hold me in the safety of your bosom as I slumber through the night. And if it is your will, I'll wake in the morning to face another new day. In Christ's name. Amen.

TUESDAY, AUGUST 31
(Read Exodus 12:1–14 and Psalm 149)
(Sing "Yes, Lord" or another familiar song)

(Morning)
Loving and gracious God, the birds are singing, the sun is smiling
down upon us, and the winds have shaken me from my slumber.
For this new day, God, I give you much thanks and praise.

(Evening)
Loving and gracious God, it was you who woke me this day,
and it is your presence that I ask for this night.
Watch over me and keep me safe in your arms of protection.

Trials and tribulations come my way, making my days bleak and my nights
long. Nonetheless, dear God, in my weariness I continue to give you thanks
and utter praises from my mouth. I know that in doing I will find the answers I seek and my soul will find peace from weariness. Christ Jesus, I
pray that my life is a living testimony of all that you are and of all that the
cross on Calvary stands for.

(Morning)
Dear God you have given us an awesome task this day.
I pray that we accomplish it with joy, thanksgiving, and praise.
And all that is before us I pray will be done pleasingly in your sight.
(Prayers of Intercession)

(Evening)
God, the day is drawing to a close. I pray that I have lived your Word,
your love, and your works this day. I pray that my life has been
an example of all that your child, Jesus, died for.
(Prayers of Intercession)

With the assurance of the promises commanded in your Word I pray.
(Pray the Prayer of Our Savior.)

(Morning)
Dear God, with the dawning of this
new day, I present myself a willing
servant here on earth. Use me, dear
God. In Christ's name. Amen.

(Evening)
Sovereign God, I rest this night with
the assurance that your angels are
keeping watch over me. Bind evil in
the walls of hell, that your child may
rest in peace. In Christ's name. Amen.

WEDNESDAY, SEPTEMBER 1
(Read Ezekiel 33:7–11 and Psalm 119:33–40)
(Sing "Have a Little Talk with Jesus" or another familiar song)

(Morning)
Giver of life, teach me this day your Word, so that I may be
of service to you and others. Guide and direct my path in all that I do.

(Evening)
Giver of life, in the stillness of the night, I confess my sins before you,
knowing that I am a sinner in need of your saving grace and direction.
I thank you for guiding and directing my path this day.

God, as we all rush through the day, doing our own thing, we sometimes
fail to find the quiet space where we can have a face-to-face talk with you.
Sometimes, God, we forget that all that we need to do is to ask for your
guidance, direction, and understanding. Righteous God, sprinkle an anointing of the Holy Spirit upon us that will bathe us in your Word and clothe us
in your righteousness.

(Morning)
Holy One, bathe me in your Word; wash me in the blood of your child,
Jesus; cleanse and restore in me a righteous heart.
(Prayers of Intercession)

(Evening)
God, I am your child, and into your care and protection I commend my soul.
(Prayers of Intercession)

**In the stillness of my talk with you, O God,
I pray to you with the assurance of your grace.**
(Pray the Prayer of Our Savior.)

(Morning)
God, you are worthy of my praises all the day long. I call the name of Jesus when I need a friend, when my body is aching, when trials and tribulations seem to be coming in all directions. God, hear this sinner's pleas for your forgiveness and love and peace. In Jesus' name. Amen.

(Evening)
On the name of Jesus I have called the whole day long. The name of Jesus has been my protector, my rock, and my strength. The name of Jesus has been my guide and my direction. With this name ever present on my lips, I rest this night. In Jesus' name. Amen.

THURSDAY, SEPTEMBER 2
(Read Matthew 18:15–20)
(Sing "Amazing Grace")

(Morning)
Loving and gracious God, I thank you for the beginning of this new day.
I thank you for the chance to start afresh and for the chance to live in peace
and harmony with my brothers and sisters.

(Evening)
Loving and gracious God, my Protector and my Shield, I give you thanks.
Thank you for another day and another chance to live as your humble servant.

God of forgiveness and mercy, sometimes it is easier to hold on to the
hurts, pain, and dissension against our brothers and sisters. We claim to
love you, whom we have not seen, yet we let hurt and anger against our
neighbors linger in our hearts. God, we claim to believe and to follow your
commandments. Yet we ignore and overlook one of your greatest commandments—to love our brothers and sisters as we love ourselves. Gracious God, help us to remember the promise and declaration that Jesus
made on the cross at Calvary. Help us to look to the Holy Spirit, who lives
within us, to forgive, love, and accept our neighbors in the name of Christ.

(Morning)
Help me to follow your commandment and to live in peace.
(Prayers of Intercession)

(Evening)
Today I have walked in the path of peace.
(Prayers of Intercession)

In the name of a living and forgiving God I pray.
(Pray the Prayer of Our Savior.)

(Morning)
Forgiving as I seek your forgiveness,
help me to forgive my brothers and
sisters this day. Cleanse my heart of
ungodliness, and help me to love as I
should, so that I can do your work here
on earth. In Christ's name. Amen.

(Evening)
Holy One, I give you thanks that I
can lie down this night with my heart
at peace. I know that as I prepare to
slumber, you have forgiven me. I
have also found from your Spirit that
the spirit of forgiveness lives within
me. In Christ's name. Amen.

FRIDAY, SEPTEMBER 3
(Read Matthew 18:15–20)
(Sing "Stand by Me" or another familiar song)

(Morning)
Forgiving and gracious God, help me to live this day mindful
to treat those around me with love and compassion.

(Evening)
Forgiving and gracious God, I thank you for healing that helped me to live this
day in peace and harmony with my brothers and sisters.
Grant me, I pray, a restful night.

Forgiving, compassionate, and loving God, sometimes in our attempt to be
right, we fail to treat our neighbors as we should. We live in turmoil need-
lessly. We fail to stop and listen to what is being said through your Word.
Grant us powers of reconciliation, so that we can all live in peace and harmony. Ever-seeing and ever-present God, we thank you for your child, Jesus
Christ. Because of Jesus' suffering, death, and resurrection we are victorious over the bondage of sin and evil. We can gather in your name and know
with assurance that you will be in our midst, guiding our paths, directing
our ways, and instructing our tongues.

(Morning)
Creator and Sovereign God, for my brothers and sisters I pray.
(Prayers of Intercession)

(Evening)
Ever-loving God and Protector, keep your children
in the bosom of your protection this night.
(Prayers of Intercession)

With faith the size of a mustard seed I pray.
(Pray the Prayer of Our Savior.)

(Morning)
God, your Word teaches us forgiveness and love for our brothers and
sisters. Help me to let your Word
abide in me, and me in your Word.
Help me to treat my neighbors with
compassion, understanding, and love.
In Christ's name. Amen.

(Evening)
Holy and ever-present Parent, tonight
as I prepare to slumber, I give you
praise and thanks for the spirit of
forgiveness and reconciliation. I pray
that your love and Word continue to
abide with me as I find rest, tucked
safely in your arms. In Christ's name.
Amen.

SATURDAY, SEPTEMBER 4
(Read Romans 13:8–14)
(Sing "Precious Lord, Take My Hand")

(Morning)
God of heaven and stars, in the dawning of this new day, I give you thanks
for a restful night and praises for all that this new day promises.

(Evening)
God of heaven and stars, let your light shine on me this night
as I slumber under your watchful eye.

Understanding and forgiving God, I stand before you in need of your direction and guidance. Direct my path, that everything I do will be pleasing and acceptable in your sight. Gracious Teacher, teach me the way that I should go, so that my life will be a living testimony to your goodness.

(Morning)
God of love, clothe your children with the armor of righteousness,
so that in everything they do, they place you at center stage.
(Prayers of Intercession)

(Evening)
Compassionate God, watch over your children as they slumber this night.
(Prayers of Intercession)

With a renewed spirit I pray.
(Pray the Prayer of Our Savior.)

(Morning)
Patient and gracious Teacher, today I will be a living testimony to someone who may need to hear your Word. Help me to answer to the challenges of this day, uplifting and praising your wondrous works. In Christ's name. Amen.

(Evening)
Holy and compassionate God, I give you thanks this day for your teachings, for your forgiveness, and for your love. I pray that I have lived this day loving and treating my neighbors as I should. Now, Holy One, as I slumber, I pray for your protection through the night. In Christ's name. Amen.

SUNDAY, SEPTEMBER 5

(Read Psalm 149 and Exodus 12:1–14)
(Sing "Oh, How I Love Jesus")

(Morning)
God of new beginnings, I thank you for another new day to be your willing
and humble servant. Use me, God. Let me be a temple of your love,
your peace, your joy, and your Word.

(Evening)
God of new beginnings, in your arms I find safety and rest for my soul.
Abide with me, gracious God.

Great is your faithfulness and worthy of our praises are you, gracious God.
For the many blessings that you have given us, God, your name will forever be lifted from my mouth. For your redemptive love and saving grace,
my heart shouts "hallelujah." For washing and cleansing me of all
unrighteousness and restoring my temple to righteousness, I give you thanks
and praise.

(Morning)
Loving God, you invite me to pray for others as well as for myself.
Hear my prayer.
(Prayers of Intercession)

(Evening)
God of peace, grant your children a safe resting place this night.
(Prayers of Intercession)

With praise and thanksgiving I pray.
(Pray the Prayer of Our Savior.)

(Morning)
God of new and wondrous beginnings, we do not know what is before
us this day. But we pray that we
answer to the tasks and challenges
before us with a willing and humble
spirit in everything we do. We pray
that our actions will be pleasing and
acceptable in your sight. In Christ's
name. Amen.

(Evening)
Trustworthy God, I slumber this night
with the assurance of your protection. I
rest this night knowing that my life is
tucked safely and securely in your
arms. In Christ's name. Amen.

MONDAY, SEPTEMBER 6
(Read Exodus 14:19–3 1)

(Morning)
O God, be with me as I seek to increase my trust in your Word
and my faith in your presence.

(Evening)
O God, I give thanks to you for abandoning neither me nor the world.

There are those moment when I doubt. It is especially true when I observe the pain and struggle in the world. Then I am reminded, God, that you move in human history in ways that amaze me. You make a way out of no way. When I am fearful and filled with anxiety, I begin to see evidences of your hand and your footprints changing the very course of events. Praise be to you, Savior God.

(Morning)
God, when I am cast down, lift me up, so that I may feel
and see your presence in the world.
(Prayers of Intercession)

(Evening)
Today I reaffirmed that you have the world in your hands.
(Prayers of Intercession)

**God does step into the human condition.
We must be open to God's actions.**

(Morning)
O God, how good it is to know that you are God! In Jesus' name. Amen.

(Evening)
Touch me and touch all peoples in the world. Make a "way" for all of us. In Jesus' name. Amen.

TUESDAY, SEPTEMBER 7
(Read Exodus 14:19–31)

(Morning)
O God, I will sing praises to you all the day long.

(Evening)
O God, thank you for all you have done. I thank you with my whole body.

God, when I think of you and remember how you reach into life and save us from the dangers of conflict, I can only exclaim your praise. Loving God, I praise you with my lips, with my hands, with songs and shouts. Let me never forget you, O God, or forget to give thanks. You are my strength when I have no strength. You are my way when I have no way.

(Morning)
Today I will sing your praise with my whole being.
(Prayers of Intercession)

(Evening)
Even as the night falls, I will continue to give you praise.
(Prayers of Intercession)

Never forget to sing God's praises.

(Morning)
I awaken to your presence with songs of praise on my lips. May they remain throughout this day. In Jesus' name. Amen.

(Evening)
As the night falls and I close my eyes, let me do so with songs of praise on my lips. In Jesus' name. Amen.

WEDNESDAY, SEPTEMBER 8
(Read Psalm 114)

(Morning)
Holy, holy, holy God, you are the holy Other. I tremble in your presence.
You are in heaven and earth.

(Evening)
Holy, holy, holy God, I bow before your presence—
you, who are before me and behind me.

Worship is a wondrous experience. I can worship while I work, while I play, when I am sitting down, and when I am standing up. When I think of you, God, and your creative genius, I am touched that I can call upon you as my personal God. I do so in awe and wonder. I tremble when I think of you, who created the universe, and yet you know me by name. Let us all praise you, omnipotent God.

(Morning)
God, you never fail me or anyone who calls upon your name in faith.
(Prayers of Intercession)

(Evening)
God, you are a great and good God. I tremble in your presence,
but I do not fear you.
(Prayers of Intercession)

God is awesome yet loving.

(Morning)
Let me come into your presence, God,
with joy and thanksgiving. In Jesus'
name. Amen.

(Evening)
You have been with me all the day
long. Let me rest myself in you. In
Jesus' name. Amen.

252

THURSDAY, SEPTEMBER 9
(Read Genesis 50:15–21)

(Morning)
God, may I have a forgiving heart this day. Jesus calls us to forgive
seventy times seven. May I live up to this counsel today.

(Evening)
God, you have forgiven me. I pray that I have forgotten
the slights and forgiven others this day.

I must always remember that what others mean for evil, God, you mean for
good. I must always pray not to return evil for evil, but to learn to forgive.
I know how to forgive because I have been forgiven by you, forgiving God,
and by others. I must remember that at the heart of the Christian life in
relation to others is the quality of my forgiving spirit.

(Morning)
A forgiving and contrite heart is what God requires of me today.
(Prayers of Intercession)

(Evening)
Have I helped someone today by forgiving him or her?
(Prayers of Intercession)

God can change evil into good.

(Morning)
God, you have shown us the way to
forgive. May I also forgive? In Jesus'
name. Amen.

(Evening)
May I not close my eyes this day
without forgiving someone. In Jesus'
name. Amen.

FRIDAY, SEPTEMBER 10
(Read Psalm 103:8–13)

(Morning)
God, I have awakened once again to the truth
that through Christ my life has been redeemed.

(Evening)
God, I pray that I have proclaimed this day, in thought,
word, and deed, that you can and do redeem us all.

God, you are a redemptive God. You judge, you forgive, and you redeem. Of all the names ascribed to you, none is more important to me than knowing that you are the Redeemer. Loving God, you do not deal with us according to our sins. I am, at times, overwhelmed that you—who know my down-sitting and my up-rising, my sins of omission as well as my sins of commission—do not deal with me according to my weakness. God, you redeem me!

(Morning)
God, you have redeemed me with your love. Let me never forget you.
(Prayers of Intercession)

(Evening)
Again I end my day as a redeemed person. I have been redeemed by God.
(Prayers of Intercession)

Touch me, O redeeming God!

(Morning)
As your child, I thank you for saving my life. In Jesus' name. Amen.

(Evening)
Let me rest this night with the knowledge that God has been good to me. In Jesus' name. Amen.

SATURDAY, SEPTEMBER 11
(Read Romans 14:1–12)

(Morning)
God, I pray that I will not be judgmental today.

(Evening)
God, may I remember as night comes that only you judge.

God, we live in a world of conflicting opinions. We often differ with one another. We must remember to differ with love. I have come to realize that in differing with another, I need not pass judgment. Whoever differs with me, I have come to understand that we are one in Christ. As brothers and sisters in Christ, there is no place for judgment.

(Morning)
I pray this day that I will see my brothers and sisters in Christ
as objects of my love, not as objects of my judgment.
(Prayers of Intercession)

(Evening)
I have left my differences with others at the altar of God.
(Prayers of Intercession)

Deliver me from being a person who judges more than loves.

(Morning)
God of love and hope, hear me when I
pray to be delivered from being
judgmental. In Jesus' name. Amen.

(Evening)
As Christ has taught, I now pray the
Prayer of Our Savior . . .

SUNDAY, SEPTEMBER 12
(Read Matthew 18:21–35)

(Morning)
Forgiving God, it is not enough for me to forgive with my lips.
I must forgive from the heart.

(Evening)
Forgiving God, I pray that I have been forgiving this day.

Forgiving God, why is it that I say I forgive and yet continue to remember the slights and the offenses caused by others? Why do I seek forgiveness while, at the same time, I do not forgive others? If I remember the slights and the perceived offenses, then I have not forgiven with my heart. Truly it is not enough to forgive with my lips. I must forgive with my heart.

(Morning)
Forgive us our sins as we forgive the sins of others.
(Prayers of Intercession)

(Evening)
I pray that no one can say of me that I have been unforgiving this day.
(Prayers of Intercession)

Help me to be a forgiving person.

(Morning)
Dear God, you have taught me how to forgive by forgiving me in Jesus Christ. In Jesus' name. Amen.

(Evening)
Wash me thoroughly, O God, so that I might sleep this night with a clean and forgiving heart. In Jesus' name. Amen.

MONDAY, SEPTEMBER 13
(Read Exodus 16:2–15)

(Morning)
Gracious God, for the opportunity to make a fresh start this week, I give you thanks. Help me not to dwell on mistakes of the past, but rather to focus on the abundant life you have promised for my present and my future.

(Evening)
Gracious God, help me to see your providence in both the joys and the trials that come my way in life, and teach me to give thanks in all things.

Jehovah-Jireh, God our Provider, I thank you for providing for me during the wilderness experiences of my life. In those periods of transition, when there was no security to be found anywhere, you continued to provide the basics of shelter, food, and clothing. In the midst of financial hardship and reversals, give us the confidence that everything we need will be provided in the timing that you choose. As the gospel song goes, "You may not come when we want you, but you're always right on time." Thank you for the many times you have intervened in the nick of time, often in ways I did not expect.

(Morning)
Eternal God, give me wisdom in dealing with difficult personalities today.
Let your light be seen in my life.
(Prayers of Intercession)

(Evening)
When the many demands of being spouse, parent, child, employee, student, entrepreneur, and disciple become too great and the unending juggling act seems impossible to keep up, remind me, dear God, that those who wait upon you will renew their strength.
(Prayers of Intercession)

"I have been young, and now am old, yet I have not seen the righteous forsaken or their children begging bread."

(Morning)
O God, who created all that we see and know, grant me creativity and resourcefulness in the exercise of my duties today. In your dear Child's name. Amen.

(Evening)
Visit my sleep, O God, inspiring me with the ideas and strategies I will need to make tomorrow successful in every way. In the name of Jesus I pray. Amen.

TUESDAY, SEPTEMBER 14
(Read Psalm 105:1–6)

(Morning)
Eternal God, help me to share with others the wonders
and miracles you have performed in my life. Use my testimony
to inspire others to want to know you better.

(Evening)
Eternal God, at the close of the day, I say "thank you" for doing
what others could not do, for opening doors that others could not open,
for closing doors that others could not close.

Teach me that praise is always appropriate and always in order, dear God. Others are not ashamed to offer high praise for mortal sports figures and movie stars. Why should I, a child of the most high God, be embarrassed to express in excited fashion what you have done for me and others? Help me to keep my priorities in order and to recognize what is really worthy of praise and really worth getting excited about.

(Morning)
Forgive me, O God, for being so focused on my own narrow concerns
that I often do not reach out to others in greater pain and greater need.
Mend broken hearts and heal wounded spirits everywhere today.
(Prayers of Intercession)

(Evening)
O God most high, give strength coupled with wisdom to our world leaders.
Enable them to make just decisions, so that more might dwell in safety and
fewer might dwell in hunger and disease.
(Prayers of Intercession)

"This is God's doing; it is marvelous in our eyes."

(Morning)
Open my spiritual eyes today, God of hosts, that I might see good in those others deem bad and envision hope for those some have dismissed as hopeless. In Jesus' name. Amen.

(Evening)
Jehovah-Ropheka, God my Healer, ease the aches, pains, and discomforts of the physical body so that my sleep might be sound and restorative. In Jesus' name. Amen.

WEDNESDAY, SEPTEMBER 15
(Read Psalm 105:37–45)

(Morning)
Jehovah-Shammah, God who is present, I begin this day making melody
in my heart to you. May I inspire others to join in my song of praise
and thanksgiving for your many blessings.

(Evening)
Jehovah-Shammah, God who is present, thank you for these moments of
solitude and reflection, and for the renewal of body, mind, and spirit
that comes from being in your presence.

Gracious God, I marvel at the fact that when you delivered your people
from slavery, they did not leave Egypt empty-handed. Loaded down with
the gold and silver of Pharaoh's realm, they exited in joy and gladness. The
Israelites rejoiced over their freedom from bondage in Egypt and the rich,
new life that awaited them in the promised land. Likewise, help me to rejoice over my freedom from both the grip and penalty of sin, secured through
Christ's atoning work on the cross. Teach me to appreciate the spiritual
riches of a life in Christ.

(Morning)
I hurriedly switched television channels last night to avoid seeing a commercial
about hungry children, O God. This morning, I pretended not to see a homeless
person in the center of town. But I saw both. Use me and reluctant others to
provide for all those in need.
(Prayers of Intercession)

(Evening)
For the battered, the broke, and the brokenhearted I pray, dear God.
Release them from their prisons of abuse, poverty, and loneliness.
(Prayers of Intercession)

"So if the Savior makes you free, you will be free indeed."

(Morning)
All-wise God, help me to take the
high road when others want to be
rude, gossipy, or argumentative. Let
Christ be seen in me. In Jesus' name.
Amen.

(Evening)
Eternal God, allow me to rise tomorrow with new vigor and energy, ready
for both the day's challenges and
blessings. In Jesus' name. Amen.

THURSDAY, SEPTEMBER 16
(Read Philippians 1:21–26)

(Morning)
Gracious God, I begin the day with the sense that, ultimately, I live and work for you. Help me to use time and resources in ways that please you.

(Evening)
Gracious God, I pause to reflect in quietness on the many ways you intervened on my behalf today. Thank you for being mindful of the various "situations" of my life and for handling them when I cannot.

The weight of the cares of this life can be so heavy at times, dear God. Like the apostle Paul, we wrestle with them. We are anxious to be in eternal peace and rest with Christ, but we are aware that there are many who need us and depend on us in the here and now. More than anyone, you depend on us to get your work done in the world. Teach us to be patient in the pains, disappointments, discomforts, and inconveniences of this life as we make sacrifices for your work and for others in Jesus' name.

(Morning)
O God, give renewed hope, joy, and sense of purpose today to those who have given up on life. Banish thoughts of suicide as you bless some with justice, others with long-overdue happiness, and still others with ways to make a positive difference in their world.
(Prayers of Intercession)

(Evening)
The sun sets now, but the Christ ever shines in the souls of those who love you, merciful God. Let the weak and defenseless who name the name of Jesus find strength and protection in you.
(Prayers of Intercession)

"For to me, living is Christ and dying is gain."

(Morning)
All-wise God, give me the wisdom to balance tough and tender approaches today as I seek to discern and do your will in my daily responsibilities. In the name of Jesus I pray. Amen.

(Evening)
God, my Protector, I commit mind, body, and soul to your safekeeping this night. Watch over everyone and everything that concerns me. In the name of Jesus I pray. Amen.

FRIDAY, SEPTEMBER 17
(Read Philippians 1:27–30)

(Morning)
O God, may newness of life and vibrancy of spirit permeate all
that you cause me to undertake today.

(Evening)
O God, for another opportunity to be alone in your presence,
I give you thanks. Give continued strength for the journey.

In doing your work, I find that I often step on toes and offend unintention-
ally those whose motives and hearts are not pure. Gracious God, help me
not to be afraid of my enemies, but rather to be steadfast in doing your will,
even when it means persecution. You are my light and my salvation, O
God. Whom shall I fear and of what shall I be afraid? When your child
returns for the church, may I be standing fast with others who labor in the
faith—all of us of one mind and of one spirit as we work to carry out your
purposes in the face of opposition.

(Morning)
In prayer, I weep with those who weep and rejoice with those who rejoice today.
Console the bereaved and brokenhearted while you help others cope with the
responsibilities and temptations that accompany fame and success.
(Prayers of Intercession)

(Evening)
Forgive me, O God, for kind words left unsaid and helpful deeds
left undone today. Send words of encouragement
and assistance of all kinds to those who desperately need them.
(Prayers of Intercession)

"You prepare a table before me in the presence of my enemies."

(Morning)
Order my steps and my affairs this
day, dear God, that I may accomplish
all that you intend. In the marvelous
name of Jesus. Amen.

(Evening)
May the morning bring new determination to follow your Spirit's leading in
all things. In the marvelous name of
Jesus. Amen.

SATURDAY, SEPTEMBER 18
(Read Matthew 20:1–11)

(Morning)
Wonderful God, give me a spirit of gratitude throughout the day,
so that I might praise you for your many blessings, both small and great.

(Evening)
Wonderful God, "All I have needed, your hand has provided." Remind me
that you have blessed me in order that I might be a blessing to others.

Generous God, you continue to give all that you have promised: salvation through your child, our daily bread, and your presence in tribulation. Yet when I look around, I often see others whom I deem less deserving enjoying more luxuries and privileges. Like the ungrateful laborers in the parable, I begin to complain that I should have more. By your Spirit, teach me that you have provided what is needed at this stage of my spiritual development and will provide more as spiritual maturity and gratitude increase.

(Morning)
I take so much for granted, O God: food, shelter, clothing, meaningful work,
and access to good medical care. Use those of us who have an abundance to take
care of those who are less fortunate, both at home and abroad.
(Prayers of Intercession)

(Evening)
Loving God, I have the freedom both to enjoy all you have given and to work to
secure more of the things that I desire over time. Grant both spiritual and actual
freedom to the unjustly incarcerated.
(Prayers of Intercession)

"Blessed be God, who daily bears us up; God is our salvation."

(Morning)	(Evening)
Open my eyes, dear God, to the needs of those around me, and open my heart to meet those that I am able. In Christ's name I pray. Amen.	Under the shadow of your wing I rest tonight, O God. Keep this home and its occupants from danger. In Christ's name I pray. Amen.

SUNDAY, SEPTEMBER 19
(Read Matthew 20:12–16)

(Morning)
Generous God, surely goodness and mercy have followed me
all the days of my life. Help me to show mercy and compassion
today to someone who needs them.

(Evening)
Generous God, inspire me with new ways for me to share cheerfully of my time,
resources, and expertise, and imbue me with the selflessness to follow through.

Sometimes it is difficult to understand your generosity, O God. You forgive the unforgivable, you heal those who hurt others, you bless those who do not deserve to be blessed. Often, you use loving-kindness to draw erring men and women to yourself. In your wisdom, you cause the sun to shine on the unjust as well as the just. Keep me from bitterness when your generosity and mercy seem unjust. Teach me to be as generous and merciful as you are. Grant me the spiritual maturity to accept the fact that your thoughts are not human thoughts, nor your ways human ways.

(Morning)
Have mercy, O God, upon the dying, the destitute, and the deserted.
(Prayers of Intercession)

(Evening)
In your infinite mercy, you have forgiven my failures, shortcomings, and
mistakes, time and again. O God, give assurance of your forgiveness to those
who cannot seem to forgive themselves for sins committed long ago.
(Prayers of Intercession)

"So the last will be first, and the first will be last."

(Morning)	(Evening)
Once again I have the opportunity to assemble with others in the house of prayer. May the joy of worship continue to energize me throughout the coming week. In Jesus' name. Amen.	I settle in for the night with a profound sense of your love and care for me. Continue to surround me and my family with your divine peace, protection, and provision. In Jesus' name. Amen.

MONDAY, SEPTEMBER 20
(Read Exodus 17:1–7)

(Morning)
Dear God, today I accept the journey that you have prepared for me.
Help me not to complain along the way.

(Evening)
Dear God, as this day draws to a close, I thank you for a wonderful journey.

Dear God, I thirst for more of you today. I confess that I don't always understand your ways, and many times I resist. Teach me this day how to trust your leading. You are faithful in guiding the steps of those who trust in you. You give living water to the thirsty. Through your many acts, you have delivered your people from destruction. Help me to be secure in your love.

(Morning)
God, keep me from contention and strife.
(Prayers of Intercession)

(Evening)
I am constantly amazed at how you care for me. I rest in your love.
(Prayers of Intercession)

As Jesus taught his disciples I now pray.
(Pray the Prayer of Our Savior.)

(Morning)	(Evening)
It is easy for me to complain because something did not go my way. I thank you for teaching me to forsake selfishness and embrace selflessness. In Jesus' name. Amen.	As I reflect on this day, O God, the realization of you as Provider becomes so clear. Teach me to trust you as Jehovah Jireh, God the Provider. In Jesus' name. Amen.

TUESDAY, SEPTEMBER 21
(Read Psalm 78:1–4)

(Morning)
Sovereign God, I arise with a hearing heart. Teach me to discern
between good and evil. Your voice, at times, has been obscure.
Do not hide your wisdom from me; I await anxiously a lighted path.

(Evening)
Sovereign God, seal in me the treasures of your wisdom.
My ears are continually attentive to your Word.

O God, by your wisdom you created the heavens and the foundation of the
earth was established. Take my life and adorn it like the beauty of your
creation. Gracious God, I open my mouth wide to declare to all your praises
and the wonderful works you have performed. I will tell generations to
come of your testimonies and your marvelous acts. Help us to teach trans-
gressors your ways and convert sinners to you. You are Sovereign of the
earth. Do not hide your wonders from us. Speak, God. Your servant listens.

(Morning)
As this day begins for me, I take this moment to meditate on your goodness.
(Prayers of Intercession)

(Evening)
Your words have been sweeter than the honeycomb.
I will meditate on your statutes during the evening.
(Prayers of Intercession)

As Jesus taught his disciples I now pray.
(Pray the Prayer of Our Savior.)

(Morning)
Guide me through this day by your
Word, O God. Grant unto me a clear
vision, so that I may walk in integrity
of heart. In Jesus' name. Amen.

(Evening)
Your instruction brings me peace. Now
I rest with confidence that your Word
preserves the faithful. Thank you for
being the God of peace. There is no
peace without your Word. In Jesus'
name. Amen.

WEDNESDAY, SEPTEMBER 22
(Read Ezekiel 18:1–4)

(Morning)
God of creation, I open my eyes and give thanks for life this day. Without the forgiveness of sin I would be eternally lost. The soul that practices sin shall surely die. I hunger and thirst for righteousness.

(Evening)
God of creation and all that is good and true, I offer to you my life and every-thing that I am. O God, mold me into a vessel of honor, fit for your use.

Great God of the universe, I celebrate your awesome sovereignty. Your holy writ says that we were clothed in sin and shaped in iniquity. Do not judge me according to my family sins, but uphold me with your hand of righteousness. Sin awaits me by crouching at my door. Your faithfulness has enabled me to overcome it. My desire is to obey your decrees and ad-here to your commandments. In doing so, I find the fullness of joy and life's pleasures forever more.

(Morning)
Open my eyes, O God. Sin is all around me. Help me to choose what is right. Righteousness exalts a nation, and sin is a reproach.
(Prayers of Intercession)

(Evening)
No other God can deliver me from sin's wages. What a great price to pay! Thank you, God, for forgiving all of my debt.
(Prayers of Intercession)

As Jesus taught his disciples I now pray.
(Pray the Prayer of Our Savior.)

(Morning)
Give me the wisdom to make right choices, and grant me the ability to live them out. Thank you, Jesus, for the Comforter, the Holy Spirit, who teaches me all things. Greater is the One that is in me than the one that is in the world. In Jesus' name. Amen.

(Evening)
For whatever is born of God over-comes the world. This is the victory that has overcome the world, our faith. Thank you, God, for delivering me from the evil one. In Jesus' name. Amen.

THURSDAY, SEPTEMBER 23
(Read Ezekiel 18:25–32)

(Morning)
Righteous and Holy One, I arise this morning with the purpose of
turning from all of my evil ways. I repent of all my wickedness.
Judge me according to your tender mercies.

(Evening)
Righteous and Holy One, thank you for extending
your scepter of righteousness. Your love and kindness have drawn
me closer. I will meditate on your justice in my sleep.

Dear God, I have missed the mark many times. I confess my sins and desire truth in my inward parts. Evil has been all around me. Renew in me, O
God, a steadfast heart. Cast me not away from your presence. You have
great pleasure in those who choose righteousness. Grant unto me entrance
into your domain. A broken spirit and a contrite heart you will not despise.
The way of God is just, and they who call on the name of God shall be
delivered from evil.

(Morning)
Merciful God, deliver me from my ways.
Help me to see clearly that the ways of humankind are right in your eyes.
(Prayers of Intercession)

(Evening)
Great Justice, help us to accept the acquittal you have granted.
Grant us the ability to receive your peace.
(Prayers of Intercession)

As Jesus taught his disciples I now pray.
(Pray the Prayer of Our Savior.)

(Morning)
We are quick to justify our actions.
Thank you for revealing to us how
wrong we have been. Continue to
wash us with hyssop and make us
cleaner than snow. In the name of
Jesus, the Anointed One. Amen.

(Evening)
Oh, how I have desired to sleep in
peace! You have delivered me from the
fruit of sin. Let your Holy Spirit
continue to instruct me in the way of
holiness. Thank you for not giving up
on me. In the name of Jesus, the
Anointed One. Amen.

FRIDAY, SEPTEMBER 24
(Read Psalm 25:1–9)

(Morning)
God of glory, I lift my hands and give you thanks for this magnificent day.
This is the day that you have made, and I will rejoice and be glad in it.

(Evening)
God of glory, show me your ways, for you are the God of my salvation.
Teach me to know your path, that I may not sin against you.

We have missed the mark many times, O God. Teach us to know the way of righteousness. What is good and upright belongs to you. Only you can instruct us in your truth. Blot out our sins that are before you, that we may enter into your presence. Those who are humble you will not turn away. You guide the humble in justice and reveal to them your ways.

(Morning)
Forgiving God, help me to run to you and not away from you when I fall.
You execute justice for those who are of a broken spirit and contrite heart.
(Prayers of Intercession)

(Evening)
Merciful God, your mercies are renewed daily. Help me to overcome
all of my mistakes. Reveal to me those hidden sins.
(Prayers of Intercession)

As Jesus taught his disciples I now pray.
(Pray the Prayer of Our Savior.)

(Morning)
It is easy to see the sins of others and overlook my own evil ways. Jesus, thank you for revealing to me the gift of forgiveness. In the name of Jesus Christ. Amen.

(Evening)
Let your Word search my heart, O God. Remove every weight that hinders your purpose for me. Help me to live out fully my destiny. Thank you, Jesus, for reconciling me. In the name of Jesus Christ. Amen.

SATURDAY, SEPTEMBER 25
(Read Philippians 2:1–13)

(Morning)
Exalted One, this morning begin your work in me for your good pleasure.
I choose to have the mind of Jesus Christ.

(Evening)
Exalted One, I embrace humility, although it is difficult at times to resist
human pride. My God, transform this proud human being into one of humility.

Joy-giver, fulfill my joy. Your joy is said to be strength. Show me the way
to this joy: it is through your love, O God, and the fellowship of the Spirit.
My eyes have been blinded by my human desires, which have led to pride.
Break me continually, so that I may find rest in your holiness. I bow, O
God, to worship at your feet. You give grace to the humble and resist those
who are proud. Teach us to clothe ourselves as Christ Jesus clothed himself
in humility and became obedient to the point of death, even the death of the
cross.

(Morning)
Merciful God, help us to prefer humility and obedience over pride.
Give us the strength and courage to suffer for righteousness.
(Prayers of Intercession)

(Evening)
Almighty One, empower me to work out my own salvation with fear
and trembling. Protect me from all false humility.
(Prayers of Intercession)

As Jesus taught his disciples I now pray.
(Pray the Prayer of Our Savior.)

(Morning)
We judge others by what they do and
judge ourselves by our intentions.
Thank you, Christ Jesus, for helping
us to see the truth. The Word proclaims, "We shall know the truth and
the truth shall make us free." Whom
the Christ has set free is free indeed.
In Jesus Christ's name. Amen.

(Evening)
You give your beloved sleep, O God.
Let your Holy Spirit make my rest
sweet. Prepare my heart for the day
that awaits my entrance, so that I may
serve you with new determination to
build your dominion. Thank you for
giving me grace. In Jesus Christ's
name. Amen.

SUNDAY, SEPTEMBER 26
(Read Matthew 21:23–32)

(Morning)
Sovereign God, rule over this new day.
I rejoice to be a servant in your sovereignty.

(Evening)
Sovereign God, deliver me from pretense and hypocrisy.
I repent of religiosity and the spirit of sectarianism.
Pure religion is from above; like a newborn babe I desire it.

Sovereign One, how many times have I resisted your authority in others. Help me to see your grace in the many sons and daughters you have in the world, though they differ in appearance and method of worship. Jesus Christ gave all disciples authority. Open my eyes to see your authority. Every believer in Jesus is ordained of you, O God. Teach me to pray for all who are in authority, that we may live a quiet and peaceable life in all godliness and holiness.

(Morning)
Loving God, teach us how not to be quick to judge others.
Reveal to us the value that you have placed in your servants.
(Prayers of Intercession)

(Evening)
Dear God, help me to review this day, that I may give
an account to those whom I have dishonored.
(Prayers of Intercession)

As Jesus taught his disciples I now pray.
(Pray the Prayer of Our Savior.)

(Morning)
Grant me the ability to obey your leaders and submit to their authority. They keep watch over us, who must give an account. Our fellowship should be joyful and not burdensome to those who lead. Discipleship should not be resisted but embraced. Thank you, God, for disciplining me. In the name of Jesus Christ. Amen.

(Evening)
The steps of a good person are ordered by you, God. Thank you for your Spirit, guiding me along the way. There are many roads that look safe, but they lead to failure. I rejoice that another day has ended with me safe in your strong tower. In the name of Jesus Christ I pray. Amen.

MONDAY, SEPTEMBER 27
(Read Exodus 20:1–4)

(Morning)
Gracious and most heavenly God, Creator of both heaven and earth,
I thank you for being God of all and allowing me to rise again.
Thank you for being God all by yourself.

(Evening)
Gracious and most heavenly God, I thank you throughout the busyness
of this day. All that I have seen, all that I have heard, and all that I have done—
nothing was so important that it overshadowed your presence in my life.

Maker of heaven and earth and those things below the earth, with great humility I come before you. I thank you, and I praise you. You have made everything, and everything is under your control. God, continue your presence in my life, so that I may keep my focus when circumstances want to rule over me. I am reminded that you blessed me to have the ability to rest in you. Thank you for reminding me that when I put you first in my life, you bless my relationships and allow me to weather the storms of this life. I know that what seems so important now eventually will pass away. Let me have nothing in my way that keeps me from seeking you first.

(Morning)
God, you who are the great "I Am" and all that I will ever need
or hope for, I have the faith to believe.
(Prayers of Intercession)

(Evening)
Gracious God, you have supplied my needs so that
I could make it through this day. Even when I did not ask, you,
by your grace and mercy, brought me through.
(Prayers of Intercession)

"Thou shalt have no other gods before me."
(Pray the Prayer of Our Savior.)

(Morning)
God, when I think about my yesterdays, I am reminded of your presence in my life. You are Deliverer, Friend, and Comforter. I pray for your continued awesome power and presence in my life. In Jesus' name. Amen.

(Evening)
The presence of the Holy Spirit was with me all day. Let your presence and the assurance of it be manifested even in my rest. In the name of Jesus Christ I pray. Amen.

TUESDAY, SEPTEMBER 28
(Read Exodus 20:7–9)

(Morning)
God, guide me this day so that I will do nothing to profane your name
or the power of your work within me.

(Evening)
God, I thank you for your guidance this day. Your Word has taught me to honor
you in all things. There is not one moment of any day when you are not with
me. Let me not leave you out of any moment in my life.

God of all, if I have forgotten to do your will in anything that you bless me
to do, if I have taken your name in vain, please forgive me. If I do not show
to others the loving-kindness you have shown me, let me be reminded that
I have lost sight of your holiness. Please, I ask for your forgiveness. If I do
not take the time to rest in your hands, not by lying down but by praising
you, please forgive me. God, I know that you have given me time to be in
this world, but do not let me be of this world. May I always take time to
worship you, to give you praise, to honor you, and, above all else, to keep
you wholly in my life.

(Morning)
As I labor throughout this day, God, keep me mindful that you have given me
each task to do so that you may be magnified in my life.
(Prayers of Intercession)

(Evening)
God, as you prepare me to complete another day, let me give you honor and
praise, so that I may rest in your loving care.
(Prayers of Intercession)

"Remember the sabbath day, and keep it holy."
(Pray the Prayer of Our Savior.)

(Morning)	(Evening)
Awaken me, as your child, to your presence, open my eyes to your ways, and influence my heart to your will. In the Savior's name. Amen.	As the day comes to a close, help me to reflect on your goodness, given today, and prepare me for tomorrow's challenges as I rest. In the Savior's name. Amen.

WEDNESDAY, SEPTEMBER 29
(Read Exodus 20:12–20)
(Reading from Psalm 80:7–15)

(Morning)
Almighty God, let me honor each person you have created
in the loving-kindness that you have blessed me to receive.

(Evening)
Almighty God, you have proven your love for me in all that I have been blessed
to receive. Continue to test me, so that I may become worthy of your realm.

Almighty God, each day I am tried by the fire, and each day you provide
for me. Each moment of my life, I am given a choice to serve you or serve
this world. Loving God, only through the trials and troubles of this world
can I become a perfected instrument for your use. In each friend or foe I
meet during my day, let your love be shown to shine through me. You are a
mighty God who is able to keep me, sustain me, and build me. In you, O
God, I have all that I will ever need or hope for. I need not want for those
things I think I should have; I know that all I need is before me every day
in you.

(Morning)
Each person I meet—my neighbor, my brother, my sister—
is as I am, a part of the body of Christ. Keep me steadfast
in the knowledge that what I do to them, I also do to the risen Savior.
(Prayers of Intercession)

(Evening)
As I have gone through this day, whether I met friends or enemies,
I pray that they have seen an example of the Christ in me.
(Prayers of Intercession)

**"Moses said to the people, "Do not be afraid;
for God has come only to test you and to put
the fear of God upon you so that you do not sin."**
(Pray the Prayer of Our Savior.)

(Morning)	(Evening)
Grant me the ability to see others through the eyes of Christ, so that others may receive blessings from you through me. In the Savior's name. Amen.	I thank you for sustaining me through today's trials and troubles, in the hope of growing strong as your servant in the world. In the Savior's name. Amen.

THURSDAY, SEPTEMBER 30
(Read Isaiah 5:1–7)
(Reading from Psalm 19)

(Morning)
Gracious God, you chose us. Let not your choice leave a sour taste in your
mouth, but let the works that I do be a sweet drink upon your lips.

(Evening)
Gracious God, I pray that the seeds I have planted this day
become sweet fruit unto you. Please find it in your favor
to increase all that you have blessed me to do.

God, you gathered your people together out of the midst of weeds and thorns.
You blessed us and fed us, that we might take your Word to those who have
not heard or shared in your glory. God, we are called by you to set an
example for those who know you not. Yet, rather than growing in the vineyard of your love, we have wasted away. We have held back, held out, and
twisted your Word. What more could you have given us when you gave us
everything we needed? Loving God, let not our shortsightedness keep you
from sustaining us. Help us to walk in and show the fruits of your love.
Guide us to grow in you, that our fruit becomes a sweet savor unto you.

(Morning)
God, help me to be reminded that you have planted in me nothing but the best.
Guide me to give the best of what you have given me.
(Prayers of Intercession)

(Evening)
Almighty God, let me not have wasted any opportunity
to quench thirst as I sought to drink from your vineyard.
(Prayers of Intercession)

**"And now, habitants of Jerusalem, and . . . of Judah, judge
between me and my vineyard. What more was there to do
for my vineyard that I have not done in it? When I expected it
to yield grapes, why did it yield wild grapes?"**
(Pray the Prayer of Our Savior.)

(Morning)
I begin this day, God, in your presence,
determined to work in your vineyard. It
is by your grace. In the Savior's name.
Amen.

(Evening)
God, I pray that my labor today was
pleasing to you. Thank you for your
pledge of protection through today's
journey. In the Savior's name. Amen.

FRIDAY, OCTOBER 1
(Read Philippians 3:4b–14)

(Morning)
O God, by your power you have granted me knowledge, wisdom, and love.
By your power I am able to do many things. This day keep me mindful that
without you, all I have been blessed with means absolutely nothing.

(Evening)
O God, if you would remove yourself from the world,
the void would be impossible to fill. With you I have the fullness of joy,
and without you I have an emptiness for which there is no relief.

God, though Paul achieved many things in his life—titles, power, and
wealth—he came to realize that without Christ he had nothing. Loving God,
remind us that there is no ribbon or medal, there is no prize or reward,
there are no scholarly achievements or financial gains that can compare to
the glory and the joy of serving you. In you, Savior God, the only thing that
counts is a serving faith. You are my crown of glory. You are my joy everlasting.

(Morning)
Though I have riches untold and have gained many things in the race you have
allowed me to run, if I have not Christ, I have already lost.
(Prayers of Intercession)

(Evening)
Today I took a step, O God, guided by you. Today I took a step on a course
that you have laid. I thank you for urging me toward the finish line
and waiting to greet me when I arrive.
(Prayers of Intercession)

**"If anyone else has reason to be confident in the flesh, I have more.
. . . Yet whatever gains I had, these I have come to regard
as loss because of Christ."**
(Pray the Prayer of Our Savior.)

(Morning)	(Evening)
Take my hand, God. Guide me by your powerful and wise Spirit. Keep me mindful of your goal, and not mine, as I press on toward the prize in Christ Jesus. In Jesus' name, I pray. Amen	Renew my strength and increase my faith, God, that I might know Christ and the power of Christ's resurrection and blessed assurance. In Jesus' name I pray. Amen.

SATURDAY, OCTOBER 2
(Read Philippians 3:9)

(Morning)
Creator God, by your suffering on the cross, I have been given one more
morning just to say thank you for this day that you have given me.
Show me how to use it to embody the power of your love.

(Evening)
Creator God, a house divided will not stand. Let me not divide my faith
between you and material things. As I rest in the comfort of your arms,
conform me to be an instrument of your use, of your peace, and of your love.

God, times are changing. The things that once were unacceptable to dis-
cuss even in the most private of circles now are open to public display.
Language that would have caused most of us to be disciplined severely is
now being spoken with such regularity that the young people who use it do
not understand the meaning of their words. People seek love through Christ,
yet marriage vows are ended in courts of law. Stand by us, that we may
have the faith to stand on your Word when the law of humankind and the
Spirit of God oppose each other. Help us to know Jesus by his love and
resurrecting power.

(Morning)
In you, O God, there is the strength to overcome.
(Prayers of Intercession)

(Evening)
God, as I have been given the privilege of going through this day,
please forgive me for the times that I used it in a faulty way
instead of under your perfect guidance.
(Prayers of Intercession)

"And be found in Jesus, not having a righteousness of my own
that comes from the law, but one that comes through faith in Christ,
the righteousness from God based on faith."
(Pray the Prayer of Our Savior.)

(Morning)	(Evening)
Give me a clean heart this day, loving God, so that I may stand ready to give love to those who seek life through Christ Jesus. In Jesus' name I pray. Amen.	Forgive me this day for losing sight of my purpose and standing outside of your righteousness. As I sleep, help me to know Jesus' love and resurrecting power. In Jesus' name I pray. Amen.

SUNDAY, OCTOBER 3
(Read Matthew 21:33–46)

(Morning)
Heavenly God, as I go through this day with each new lesson that I have taught,
let me use it wisely to build up your realm.

(Evening)
Heavenly God, this day you have provided me with the ability to be more than a
conqueror. I pray that all that I do gives praise, glory, and honor to your name.

Sustainer God, we continuously have been given your best, only to destroy
it, as disobedient children, by our words and our actions. As we look at the
world around us, we seemed to be bent on killing what you have so lovingly given life. When you created the earth, you said "it was good"; and
when you created humankind, you said "it was very good." God, let us take
the very goodness of what you have built and build on what you have created. Let us take your Word forth unto those who have not heard and those
who have not seen. May we take what you have given to us abundantly and
build it up to be a shining tribute to who you are in our lives.

(Morning)
God, help me to see those whom you have placed in my path as my guides to
glory. And let me be used so that I may guide someone to you.
(Prayers of Intercession)

(Evening)
Savior, as I end this day, you have blessed me to be in contact with friend and
foe alike. Let me not become so confused by the challenges of this world that I
lose sight of the source of all my blessings.
(Prayers of Intercession)

**"The realm of God will be taken away from you
and given to a people that produces the fruits of the realm."**
(Pray the Prayer of Our Savior.)

(Morning)	(Evening)
Help me to see the value in my person as it is equipped to yield much fruit for the building of your realm. In the Savior's name. Amen.	God, in me you have created greatness and goodness for all to see. Help me to create an attitude of continuous praise as I yield to your Spirit of guidance, even as I sleep. In the Savior's name. Amen.

MONDAY, OCTOBER 4
(Read Psalm 23)

(Morning)
Loving Shepherd, wherever you lead today,
may I ever be aware that I am at home in you.

(Evening)
Loving Shepherd, I pause at day's end to give you thanks
for seeing me through the day.

Gracious God, there are moments when I find it hard to think of myself as a sheep in need of a shepherd. Yet I know that I need your guidance and your care, your protection and your nurture. It is so easy to slip into the false assuredness of this age and to forget those needs. My greatest confidence, then, is in my own ability to face the challenges of the days and the shadowy valleys of my nights. At that very moment, I come face to face with the limited scope of my abilities and the infinite expanse of your care. A sheep I am!

(Morning)
May I be aware of green pastures and still waters as I go about the activity of this day, that others may catch a glimpse of my Shepherd in what I say and do.
(Prayers of Intercession)

(Evening)
Now, Good and Merciful One, as I prepare to rest,
I entrust my spirit to your care.
(Prayers of Intercession)

"God is my Shepherd, I shall not want."

(Morning)
Jesus, good Shepherd, open our minds to your guidance and continue to feed us the bread of life. In your name I pray. Amen.

(Evening)
For the leading of your Holy Spirit this day, thank you, loving God. In the name of Jesus I pray. Amen.

TUESDAY, OCTOBER 5
(Read Exodus 32:1–14)

(Morning)
All-knowing One, with anticipation I greet this day.
I await the many ways that you will reveal your will to me.

(Evening)
All-knowing One, as I reflect on the events of this day
I seek your counsel. Sharpen my perception, I pray.
Enable me to see where your will has been at work.

Liberating God, waiting for a word from you is not something your children of earth do well. We want what we want, when we want it! Surely our impatience and faithlessness are enough to tempt you to anger. Yet we only know you to be merciful and gracious in your kindness. Forgive us, we pray, for our shortsightedness and for those times when we create other gods and worship them. Free us from the anxiety of the moment. Bless us with courageous patience for your word, in the midst of a world that is intent on finding its own way to a sure thing.

(Morning)
In the sacredness of your presence, I greet you this day, O God, with hope that rests solely on your promise fulfilled in Jesus.
(Prayers of Intercession)

(Evening)
O Forgiving, Holy One, for every blessing of this day, I give you thanks.
For each manifestation of your love, I praise you.
(Prayers of Intercession)

**"Turn from your fierce wrath; change your mind
and do not bring disaster on your people."**

(Morning)
As I return to your world from the mountain after sharing moments with you, O God, sustain me throughout the day. Be an ever-present Holy Spirit. In Jesus' name. Amen.

(Evening)
Gracious God, as I rest tonight, let your Spirit nourish and strengthen my resolve to patiently attend to your Word. In Jesus' name. Amen.

WEDNESDAY, OCTOBER 6
(Read Matthew 22:1–14)

(Morning)
Gracious Creator, as I prepare for an active day of labor and business,
may I be reminded that as worthy as these endeavors may be,
they take no precedence over being at one with you.

(Evening)
Gracious Creator, your invitation to the feast of your blessings has been with
me. I thank you for including even me to be among those you seek to welcome.

Inviting God, the banquet that you have prepared is a feast of rejoicing,
where anyone is welcome—the good and the bad. Yet in serving you, we
sometimes corrupt the invitation by including those like us, those with whom
we are comfortable, those who share our economic status or our positions
on issues. As we proclaim the good news of Jesus, the gracious gift of your
realm, open our hearts so that our invitation will be true to your invitation
to all.

(Morning)
Beyond the walls of sacred spaces, you send your servants to invite. Encourage
all who claim discipleship of Jesus, that we may reflect your love and your
grace in the difficult places where your Word is not welcome.
(Prayers of Intercession)

(Evening)
For opportunities to serve and for sisters and brothers in discipleship and
service, I give you thanks and praise.
(Prayers of Intercession)

"Go to the street corners and invite anyone you find."

(Morning)
Expand my vision, O God, that I might
see your realm as it truly exists,
comprising any and all. In the name of
the Christ. Amen.

(Evening)
May the rest you give this night
refresh and strengthen me to serve
you all the more tomorrow. In the
name of the Christ. Amen.

THURSDAY, OCTOBER 7
(Read Isaiah 25:1–9)

(Morning)
Living God, Eternal One, already with the dawning of the day,
you have done a wonderful thing.

(Evening)
Living God, Eternal One, before I rest, I turn to you.
Hear my prayer and the prayers of all who call on you this night.

Strong Deliverer, God of the ages, your prophet recalls the expressions of praise that rise out of your people. For you have granted deliverance throughout time. We know that your plans continually unfold in our day. And by the examples of your faithful ones, we are reminded to wait. Grant us resilience of spirit so that our waiting will not be filled with passive resignation. Strengthen our faith; fill us with hope and expectation so that our wait is rendered through active lives of devoted service to you. Bless us, O God, that we may be shelter and shade for those who are forced to go without.

(Morning)
The tear-stained faces of the world look to you because you remain
the source of consolation and hope. Fill my spirit with compassion,
so that my life becomes an expression of your love.
(Prayers of Intercession)

(Evening)
In you, O God, I rejoice as I consider all the ways
that you continually bless and sustain your creation.
(Prayers of Intercession)

"O God, you are my God; I will exalt you, I will praise your name."

(Morning)
Bless the endeavors of this day; let the faithful work of those who serve be attributed to your empowering presence. In Christ's name. Amen.

(Evening)
From the stress and busy periods of this day, Exalted One, I come. Grant that your peace will accompany me through the night. In Christ's name. Amen.

FRIDAY, OCTOBER 8
(Read Psalm 106:1–6, 19–23)

(Morning)
Holy One, as you awaken me to the glory of your creation,
bless this day with reminders of your faithfulness.

(Evening)
Holy One, the evening has come, and the day has passed. In the delights of this
day, I have seen your goodness; in its challenges, your gracious hand at work.

Gracious God, the psalmist reminds us that we trust in you to remember,
while our tendency is to forget. In so doing, she not only acknowledges the
sins of her ancestors; she confesses the sins of her own day and time. Before you, O God, we must acknowledge our own forgetfulness. Like your
chosen children in Israel, we willingly allow your wondrous acts of compassion and deliverance to recede into the substrata of our consciousness.
Forgive us, O God, we pray! Rekindle our awareness of your steadfast and
enduring love and your unfailing mercy.

(Morning)
Your unfailing quest for our salvation brought Jesus into the world.
May we find in Jesus, your Anointed One, the intentionality
of your love and a living reminder of your presence.
(Prayers of Intercession)

(Evening)
God, we need reminders to help us remain attuned to your eternal reality.
We forget your works and wait not for your counsel. Thank you for Jesus,
who calls us to renewed awareness of your mercy and your grace.
(Prayers of Intercession)

"O give thanks to God, for God is good."

(Morning)
Throughout this day, may I be ever
aware of your abiding presence and the
wonders of your works. In Jesus' name.
Amen.

(Evening)
Remember me. Remember me. O
Sovereign One, remember me! In
Jesus' name. Amen.

SATURDAY, OCTOBER 9
(Read Psalm 23)

(Morning)
Blessed One, I awaken to the opportunities of this day
fully assured of your leading presence.

(Evening)
Blessed One, by your goodness and your mercy, I have been blessed
throughout this day. To you I give thanks and praise.

To you, Holy One, we bring the questions and negations that haunt us as individuals: "Am I an acceptable person?" "Do I have what it takes?" "What will become of me, if . . .?" "I give up; trying is useless." Doubt, insecurity, fear, and hopelessness persist with us, O God. We live in the presence of these enemies. These are the shadowy valleys of death through which we sojourn. Thank you for the infectious spirit of your psalmist, whose confidence in you inspires us today. We are reminded that you provide, lead, and accompany; that you spread the table, anoint the head, and fill the cup. You provide the dwelling place, now and for all the years to come. What more do we need to know?

(Morning)
The challenges that I encounter in living are many and varied, O God.
In every way, I look to you to be my help and guide.
(Prayers of Intercession)

(Evening)
With confidence that you are able, I bring to you, O Listening One,
the concerns of my heart today. Bless my prayers with quiet moments,
that I might hear you when you answer.
(Prayers of Intercession)

**"Even though I walk through the shadowed valley,
I fear no evil; for you are with me."**

(Morning)	(Evening)
Blessed One, let your paths of righteousness be mine this day. In Jesus' name. Amen.	Loving God, with the rest that you provide, restore my soul, I pray. In Jesus' name. Amen.

SUNDAY, OCTOBER 10
(Read Philippians 4:1–9)

(Morning)
Gracious God, there is a simple and tremendous joy that comes as I begin
this day, because the beginning, as always, is with you.

(Evening)
Gracious God, thank you for the blessing of companionship in discipleship
and ministry, and for brothers and sisters who share in
"struggle for the cause of the gospel."

Precious God, your apostle had it right: whatever the differences between
Euodia and Syntyche, they could be of one mind concerning Jesus; and
that oneness could be the source of reconciliation for them. Discipleship is
not always a harmonious walk. God, we need your help to stay focused in
mission and ministry. Redirect our attention to that which is true, honor-
able, just, pure, pleasing, commendable, excellent, and worthy of praise.
In doing this, we will see our Savior, dear God. The Christ is the center of
all things and the One in whom we are made one.

(Morning)
Holy One, the need of this world for peace and reconciliation is so great
that at times it overwhelms. Inspiring One, dwell in us today.
(Prayers of Intercession)

(Evening)
God of peace, with your healing presence,
be in all of the places where discord reigns this night.
(Prayers of Intercession)

"Rejoice in God always, again I will say, 'Rejoice.' "

(Morning)	(Evening)
God, let the joy of your presence	Healing God, cure our anxieties this
refresh my spirit throughout this day.	night. Let your peace which passes all
In Jesus' name. Amen.	understanding guard our hearts and
	thoughts. In Jesus' name. Amen.

MONDAY, OCTOBER 11
(Read Matthew 22:15–22)

(Morning)
God over all commerce, may I honor you as I enter today's work.

(Evening)
God over all commerce, may my life and my life's work be an offering to you.

It is so easy, O Provider God, to lose sight of purpose, integrity, your teaching, and your truth. We often are trapped and swayed by the systems of trade, commerce, and currency. But Jesus, our example, made no distinction between common living and the reign of your sovereignty. Help us to offer, as Jesus did, all our lives, all our doings, as a praise to you. Help us to give wholly our work in the world of commerce as worship. May even our "daily grind" be made holy by your presence.

(Morning)
Provider God, help me to work with your intentions in sight.
Give me the courage of integrity.
(Prayers of Intercession)

(Evening)
Provider God, as I review my day, forgive my failures to trust you
or to walk in integrity. Give me grace for the next opportunity.
(Prayers of Intercession)

"Render even to Caesar as unto God"
(Pray the Prayer of Our Savior.)

(Morning)
It is so easy to work for work's sake. Teach me, O God, to work with your reign in view. Remind me that jobs and civic responsibilities are merely places in which I may serve you better. In Jesus' name. Amen.

(Evening)
As I rest in your provision of sleep, O God, may I rest knowing that all that I am and all that I do are in your care. Remind me that jobs and civic responsibilities are merely places in which I may serve you better. In Jesus' name. Amen.

TUESDAY, OCTOBER 12
(Read Exodus 33:12–23)

(Morning)
Great God of glory, I wake to experience your presence anew.
Throughout this day, may I know your grace and favor.

(Evening)
Great God of glory, thank you for your presence,
which has attended me today, and for the rest you now give.

Leadership is hard, gracious Leader. While it is sometimes a lonely job, none of us is able to lead alone. In all our endeavors, we need at least two things: able helpers to ensure that the tasks of life are done, and the assurance that your own presence will be our guide and aid. How else can we be assured that the tasks of parenting or pastoring, supervising or supporting, will be done with your favor? We do not want only to get the job done by brute force or human effort. But, gracious Leader, we want the wind of your compassion and mercy, your glory, to be the power in all we do.

(Morning)
God of goodness, declare your name and presence in my life today.
May I be a conduit of your glory in the earth.
(Prayers of Intercession)

(Evening)
God of goodness, shelter me safely in your care, covering me with your loving hand. May I know the afterglow of your presence.
(Prayers of Intercession)

"My presence will go with you, and I will give you rest."
(Pray the Prayer of Our Savior.)

(Morning)
This day I long for your glory, the assurance that you are with me, and the faith and confidence that you are pleased with me, O God of mercy and compassion. In Jesus' name. Amen.

(Evening)
As I yield my mind and body to your care in the night, thank you for your steadfast loving-kindness, your mercy and compassion, O God of glory. In Jesus' name. Amen.

WEDNESDAY, OCTOBER 13
(Read Psalm 99:1–5)

(Morning)
Sovereign Creator, give us your perspective on the governments
and leaders of the earth. You are the ultimate authority.
May we bow to your awesome and holy name.

(Evening)
Sovereign Creator, we exalt you as governor of our lives
and of the life of all your people. Indeed, you are
the ultimate authority who loves justice and equality.

Almighty God, in whose presence the natural order gives reverence, we praise you for your great and awesome name. Especially we praise you for the characteristic of holiness, by which you measure justice and establish equality. Sometimes, O God, we cannot see what is just and right. We cannot see how great you are in all the earth. All around us are famine and poverty, chaos and war. We cannot experience the holy. Nations and their leaders do not acknowledge your presence in the affairs of all people. Often we are guilty of the same. Help us to live with the perspective of exalting you and bowing humbly at your feet as we share the stewardship of all creation.

(Morning)
God, exalted over all the nations, teach me what is just and right,
then enable me to live my life governed by your justice.
(Prayers of Intercession)

(Evening)
I rest tonight on the footstool of your mercy, holy God.
Be enthroned in my life, and be ruler of my heart and actions.
(Prayers of Intercession)

Let us praise God's great and awesome name for God is holy.
(Pray the Prayer of Our Savior.)

(Morning)
As the morning dawns to new responsibilities and possibilities, help me experience the day in your holiness. May I set this day aside as belonging to you, O God of all creation. In Jesus' name. Amen.

(Evening)
Sleep comes to my eyes, O God of all creation, as to all creatures. Yet you do not sleep. Watching over me is your care. Be exalted, even in my dream state. In Jesus' name. Amen.

THURSDAY, OCTOBER 14
(Read Psalm 99:6–9)

(Morning)
Choosing God, as you chose Moses, Aaron, and Miriam
in times past to represent you in the world, choose me.
May I be as Samuel and Huldah, who called on your name.

(Evening)
Choosing God, thank you for giving me the opportunity to be your emissary in
the world. Thank you for the gifts of your instructions and commands.

The world is such a busy and noisy place. We can be distracted so easily by
all that demands our attention. God, it is easy to miss your voice, directing
and leading us. And your "statutes and decrees" do not seem so readily
clear-cut at times. The best we can do is to be as those leaders of old who
found a quiet place or sanctuary, or the dead of night, in order to clear the
space of noise and people. From these quiet places and times, we emerge
with an answer—though not always a distinct one—because it is your nature to answer those who call upon you. And loving God, it is your character to forgive us our misdeeds, though we still face the consequences of our
actions. For directions and answers and consequences we give thanks to
you, O God.

(Morning)
As you have directed in the past, make your way clear before us today,
O Guiding Pillar.
(Prayers of Intercession)

(Evening)
Exalted and wondrous God, you have spoken by and to your people.
We worship you in the place of your choosing.
(Prayers of Intercession)

**"There is no question too great for God;
there is no answer too insignificant."**
(Pray the Prayer of Our Savior.)

(Morning)	(Evening)
You are a forgiving God who listens when we pray. I bless you for answering us day by day in expected and unexpected ways. In Jesus' name. Amen.	In the calm of night, O God, speak clearly to my heart of peace and purpose, of forgiveness and fortitude, of grace and grit. In Jesus' name. Amen.

FRIDAY, OCTOBER 15
(Read Isaiah 45:1–7)

(Morning)
Undisputed God of all creation, remind me in this day
that you choose the most unlikely people in order to carry out your will.
May I not turn away from anyone, thinking you could never
speak to me or change my life through such a person.

(Evening)
Undisputed God of all creation, I am reminded that you choose
the most unlikely people in order to carry out your will.
May I be among those who honor you with my life.

God, we believe that you are for peace and not war. Yet today we read of war. Cyrus was chosen to become the ruler of Syria and did not know it. What a thought: that you may use someone I consider a foreigner and an enemy to show that you are sovereign over all. As we realize this, how do we address the world where we live, when we are told to choose sides constantly? How do we do the work of justice? Teach us, O God.

(Morning)
God, we acknowledge you as the one and only God of all creation,
who through ordinary and obscure people show yourself to be mighty.
(Prayers of Intercession)

(Evening)
God, may we acknowledge that you have strengthened us.
For the sake of your people, we respond to your call.
(Prayers of Intercession)

**"From the rising of the sun until the place where it sets,
people will know there is none besides God."**
(Pray the Prayer of Our Savior.)

(Morning)
It is easy to dismiss people as insignificant or unimportant. Yet, God, you choose the most unlikely people for your own good purposes. I do not want to be guilty of missing your hand in my life or in the lives of those around me. In Jesus' name. Amen.

(Evening)
If I missed your presence in an unlikely source today, O God, forgive me. Increase understanding that you are not bound by my human ideas of who should or should not be chosen. Help me to acknowledge you in faces around the world. In Jesus' name. Amen.

SATURDAY, OCTOBER 16
(Read Psalm 96:1–13)

(Morning)
Majestic God, we worship you in great humility.

(Evening)
Majestic God, we honor your great and glorious strength.

All creation is singing praise to you, Maker of all the heavens and earth. Help us not to destroy your witness among the created order by our own selfish abuse of nature. Your name is a declaration of salvation day by day, and your deeds are marvelous among all peoples. You alone are to be reverenced and honored. For in spite of injustices, troubles, and turmoil, the world is firmly established by your love, and you, O God, will judge every action of humanity with equality and justice. You are a righteous judge in an unseemly world. In a world of falsehoods, your truth will prevail in righteousness. May these realities be my song both day and night.

(Morning)
Giver of songs, as wind whispers of your splendor
among treetops, so I offer my songs up to you.
(Prayers of Intercession)

(Evening)
Giver of songs, I turn from all my idolatries
and worship you in all your splendor and glory.
(Prayers of Intercession)

**"Declare God's glory among the nations,
God's marvelous works among all the peoples."**
(Pray the Prayer of Our Savior.)

(Morning)
Our world is so full of ugliness, horror, and pain. It is difficult to see your glory in the midst of it all, O God. Today help me to sing of your grace and righteousness even in the presence of unrighteousness. In Jesus' name. Amen.

(Evening)
Our world has so much possibility. Nature sings of it. May my heart sing along. In Jesus' name. Amen.

SUNDAY, OCTOBER 17
(Read 1 Thessalonians 1:1–10)

(Morning)
Living and true God, help me to be a model of one
who believes in your active presence in our world.

(Evening)
Living and true God, help me to model
with full conviction your sustaining grace.

In the pressures of living are we known, Living Presence. Authentic witness to Jesus the Christ must be made with more than words; it also must be made in power and in Holy Spirit and with full conviction. Deliver us from lip service and half-hearted devotion. May our work be in faith. May it be a labor of love. May we have a tenacious hope in Jesus the Christ. Increase our joy in service, so that the love of Christ is evident to all who are greeted by us. We wait expectantly for your divine interruption in our lives. In the meantime, help us imitate our Savior in every way.

(Morning)
Divine Joy and Hope of Heaven, give us grace
and peace to enter the world with full conviction.
(Prayers of Intercession)

(Evening)
Divine Joy and Hope of Heaven, give us peace
and grace to share your gospel with full conviction.
(Prayers of Intercession)

**"We always give thanks to God for all of you
and mention you in our prayers."**
(Pray the Prayer of Our Savior.)

(Morning)
I want to be an imitator of you, gracious God. I want to imitate your love and care and power for and in the world. May I welcome those whom you welcome to serve you, living and true God. In Jesus' name. Amen.

(Evening)
I wait for your interruption into my life, O God. I want to experience your resurrection power each day and labor in love toward your destiny. In Jesus' name. Amen.

MONDAY, OCTOBER 18
(Read Deuteronomy 34:1–2)

(Morning)
Eternal One, who granted life to our human forms, you have given
us this earth in all of its abundance to use according to your guidelines:
that we should honor and respect its quality, for ourselves
and for our descendants. Thank you for your gift.

(Evening)
Eternal One, today another day has passed.
I pray that for every end, there is a beginning.

Great-grandfather, I was there when you sat me on your knee and told me
of the time when you were young like me. You took my hand in yours so
that I could feel the pressure of your grip, and you let me touch the lines on
your face and see the wisdom in your smile. In all of the world, God, there
has never been one such as this, such as my grandfather, my great-grandfather.
You must pass, as all things must pass, but the words from your lips live on.

(Morning)
Too often we say our *thank-you*s with the hope of obtaining something more.
This morning I wish to give thanks to you.
(Prayers of Intercession)

(Evening)
I pray, God, that you let today be an affirmation of the world
you have given and of our place in it.
(Prayers of Intercession)

**Help us to find meaning in the things that surround us—
the branch of a tree or the flight of a bluebird.
For all of these works, which are displayed before us, I give thanks.**

(Morning)
Omnipotent Being, I praise and give
thanks to you for the knowledge to
meet today's challenges. Truly you are
in all things. Through the wisdom of
my brothers and sisters, you have
imparted the guidance to live, to rest
with the hope of a tomorrow. In
Christ's name. Amen.

(Evening)
God, surely you spoke from the
mouth of Moses and just as surely
from Moses to Joshua and throughout
all who have spoken and all who have
received the Word. Your wisdom lives
on in all that you are. Help us to
listen, divine Creator, when you
speak. In Christ's name. Amen.

TUESDAY, OCTOBER 19
(Read Psalm 90:1–6)

(Morning)
Creator God, how much greater you are than your creation! Your
power and might are so beyond our understanding, like a light that is blinding.
Thank you for giving us the strength to look, even if only for an instant.

(Evening)
Creator God, as we look to the night sky, the darkness gives birth to the countless stars cradled in the arms of the Milky Way. Our best telescopes,
when pointed at regions among those stars, extending their grasp as far as they
can, reveal galaxies as innumerable as the stars themselves.
What lies beyond even these?

Heavenly God, there is a daffodil that grows on a rock lying near a brook
that runs through the countryside in a state called Michigan on a continent
of land surrounded by ocean on the third planet from a star located in an
arm of the Milky Way galaxy. The Milky Way is but one of many that lie in
clusters of galaxies in one of the many habitable universes that coalesce in
bundles, pulled by the strength of their origin. These quarks and leptons
make up the atoms that compose the molecules of a daffodil that grows on
a rock lying near a brook that runs through the countryside.

(Morning)
Creator of all that is, help the dawn of understanding come,
that every ant or bee or moth has a name.
(Prayers of Intercession)

(Evening)
God, your relative power and might are beyond our understanding,
like a light that is blinding. Thank you for giving us the strength to look,
even if only for an instant.
(Prayers of Intercession)

**May I continue to be a part of what you are, so tomorrow your Word from
my lips might help to guide another part of you, as you have guided me.**

(Morning)
God, when we find ourselves trapped
in our own tiny worlds, whether
caving in or expanding, help us to see
the bigger picture, that we might find
solace in you. In Christ's name.
Amen.

(Evening)
Often, God—too often—we dream to
forget, dream to wake up and never
remember. Help us tonight to remember our dreams, so that tomorrow we
may rise and give thanks for them. In
Christ's name. Amen.

WEDNESDAY, OCTOBER 20
(Read Psalm 90:13–17)

(Morning)
God, as this new dawn lights our world, small in comparison to your majesty and might, I give thanks and praise to you in the hope that when dusk arrives, you will find favor in the works of the day.

(Evening)
God, even as the darkness falls in solemnity around us, so your power awes us into the feared unknown. With all that you are and all that you have promised, I ask that you help us to find resolve in the good that you are.

God Almighty, as the millennium approaches, we scurry like ants from the stomp of a footstep, ever awaiting your judgment. If we have been given the power to control our own destiny, as our own freedom is perceived in the things that we do, give us the strength to evolve not into the silent terror of the newspaper headline but into the Godly beings we are—beings of love and of light. Help to clear our paths not with fire, God, but with love. Grant us this wish, that this earth and these heavens might remain one in your grace and forgiveness.

(Morning)
You who are larger than we can conceive, I ask that in accounting for our deeds, you remember your creation. Give us hope in the midst of your vastness.
(Prayers of Intercession)

(Evening)
A pardon, Awakened One, for those of us who have been frightened into sleep.
(Prayers of Intercession)

If you believe in the good of even one of our kind, if for only a millisecond potential exists for one of us to find the path you have sought for us, then surely we must be worthy of redemption.

(Morning)
Every day we arise and brush our teeth and comb our hair with the knowledge that the day we are about to confront means something—that we are not rising from sleep in vain. May the truth and godliness of this path continue. In Christ's name. Amen.

(Evening)
Though the history of the world has shown that your justice is not always revealed to human benefit, I pray that history's lessons be like the lessons of today—new to our minds and full of the sincerity of our hearts. In Christ's name. Amen.

THURSDAY, OCTOBER 21
(Read Leviticus 19:1–2, 15–18)

(Morning)
Origin of the World, I praise you for this day, as the breath of the world.
As this day's Provider, do we see as the eyes of the world?
Do we see all as love? Sorrow? Pain? Joy? Do we feel?
As one who is truly blessed, so we, in all that we do, are blessed.

(Evening)
Origin of the World, today has truly been a divine day,
for here I am in you. Through everything I do, another origin.

Somehow, God, we are here. Of that, given our sensibilities and the capacity for reason, there can be no doubt. Creator, I am because you are. And I am not alone. From horizon to horizon, my senses reveal the truth of this. I am thankful for the life that you have given us. Our reality, for all of the assurance in the joy it brings, in all of the confusion of violence and hate, is wondrous because it is. I am thankful for the nightmares as well as the dreams, because without the nightmare I would not have recognized the dream. That which my perception reveals I call holy, for in sorrow we grasp the yearning for change, in change we realize our potential for freedom, and in true joy we are created anew every moment of our lives.

(Morning)
Share with us the precedent set by the birds in the sky, by the creatures
that inhabit the earth, not for profit or gain but by the sheer instinct
that you have given, for the love of life—to survive.
(Prayers of Intercession)

(Evening)
As we look to the other members of our race, we can see at times
so much cruelty. Give us the hearts and minds to endure ourselves
and not to uproot the garden while tending to the weeds.
(Prayers of Intercession)

**Divine Maker, as you love us, help us to learn
from the wisdom of your earthly temple.**

(Morning)	(Evening)
Thank you for the abundance of diversity, God, with which you help me learn. Grant me the peace of mind to stare not in judgment but in understanding. In Christ's name. Amen.	In the comfort and knowledge that I am part and parcel of you, God, one with the dreams of all that is holy and good, I lay myself down to sleep. In Christ's name. Amen.

FRIDAY, OCTOBER 22
(Read Psalm 1)

(Morning)
Founder God, this morning, I wake with gladness in my heart that
I have so much to delight in being who I am.

(Evening)
Founder God, I ask for your forgiveness of my shortcomings,
for your patience when my ignorance seems trying,
and for your love to guide me through the storm.

When a hate grows so strong that it obliterates all in its path, it has nothing left to obliterate but itself. But when a love grows so strong that it creates love in another, it multiplies a thousandfold and beyond. Let nature take its course, Father, for I have trusted it this far. Let nature take its course, Mother, for you loved existence enough that you created destruction with the capacity to destroy itself and creation with the capacity to live on.

(Morning)
Help me, God, with the freedom you have given to make the right choices
at the right times, so that the fruit of my deeds may multiply.
(Prayers of Intercession)

(Evening)
Jesus, in all that you have done, over the years
and across cultures, I remember you.
(Prayers of Intercession)

The days are countless grains of sand.

(Morning)
Creator, how long has your creation
gone on? Surely the love and joy of
creation of the past have brought
before us what we see today. I arise
and give thanks to it. In Christ's name.
Amen.

(Evening)
May your Word be clearly heard, that
we might follow—on this night,
tomorrow, and in life everlasting. In
Christ's name. Amen.

SATURDAY, OCTOBER 23
(Read 1 Thessalonians 2:1–8)

(Morning)
Loving Creator, as I wipe the sleep from my eyes, my newfound focus
becomes sharper. The day lights up before me. Give my spirit
comprehension, so that I might recognize your Spirit today.

(Evening)
Loving Creator, when you speak to me through others,
there is no ulterior motive—it is speech, and that is all.
Your Word speaks of love, of joy, and of caring, and in the blanket
of the comfort of this Word do I prepare myself for sleep tonight.

Throughout history, God, your message often has been misconstrued. Your
messengers have toiled, often to encounter only anger and fear. Long ago
you sent your child to us to deliver a message of truth. Jesus was beaten
and torn down and executed—all for the sake of the truth. Daily you remind us that to love one another is better than to hate, that we have only to
believe in you to feel the power of your Spirit, and that to do so is the
promise of everlasting life. Too often the problems of the day control us.
Help us to hear those who toil to speak the truth. Fill us with compassion
and serenity, in the name of our Teacher's Teacher.

(Morning)
To those who are willing to speak to me today,
I will listen. May those I speak to hear.
(Prayers of Intercession)

(Evening)
Thank you, God, for your sacrifice. Help me to learn from you
the meaning of the penance you have placed before me,
so that through my sacrifices and your Word, I may be fulfilled.
(Prayers of Intercession)

**Please soften the hardened hearts of your children with your Word. May it
be gentle and filled with the caring I know you possess.**

(Morning)	(Evening)
This day, like the others that came before, speaks to me both of burden times and of contentment. Help me to understand the meaning of both, God, as your purpose fills my being. In Christ's name. Amen.	Holy One, as I lay me down to sleep, I ask for forgiveness for those times I failed to listen when you spoke; for those times I reviled any messengers sent to warn me, to comfort me, that I might abide. In Christ's name. Amen.

SUNDAY, OCTOBER 24
(Read Matthew 22:34–46)

(Morning)
God of the earth and heavens, today let me ask no questions of you.
Help me to surrender to your love.

(Evening)
God of the earth and heavens, forgive us for our questions as we search for the underlying meaning of it all. However much we know, still there will be so much more we do not know. In our longing to grasp and pin down the infinite, may we be filled with the grace and beauty of our mortality, in your sight.

There, from dawn until dusk Jesus stood, wondering at the sun as if, in the hours that passed, looking with eyes wide and curious, true meaning would surely come. The heat and the blaze of the light were great. Still his stance did not abate, looking for the meaning of the why and the how of things.

(Morning)
God, Forgiver, I ask that when I have doubts, looking for answers
to questions larger than myself, you forgive me. Help me to find
not the right answers but the right questions.
(Prayers of Intercession)

(Evening)
God, I yearn for contentment, the solace of pinning down that in life which cannot be pinned down. Grant me the understanding that though I will never comprehend your divine nature, I may yet succumb to your divine love.
(Prayers of Intercession)

The man made demands, held his glance, made his stand, until all that was left was a man full of pride, blinded by a day in the sun.

(Morning)
Thank you, Maker, for allowing me to serve, for bestowing upon me the urge to believe in you, my perception granting no clues save for love. In Christ's name. Amen.

(Evening)
My God, we are connected. All people are connected. Help us to see the truth in this and move on. In Christ's name. Amen.

MONDAY, OCTOBER 25
(Read Joshua 3:7–17)

(Morning)
God of difficult crossings, I arise,
rejoicing that you exalt my precious humanity.

(Evening)
God of difficult crossings, I rest, thankful that you held back
this day's concerns and troubles from swamping me.

Guide me as you guided Joshua and the people of Israel, through transitions: birth or death; new jobs or retirement; the first months of kindergarten, college, or a nursing home; marriage, divorce, or the death of a spouse; new towns, new churches, new colleagues, new goals. Each of these frightens me. Help me to stand still, clutching my faith, as the Israelites did the ark, and expecting the way to be clear.

(Morning)
I pray for those, particularly adolescents, who need a sign to believe in their
possibilities for going forward.
(Prayers of Intercession)

(Evening)
I pray for those who need your protection
"going over Jordan" into death this night.
(Prayers of Intercession)

Wherever we go, you guide our paths and steady our feet.

(Morning)
Holy God, for myself and for others, I pray that this day will be filled with large and small transitions. May they become opportunities for your blessing. In the name of the Christ. Amen.

(Evening)
Holy God, restrain the flood of my confusions, yet bathe me in the river of sleep. In the name of the Christ. Amen.

TUESDAY, OCTOBER 26
(Read Psalm 107:1–7)

(Morning)
Loving God, open my mind, heart, spirit, and body to thankfulness,
so that everything I do today may be rooted in gratitude
for creation's wonder and the intimacy of your saving presence.

(Evening)
Loving God, as I prepare for sleep, let me count out thanks
for the particular blessings of this day.

Your song is found in the rhythms of the psalmist, in the heartbeat of an infant, and in thousand-year-old light pulsing from a distant star. And yet you know each one of us. You have always been, you are now, and you always will be a source of limitless caring. However faint, lost, needy, or frightened your people are, you sustain them. Forgive me when I don't remember your love for me. Forgive me when I don't volunteer to be a love-sharer with others.

(Morning)
I pray for the thirsty, and I pray to be empowered to give the living water.
(Prayers of Intercession)

(Evening)
I pray for the hungry, and I pray to be empowered to give physical sustenance.
(Prayers of Intercession)

I know what it is to be lost. Seek those who are lost this day.

(Morning)
Send me, one of your found children, out into this day willing to share my faith and your love. In the name of the Christ. Amen.

(Evening)
As one of your found children, I relax secure in your grace and expectant of the blessing shadow of the night. In the name of the Christ. Amen.

WEDNESDAY, OCTOBER 27
(Read Psalm 107:33–37)

(Morning)
God of river blessing, soak into the parched desert soil of my life today,
so that I may be an oasis to all who pass my way.

(Evening)
God of river blessing, I give you thanks for the fruitfulness
of my day in work, friendship, family, community, and church.
Now I am thirsty for the deep drink of silence.

Some of the parched, barren, desert places in our society are the results of
human wickedness. I confess that sometimes I wait to ride the wave of
some miraculous ever-flowing stream when I could be planning an irriga-
tion system with pipelines through school boards, town meetings, ballot
boxes, community centers, urban gardens, youth outreach, prison visita-
tion, and my own congregation.

(Morning)
I pray for those whose experience is life as a salty waste
because of discrimination based on race, age,
ability, gender, sexual orientation, or ethnic background.
(Prayers of Intercession)

(Evening)
I pray for the small settlements where justice is bubbling up
in secret this night. Some of them are churches.
(Prayers of Intercession)

We all "follow the drinking gourd" as we take your path to freedom.

(Morning)
Today I am wet with love of you, love
of all your children, and love of
myself. Splash me. In the name of the
Christ. Amen.

(Evening)
Tonight I am wet with love of you,
love of all your children, and love of
myself. Let my surface reflect your
face. In the name of the Christ. Amen.

THURSDAY, OCTOBER 28
(Read 1 Thessalonians 2:9–13)

(Morning)
Voice in my heart, Word of God, I awaken and know you have been speaking in my dreams. I turn to Scripture, expecting you again.

(Evening)
Voice in my heart, Word of God, I reflect on this day and know you have spoken in nature, friend, and event. I turn to scripture, expecting you again.

Day and night, light and darkness, creatures and breath—all are your words. The Christ child of Mary, Wisdom of creation, Healer, Bread-breaker, and Star-namer are your words. Teach me to listen. Teach me, as well, to trust my own fragile words to share your love, even when I know they are imperfect. And teach me, like Paul, not to burden with my gospel words but to witness, lift up, and encourage.

(Morning)
I pray for those who have been damaged because your Word was enslaved by bigoted, judgmental, or fanatic human words.
(Prayers of Intercession)

(Evening)
I pray for those who have lost interest because your Word was masked by boring, trivial, or repetitious human words.
(Prayers of Intercession)

Your Word is a lamp to my feet; let me be a wise keeper of oil.

(Morning)
Open my lips, that I may praise you. Let your Word work in me today, that I may be worthy of the life you have given me. In the name of the Christ. Amen.

(Evening)
Hear my prayers and then close my mouth, so that I may listen to your whisper before I speak. In the name of the Christ. Amen.

FRIDAY, OCTOBER 29
(Read Micah 3:5–12)

(Morning)
Prophet-maker God, I rise this morning willing to face my situation
with honesty. Confront me with what I should do and say.

(Evening)
Prophet-maker God, I rest the struggles of this day in your care.
As you have stirred my spirit, now ease my weariness.

You call me to unflinching evaluation of my political, social, and economic
environment. I confess that sometimes I avoid challenging the injustices
that create a society in which I am silent when others are harmed, unless I
or someone close to me is threatened. Shake me with your Spirit and pour
into me your call for justice, so that I may never be tempted to murmur a
false "peace" instead of an uncomfortable prophecy.

(Morning)
I pray for journalists, preachers, and politicians,
all in their own ways called to be prophets.
(Prayers of Intercession)

(Evening)
I pray for elementary-school teachers, lawyers, and artists,
each in their own ways entrusted with the preservation of truth-telling.
(Prayers of Intercession)

**Teach me to live with honesty and justice in my own home
and family before I confront the larger world.**

(Morning)
Open me to your will this day, Creator
of true peace, Christ of the dispossessed, Spirit of urgent answers. In
the name of the Christ. Amen.

(Evening)
Let the sun go down on false prophecy,
compromise, and faithlessness. May I
discover your clarity under the night
wings. In the name of the Christ.
Amen.

SATURDAY, OCTOBER 30
(Read Psalm 43)

(Morning)
Light-sender, Hope-sealer, Morning Joy, I praise you with the harp of my soul-strings, and I dance to the altar of your dwelling in my heart.

(Evening)
Light-sender, Hope-sealer, Evening Refuge, I praise you again for the plucked tunes of this day's music. I climb the holy hill of your nightfall.

Sometimes I am unsure of your presence, particularly when I am buffeted by the opinions of others. I defend you against arguments and indifference. When I do not feel your constant warm assurance because of personal suffering and grief or the random violence and oppression of the world, I am resentful and petulant. Help me to welcome you into the depths of pain as well as good fortune, so that I can understand your love of me. With joy and sorrow, teach me to be more fully human.

(Morning)
I pray for those who will face this day the diagnosis of an illness, the death of a spouse, the loss of a job. Give them strength for their mournful walking.
(Prayers of Intercession)

(Evening)
I pray for those who are depressed this evening, especially those tempted to end their lives. Be their dwelling place of safety.
(Prayers of Intercession)

**"Why are you cast down, O my soul,
and why are you disquieted within me?"**

(Morning)
Send out your light and your truth, and let them lead me through this day. In the name of the Christ. Amen.

(Evening)
So assure me of your love that my doubt may melt away and my hope may shine brightly enough to be seen by others. In the name of the Christ. Amen.

SUNDAY, OCTOBER 31
(Read Matthew 23:1–12)

(Morning)
God, I awaken humble before sunshine and rain, humble before the magic
of time and the treasure of space, humble before the beauty of body and
the quicksilver of mind, humble before the bounty of human diversity and
the kaleidoscope of human behavior.

(Evening)
God, I lay down the burdens other people have pressed on me today
and those I foolishly have chosen for myself. I lay down the burden of
sinfulness and that of self-righteousness. I lay down the burden of rules
and that of freedom. I float into your embrace.

You, O God, are all the authority I need. Protect me from religious doc-
trines and observances that squeeze the joy out of faith. Shut my ears to
self-appointed judges, and help me recognize my own tendency to place
obligations on others. Save my faith community from being stifled under
committees, traditions, insider groups, deadening liturgy, or endowment
funds. Let us travel light.

(Morning)
I pray for surgeons, psychotherapists, CEOs, foster parents, who are given
authority and may choose to be servants.
(Prayers of Intercession)

(Evening)
I pray for fast-food handlers, assembly-line workers,
and nursing-home aides, that within their servant roles,
they may discover a deep authority.
(Prayers of Intercession)

**"All who exalt themselves will be humbled,
and all who humble themselves will be exalted."**

(Morning)
Christ, stern and gentle Teacher,
remind me every hour, whether I like
it or not, that I am called to be a
servant. In the name of the Christ.
Amen.

(Evening)
Christ, stern and gentle Teacher, I am
exalted by your love. No honor, no
respect, no celebration I have ever
known compares to the sheer exalta-
tion of resting in your grace. In the
name of the Christ. Amen.

MONDAY, NOVEMBER 1
(Read Joshua 24:1–3, 14–25)

(Morning)
God, take me in your hands; help me to yield to your shaping and molding.
Empower me to be faithful to what you have called me to be and to do today.

(Evening)
God of the universe, you ordered this day for all creation according to
your plan. Today you held my hand over rough places and calmed
the tumults of my heart. Grant rest to my body and peace to my soul,
for in your love alone are absolute acceptance and joy.

Sovereign God, thank you for people of faith like Joshua. By his story, you help me see more keenly whose I am. Turn Joshua's words into a sword to slay the idols in my life. Remind me of your love and the certainty of your judgment. Teach me to be grateful, and in my gratitude empower me to serve you. Help me to extend a life of service beyond myself by living out my faith, so that my household and my friends will recognize you as their God and themselves as your servants. Grant me the courage of Joshua, and remind me of your sacrificial love through Jesus Christ.

(Morning)
God, in this world of many choices, help me to choose you above all else,
with all my heart, with all my soul, and with all my mind.
(Prayers of Intercession)

(Evening)
God, write in my heart an everlasting covenant with you.
Grant that my life seeks, above all, to fulfill it.
(Prayers of Intercession)

"But as for me and my household, we will serve God."
(Pray the Prayer of Our Savior.)

(Morning)
Loving God, enable me to live Joshua's story today. In Jesus' name. Amen.

(Evening)
Loving God, I rest in your love and unconditional acceptance. In Jesus' name. Amen.

TUESDAY, NOVEMBER 2
(Read Psalm 78:1–7)

(Morning)
Divine Teacher, your wisdom and power are boundless,
and your mercy is beyond measure. Wash me anew of my sins,
and refresh my soul with the lessons of all generations.

(Evening)
Divine Teacher, thank you for your lessons. I learn slowly, and the tests
are not easy. But the faithful you always pass. God of mercy, hallelujah!

Gracious God, thank you for your commandments and teachings in my lifetime and over all generations. You wrote them in my conscience, in the laws of your creation, and in the lives of your faithful witnesses. The wonders of your deeds fill the Scriptures. My sins and the sins of humankind are many, and only the saving blood of Jesus can satisfy your justice and holiness. Help me to learn my lessons well and to share your love with people I meet through the power of your Holy Spirit.

(Morning)
Divine Teacher, make me teachable and empower me
to be a model to the people I love.
(Prayers of Intercession)

(Evening)
God, give me a holy memory to remember your glorious deeds.
(Prayers of Intercession)

"We will tell to the coming generation the glorious deeds of God."
(Pray the Prayer of Our Savior.)

(Morning)
Loving God, enable me to live out
your teachings. Help me to brighten a
young person's day. In Jesus' name.
Amen.

(Evening)
Loving God, continue to create in my
consciousness love for your ways and
obedience to your laws. In Jesus'
name. Amen.

WEDNESDAY, NOVEMBER 3
(Read Amos 5:18–24)

(Morning)
Loving God, I tremble in the face of your disapproval and judgment.
But morning always brings the hope of a new day. By the power of your
renewing Spirit, help me to have a fresh start today.

(Evening)
Loving God, I offer my life as a continuing act of worship to you.
May it be pleasing in your sight.

Holy God, you call your people to a life of wholeness and integrity. You
require that the words of our prayers match the deeds of our lives. You ask
your people to offer their lives as a living sacrifice and worship to you.
You call us to a life of serving and caring, not acquiring and using. Help
me to serve you by caring for the weak and the poor and by working for
justice in a society that favors the rich and the powerful. Forgive my sins
of inaction and timidity and the injustices of my generation.

(Morning)
Holy God, bless your people with personal righteousness and social justice.
(Prayers of Intercession)

(Evening)
Holy God, may the words of your people, the meditations of their hearts,
and the deeds of their hands be pleasing in your sight.
(Prayers of Intercession)

**Let justice roll down like waters and righteousness
like an ever-flowing stream.**
(Pray the Prayer of Our Savior.)

(Morning)
Holy God, make me an instrument of
your justice and righteousness. In
Jesus' name. Amen.

(Evening)
Holy God, refresh me in the shower
of your justice, and nourish me in the
spring of your righteousness. In
Jesus' name. Amen.

THURSDAY, NOVEMBER 4
(Read Proverbs 6:17–20)

(Morning)
Holy God, your holiness reveals the reality of my sinfulness.
Forgive my sins, and help me celebrate this day as a forgiven
and beloved child of a gracious God.

(Evening)
Gracious God, forgive my sins again. Is it ever possible not to sin? Ah, I can
only rest in your assurance that nothing can separate me from your love.

Holy God, you know me so well. You know that I have feet of clay. My
experiences with other people have taught me to be defensive and mis-
trustful, and I have learned to put myself first above others. Thank you,
gracious God, for not giving up on me. You forgive my sins and cast them
away as far as the East is from the West. Your love for me is as great as the
heavens are far from the earth. Bless me with friends and mentors who
would be willing to point out my errors and show me your way. Grant me
an obedient and forgiving heart.

(Morning)
Holy God, I pray that I may be as ready to forgive myself
and others as you are to forgive me.
(Prayers of Intercession)

(Evening)
Create in me, O God, a real and abiding consciousness
that I am holy just because I am your child.
(Prayers of Intercession)

"The righteous will live by faith."
(Pray the Prayer of Our Savior.)

(Morning)
Holy God, help me to be righteous
and keep me from being judgmental
of others. In Jesus' name. Amen.

(Evening)
Gracious God, your righteousness is
with those who love you and obey
your commandments. In Jesus' name.
Amen.

FRIDAY, NOVEMBER 5
(Read Psalm 70)

(Morning)
Thank you, God, for being my Protector. Your power is absolute,
and your reliability is sure. Whom shall I fear?

(Evening)
Thank you, God, for the sun has set and my enemies lurk in the shadows.
But your light will reveal their injustice and protect me from their evil plot.

Almighty God, when I make a stand for what is right, help me to be steadfast. Remind me that the loss of my earthly possessions, my job, my friends,
or my social status does not compare to the gain of your heavenly realm.
Protect me from the enemies of justice and righteousness by thwarting their
plans. Bring to my side sisters and brothers of wisdom and courage. Bring
down failure to my enemies and deliver me success, so that your name will
be glorified and your people encouraged.

(Morning)
Great God, I pray for courage and faith for all in the world
who suffer persecution for the sake of justice and righteousness.
(Prayers of Intercession)

(Evening)
Triumphant God, the war is won, and you are the victor.
May I rest in the assurance of your final victory.
(Prayers of Intercession)

"Let all who seek you rejoice and be glad in you."
(Pray the Prayer of Our Savior.)

(Morning)
Almighty God, deliver us from evil.
In Jesus' name. Amen.

(Evening)
Almighty God, you are my Shield and
my Deliverer. In you do I trust. In
Jesus' name. Amen.

SATURDAY, NOVEMBER 6
(Read 1 Thessalonians 4:13–18)

(Morning)
Glorious God, thank you for the assurance of life everlasting
with you in the company of your people in glory.

(Evening)
Glorious God, remind me of the faith stories from the life
of my departed loved ones.

Glorious God, thank you that death is not the finality of life. But, God, I dread death even though it seems to be the threshold to eternal life. The loss of a loved one in death feels so final and the loss so great to bear. Thank you, God, for your assurance in the Bible that the saints who died are with you and that we will have a reunion in heaven at your appointed time. There is no greater comfort than this. Thank you, Jesus, for your sacrifice on the cross, which opened the doors of heaven for your people. In response to your sacrificial love, help me to live a life that will bring a little bit of heaven on earth through the power of your Holy Spirit.

(Morning)
Loving God, I pray for your comfort for grieving people in the world.
(Prayers of Intercession)

(Evening)
Loving God, grant that your people may sleep in heavenly peace.
(Prayers of Intercession)

"Do not grieve for those who have died as others do who have no hope."
(Pray the Prayer of Our Savior.)

(Morning)
Loving God, help us to be thankful and to celebrate the life of our loved ones. In Jesus' name. Amen.

(Evening)
Loving God, thank you for the cloud of witnesses. Teach us the lessons of their faith. In Jesus' name. Amen.

SUNDAY, NOVEMBER 7
(Read Matthew 25:1–13)

(Morning)
Jesus, help me to make ready for your coming.
May each breaking dawn serve as a reminder of your glorious return.

(Evening)
Jesus, as I switch on the lights each evening,
teach me anew the lessons of the parable of the ten bridesmaids.

Jesus, thank you for coming into the world and into my life. You first came as a helpless baby, unknown and unwanted by the world. But you will come again as a triumphant ruler, and every knee will bow before you, and every tongue will sing praises of your glory. Jesus, allow me to take part in the welcoming chorus. As you have written your laws in my heart, let my life be an anthem of faith and obedience. As you have washed my sins away by your sacrifice on the cross, let me be part of the clean-up crew to get things ready for your arrival. Jesus, I am not worthy, but just say the word and my spirit will be made whole.

(Morning)
Jesus, I do not know when you will come; help me to be ready always.
(Prayers of Intercession)

(Evening)
Jesus, as I lie down to sleep, grant me peace and joy,
knowing that I may wake up in heaven.
(Prayers of Intercession)

"Keep awake, therefore, for you know neither the day nor the hour."
(Pray the Prayer of Our Savior.)

(Morning)
Jesus, thank you for the anticipation of your coming. In your precious name. Amen.

(Evening)
Jesus, bless my soul and let your Word be a lamp to my feet. In your precious name. Amen.

MONDAY, NOVEMBER 8
(Read Psalm 123)
(Sing "God of Grace and God of Glory" or another familiar song)

(Morning)
Dearest Jesus, as I open my eyes to behold a new day,
may they fall on you and only you.

(Evening)
Dearest Jesus, as dusk settles in, may your mercy surround me.
Enable me to extend your mercy to others.

Ever-abiding God, when I search for you, I find that you have always been with me. In the midst of my searching, I learn what is most important, enabling me to let go of all the scorn and contempt that I have endured from others. Help me always to remember that in the midst of those who would scorn and speak evil of me, you will never leave my side. For your supporting presence, my focus will always remain on your mercy and love for me.

(Morning)
Most merciful God, you have shown me your mercy and love.
Help me to pass that love and mercy on to others.
(Prayers of Intercession)

(Evening)
Today, I walked aware of your goodness and mercy. Grant me the courage and wisdom to be always aware of the need to reach out to others.
(Prayers of Intercession)

**Remaining in your presence, my searching ends.
In your mercy and love, I find peace.**
(Pray the Prayer of Our Savior.)

(Morning)
How great is your faithfulness, most merciful God. Morning after morning, new mercies I see. In Jesus' name. Amen.

(Evening)
As I close my eyes, I rest filled with your love, mercy, and a grateful heart. In Jesus' name. Amen.

TUESDAY, NOVEMBER 9
(Read Psalm 90:1–8)

(Morning)
Eternal and everlasting God, your voice wakes and summons me to rise and begin this new day. I give thanks to the One who calls me by name.

(Evening)
Eternal and everlasting God, Rock of Ages, cleft for me,
let me hide myself in thee.

Never-changing God of the ages, throughout all generations you have been a safe dwelling place. You existed before the beginning of time and will continue to exist beyond what I could ever think or imagine. Knowing that you are omnipresent—everywhere at once—I can hide myself in you, in the bosom of your safety. I never will escape trials and tribulations, but I can accept them with joy, knowing that I am in your great love.

(Morning)
With wisdom and power, our Redeemer reigns. What an awesome God we serve! Sing hallelujah to our Parent, Teacher, and Sovereign God.
(Prayers of Intercession)

(Evening)
Where God leads me I will follow, knowing that God gives me grace and glory and goes with me every step of the way.
(Prayers of Intercession)

From everlasting to everlasting, you are God, the Alpha and Omega.
(Pray the Prayer of Our Savior.)

(Morning)
Omnipotent and forgiving God, who reproves me with righteous anger when I need it, wash away my sins. In Jesus' name. Amen.

(Evening)
Protector, I close my eyes in sweet rest, knowing that as long as I cling to you in love, you will keep and surround me in your protection. In Jesus' name. Amen.

WEDNESDAY, NOVEMBER 10
(Read Psalm 90:9–12)

(Morning)
Ancient One of days, satisfy me in the morning with your steadfast love,
so that I may rejoice and be glad all of my days.

(Evening)
Ancient One of days, teach me to be aware of my limited number of days,
in order that I might use them wisely.

God, teach me to make the most of my days here on earth, so that I may not waste an hour or minute of the day. Christ, from your teachings you have shown us the importance of placing nothing before our relationship with you and others. Help me to make the most of my relationships, realizing that when I leave this temporary home and enter into my heavenly home, you are all that I will take with me.

(Morning)
As the rising of the sun extinguishes the darkness of the night,
allow me to live this day to its fullest as if it were the last.
(Prayers of Intercession)

(Evening)
Praise and glory to you, most Holy One, for another day in your service.
(Prayers of Intercession)

Make us glad as many days as you have afflicted us.
(Pray the Prayer of Our Savior.)

(Morning)
I rise this day begging for forgiveness of my sins, that the few days of my life may be spent seeking your wisdom. In Jesus' name. Amen.

(Evening)
As this day draws to a close, may your Spirit descend upon me, that I might feel your presence now and forever. I await the Holy Spirit! In Jesus' name. Amen.

THURSDAY, NOVEMBER 11
(Read Matthew 25:14–30)

(Morning)
Creator of all that is, I arise this day asking for your help. Help me to invest my services for the betterment of your dominion here on earth.

(Evening)
Creator of all that is, I pray that the fruits of my labor have been beneficial. This increase I gladly give to you.

Giver of life, I raise my voice and lift my hands in praise to you, for your presence in my life means more to me than life itself. I pray that the gifts and talents you have so richly blessed me with will be used for the uplifting of your realm here on earth. Use me, God, for I am your willing and faithful servant.

(Morning)
Granter of talents and gifts, help me to realize the magnitude of the many talents and gifts you have bestowed upon me. Help me to use them, share them, and sharpen them, for I know that my doing so will be pleasing in your sight.
(Prayers of Intercession)

(Evening)
Gracious and compassionate God, this day I pray that the fruits of my labor are acceptable in your eyes. Grant that I may hear, "Well done, good, trustworthy, and faithful servant. Enter into the joy of my arms."
(Prayers of Intercession)

We are accountable!
(Pray the Prayer of Our Savior.)

(Morning)
I work hard, loving Parent, to apply my meager talents in the fashion that you set before me. Bless my efforts, that you may enjoy the work I have done. In Jesus' name. Amen.

(Evening)
As I prepare to rest my physical body, I bring to you, my Parent, Teacher, and Instructor, the interest from my talents. The spoken and unspoken word, the touch of kindness, the smile of your presence in my life as it lightened one heart, comforted one soul, and brought relief to one wayfarer are my love offerings to you. In Jesus' name. Amen.

FRIDAY, NOVEMBER 12
(Read 1 Thessalonians 5:1–11)

(Morning)
Almighty and everlasting God, thanks be to you, who save me! As I awaken,
I rise from my gloom with the assurance that if I remain faithful to you,
gracious God, I will see the glory of the coming Christ.

(Evening)
Almighty and everlasting God, I pray that all who are separated from you
because of the sins of this world will turn to you and walk in obedience.

God, you paid a great price to redeem me, and I give you my life and my
loyalty. Because Christ Jesus died for my sins, I will choose daily to love
and serve you. I wait fearlessly, patiently, and with peace and confidence,
for your second coming, because I know that you have delivered me from
my sins and I now walk in obedience. Hallelujah, for the reward of obedience is waiting for me!

(Morning)
Send your light, merciful God, that I might find my way.
Lead and guide me along my journey.
(Prayers of Intercession)

(Evening)
Redeeming God, help me to keep my eyes on the path of righteousness.
I want to follow you each step of the way. Order my steps in your Word;
I want to walk worthy!
(Prayers of Intercession)

**"Encourage one another and build up one another,
as you are indeed doing."**
(Pray the Prayer of Our Savior.)

(Morning)
Understanding and forgiving God, I
thank you for your redemptive love
and place all my hope in you. Help
me as I strive to walk in your way,
encouraging my brothers and sisters
along my journey. In Jesus' name.
Amen.

(Evening)
Abide with me, fast falls the eventide,
the darkness deepens. God, with me
abide. In Jesus' name. Amen.

SATURDAY, NOVEMBER 13
(Read Judges 4:1–7)

(Morning)
God, yesterday's mistakes are behind me. Grant that I might listen
to the Holy Spirit's instructions and with renewed strength stand!

(Evening)
God, allow your given victories of this day
to strengthen my efforts to walk in the way of righteousness.

When the turmoil and turbulence of this life cause me to drift away from
you, bring judgment into my life to direct its course back to you. With
faith, I know that you will hear my cries and guide me. You will deliver me
from the enemy of my soul and cause me to be victorious. Your love and
faithfulness endure forever.

(Morning)
Gracious God, give me the wisdom to hear your instruction.
Direct my life in accordance with your desire.
(Prayers of Intercession)

(Evening)
My soul rejoices in praises for your unending direction and guidance.
(Prayers of Intercession)

**I seek divine judgment. If I but listen, you will set
my feet on the path of righteousness. I will listen and obey.**
(Pray the Prayer of Our Savior.)

(Morning)
I will not find you in the voices of
contemporary society. However, I will
find you in the most unexpected
places. From the lips of strangers, I
will hear your still, small voice. And I
will obey your command. In Jesus'
name. Amen.

(Evening)
Did I listen? Did I hear myself? Did I
obey? Did I close my ears to the
deafening sounds of this world? Did I
shut them out and hear your words?
Did I stand for Christ? As I prepare to
slumber this night, I pray that I heard
and obeyed. In Jesus' name. Amen.

SUNDAY, NOVEMBER 14
(Read Zephaniah 1:7, 12–18)

(Morning)
Compassionate and forgiving God, I have sinned and do not deserve your grace. I pray for your forgiveness, that I might be a willing and able servant.

(Evening)
Compassionate and forgiving God, I prostrate myself before you. Forgive me for conforming to the materialistic path of society. Teach me your ways.

God, your day is coming. I will be commanded to stand accountable for my sins before you, a God who is omnipotent, all-knowing, compassionate, and merciful. Sinner that I am, I seek this day and every day the forgiving grace of Jesus Christ, knowing that Jesus is a forgiving and loving parent. Cleanse me of all unrighteousness and anoint me from head to toe with your Holy Spirit, in order that I might be a willing and able servant.

(Morning)
Search me, God, that I may rid myself of the hidden sins
that I do not want to see.
(Prayers of Intercession)

(Evening)
Bring your lamp, your light, the light of the world, and save me from my sins.
(Prayers of Intercession)

The light of the world is Jesus.
(Pray the Prayer of Our Savior.)

(Morning)
Out of the chaos of the world, wandering on its willful way, let the light of your grace fall on me. In Jesus' name. Amen.

(Evening)
I have no fear. My life is founded on the rock of Jesus Christ. When the day of God comes, I will be victorious. In Jesus' name. Amen.

MONDAY, NOVEMBER 15
(Read Ezekiel 34:11–16)
(Sing "Savior, like a Shepherd Lead Us" or another familiar hymn)

(Morning)
Loving God of day, you call all of your sheep by name.
May I hear you call my name, and may I have the courage to answer.

(Evening)
Loving God of the night, as I lie down to sleep, give me the comforting
assurance that you are watching over the flock and guarding your fold.

Loving God, a psalmist who was also a shepherd once contemplated the
relationship with you, comparing it to a shepherd's relationship with sheep.
The psalmist proclaimed, "God is my shepherd, I shall not want." Throughout the years, you have called men and women to care for your flock; yet
the care of a hireling cannot match the care of the owner. In your great
might, you declare your intention to search for your sheep, to gather your
flock, and again to be the great shepherd of your people. God, I want you
to be my shepherd, for your voice is the only one I can trust in this world.

(Morning)
Living God, let me be as a little lamb today,
trusting you for all my needs and the needs of others.
(Prayers of Intercession)

(Evening)
As I remember my day, help me to see how I have responded
to your care as my shepherd.
(Prayers of Intercession)

With boldness and confidence I now pray.
(Pray the Prayer of Our Savior.)

(Morning)
God, lead me in your righteousness;
make the way plain before me. It is you,
God, who makes me dwell in safety. In
the name of Jesus. Amen.

(Evening)
At the close of this day, into your
hand I commit my spirit. In the name
of Jesus. Amen.

TUESDAY, NOVEMBER 16
(Read Ezekiel 34:20–24)
(Sing "Where He Leads Me" or another familiar hymn)

(Morning)
God of mercy and grace, you seek out your sheep, and you judge between the good and the bad. May I experience your mercy in my judgment today.

(Evening)
God of mercy and grace, I am responsible for my own thoughts, words, and deeds. May I commit myself so completely to you that my thoughts, words, deeds, and even my dreams may be grounded and rooted in you.

Gracious God, you confront me with a most unpleasant side of my nature today. Your flock has been scattered because individuals have exercised their power to intimidate other sheep. I often think that I have no power, but perhaps even I have exploited those who are weaker than I. I cannot stand in my self-righteousness and present myself as faultless before you. Even though I may consider myself one of the weaker sheep, there are others weaker than I. Teach me how to love those who are weak, so that they might experience the bounty of your love. Send David, the shepherd, not only to lead the flock, but to teach me my responsibility toward other members of the fold. Teach me to be merciful, so that I might obtain mercy.

(Morning)
Dear Savior of all, forgive my foolish ways. Reclothe me this day so that the world may see you living in me and me living in you.
(Prayers of Intercession)

(Evening)
God of Abraham and Sarah, Isaac and Rebecca, Jacob and Rachel,
as you led their children by pillar of cloud and pillar of fire,
so, too, may you lead me to your promised land.
(Prayers of Intercession)

With boldness and confidence I now pray.
(Pray the Prayer of Our Savior.)

(Morning)
As I go forth today, Gracious God, let me not go forth to push with flank and shoulder, scattering your flock. Rather, let me go forth committed to the restoration of your flock. In the name of Jesus I pray. Amen.

(Evening)
As the sheep settled under the stars, committed to the care of the shepherd, so, too, may my spirit be committed to your care this night. In the name of Jesus I pray. Amen.

WEDNESDAY, NOVEMBER 17

(Read Psalm 95:1–7a)

(Sing "Joyful, Joyful, We Adore Thee" or another familiar hymn)

(Morning)
Sovereign God, to you I bring the sacrifice of praise today.
With joy and thanksgiving I come to you, bowing to you, Creator of all.
Receive, I pray, my offerings to you.

(Evening)
Sovereign God, land and sea, mountain and valley, heights and depths
of the earth you have made, and you even made me. When I consider
the works of your hands, my soul sings just how great you are.

In my daily worship, Sovereign Shepherd, I acknowledge who you are. As your presence engulfs and envelops me, I am moved to praise and thanksgiving. I remember who you are and what you have done; I remember who I am and whose I am. You have made me, designed me to worship you and to shout joyfully to your name. I am awed by your vastness, the multifacetedness of your being. And yet, in the midst of this vastness, you know me individually, even holding me in the palm of your hand. No one is able to snatch me out of that hand. Such knowledge is too wonderful for me. I will sing and praise your name.

(Morning)
Loving God, what may be noise to human ears is music to yours.
With joy I will tell of your mighty acts in my life. As I bow before you,
I lay before you concerns for my life and those around me.
(Prayers of Intercession)

(Evening)
Sovereign Shepherd, you have led me beside the still waters and paths of
righteousness today. In this nighttime, may I lie down in green pastures.
(Prayers of Intercession)

With boldness and confidence I now pray.
(Pray the Prayer of Our Savior.)

(Morning)
Gracious God, you have given this day
to me as a gift. My service today is my
gift to you. May it be like that of
Abel—acceptable to you. In the name
of Christ. Amen.

(Evening)
As I lay my head in sleep tonight,
tender Shepherd, into your care I
commit my spirit. In the name of
Christ. Amen.

THURSDAY, NOVEMBER 18

(Read Ephesians 1:15–23)
(Sing "My Faith Looks Up to Thee" or another familiar hymn)

(Morning)
Gracious and glorious God, give me a spirit of wisdom and revelation,
that I may know you and the hope to which you have called me.

(Evening)
Gracious and glorious God, your power and might have been given to me
this day. Help me to sing about the faith that the somber past has taught me
and a song full of the hope that the present has brought me.

Dear God, were you trying to tell us more about your love for us when your
child died on the cross? Certainly other means of execution existed. Yet
you chose the first century, when Rome ruled much of the world. What
were you trying to say with the cross—its vertical post pointing to you and
its horizontal arm seemingly reaching out to embrace the world? Is it that
the true church is characterized by loyalty to you and love of humanity?
Paul tells the church at Ephesus that he has heard of their faith in Jesus and
their love for the saints. He rejoices because they got the point. Help me to
get the point and learn to love you and all that you have created.

(Morning)
As I pray for others, loving God, I discover my need for others to pray for me.
As Paul prayed for the faith of the Ephesians, I pray for my faith and the faith
of others. May I be lifted in prayer by those for whom I pray.
(Prayers of Intercession)

(Evening)
As I remember this day, I do not cease to give thanks to you,
Sovereign God, for all that you have done on my behalf.
(Prayers of Intercession)

With boldness and confidence I now pray.
(Pray the Prayer of Our Savior.)

(Morning)
God of the day, let your immeasurable
power be at work within me this day.
I offer myself into your hands, that I
might do your bidding. In Christ's
name. Amen.

(Evening)
God of the night, I am weary. As I
prepare to rest this night, into your
hands I commit my spirit. In Christ's
name. Amen.

FRIDAY, NOVEMBER 19
(Read Ephesians 1:15–23)
(Sing "One Bread, One Body" or another familiar hymn)

(Morning)
O Holy One, after a night of rest, you awaken me to rise to greet the day.
May soundness of body, mind, and spirit be mine.

(Evening)
O Holy One, with Jesus as the cornerstone, I become a valuable piece
as you reign upon the earth. Remind me that my value is directly
related to my relationship with Jesus. May I strive to deepen that
relationship with every moment that you give to me.

O Beloved One, you have set Jesus as the head of the church, and we are
Christ's body. Our world stands in disunity and chaos. Paul believes that
you sent Jesus to bring dissonant strands together. Christ becomes the head,
and the church is literally and figuratively the hands, the feet, the voice to
do Christ's bidding. We only need to remember one thing: "Go therefore
and make disciples of all nations, baptizing them in the name of the Father,
the Son, and the Holy Spirit, teaching them to obey everything I have commanded you. And remember, I am with you always, to the end of the age."

(Morning)
We are one in the Spirit with God, and we pray that all unity
may one day be restored. In prayer with others today,
loving God, let me experience unity in community.
(Prayers of Intercession)

(Evening)
Working with others can sometimes be difficult, O Holy One. Sometimes
I have to subordinate my wishes and desires by having a yielding spirit.
Help me to blend with others, to walk hand in hand with them.
(Prayers of Intercession)

With boldness and confidence I now pray.
(Pray the Prayer of Our Savior.)

(Morning)
Gracious God, make me part of that
one great community throughout the
whole wide earth. In the name of the
Christ. Amen.

(Evening)
I am bound with you tonight, my
God, and it is into your hands that I
commit my spirit. In the name of the
Christ. Amen.

SATURDAY, NOVEMBER 20
(Read Matthew 25:31–46)
(Sing "The King of Love My Shepherd Is" or another familiar hymn)

(Morning)
Savior God, at the beginning of the day you lead me to consider
the end of time. I pray that you would direct my steps according
to your precepts, that I might serve you this day.

(Evening)
Savior God, at the close of the day, I ask you to stay with me,
even though I might have failed you during the day.

God, you are so amazing! How strange that the Christ, abundant in power
and glory, should identify with the poor, the downtrodden, the disenfran-
chised. Too often we look to help those who can help us, the old "I'll scratch
your back if you scratch mine" routine. Yet the underlying theme of your
Word today is that giving for recognition is unwholesome and unhealthy. It
is good to give when asked, but somehow I feel that it is even better to give
unasked, to discern the needs of those around me, survey the resources you
have provided me, and then rise to meet the presented need. Remind me
that in either my abundance or my meagerness, you have provided for me
to meet someone else's emptiness. Make me worthy to be a giver and an
instrument of giving.

(Morning)
Today, loving God, let me go beyond seeing the needs of those around me
and let me feel them. I begin by praying for myself and others.
(Prayers of Intercession)

(Evening)
This night, as I reflect on the activity of the day, I pray, Sovereign God,
that of all that I gave this day, I truly gave of myself to all.
(Prayers of Intercession)

With boldness and confidence I now pray.
(Pray the Prayer of Our Savior.)

(Morning)
I am created in your image, as is every
man, woman, boy, and girl. Help me
to see you in everyone I meet today. In
the matchless name of Jesus. Amen.

(Evening)
As the shadows draw around me, into
your hands I commit my spirit. In the
matchless name of Jesus. Amen.

SUNDAY, NOVEMBER 21
(Read Matthew 25:31–46)
(Sing "How Great Thou Art" or another familiar hymn)

(Morning)
Sovereign God, as I bow before you this day, remind me that you are
also a righteous judge and that one day I must stand before you.
Help me to prepare for that day, beginning today.

(Evening)
Sovereign God, be merciful to me, for I am a sinner. Help me to see myself
as I truly am, the way you see me. Help me to confront the unpleasant sides
of who I am and then transform me into who you have created me to be.

Gracious God, life presents us with many opportunities to reveal the love
we have for you and for humanity, yet our biographies are filled with blown
opportunities. Too often we delude ourselves by saying, "I'm not really
that bad," or "I am not as bad as they," or "I know I'm not that good, but
God will forgive me." The harsh realities of judgment and punishment are
before me today. I pray that I will not presume your goodness, mercy, and
grace.

(Morning)
In this new day, help me to be honest with myself and acknowledge
that I am not all that you have meant for me to be. May you reign in me
as I pray for myself and others.
(Prayers of Intercession)

(Evening)
As I lie down to sleep tonight, should judgment time come,
may I be numbered among the righteous and enter into eternal life with you.
(Prayers of Intercession)

With boldness and confidence I now pray.
(Pray the Prayer of Our Savior.)

(Morning)
You have prepared for me an inheritance from the foundation of the world.
Let me live today that I might receive
my place in your realm. In Christ's
name. Amen.

(Evening)
Into your hands I commit my spirit. I
can do nothing more. In Christ's
name. Amen.

MONDAY, NOVEMBER 22
(Read Isaiah 64:1–7)

(Morning)
O God of awakening and peace, your presence is everywhere. Help me this day
to open my eyes, my ears, and my heart to awareness of all of your blessings.

(Evening)
O God of rest and peace, grant that my spirit may enjoy the rest
and the peace as the night tenderly enfolds me. So may it be.

God, the prophet Isaiah reminds the people of Israel of their many shortcomings. They were, no doubt, surprised at such a drastic comparison of
their "goodness" with filthy rags. In today's world, the average Christian's
lifestyle deserves the same comparison. Our whole society reflects the fact
that we have all sinned and fall short of the real and forgiving goodness of
our Creator. O God, help me to clear my vision to see myself as I really am,
right now!

(Morning)
Help me, O God, to see and recognize your loving and forgiving hand
at work in my life. Permit me the joy of your amazing grace.
(Prayers of Intercession)

(Evening)
God, it is my sincere prayer that your forgiving grace may comfort
and renew me this very night and on the morrow.
(Prayers of Intercession)

As Jesus taught his disciples I pray
(Pray the Prayer of Our Savior.)

(Morning)	(Evening)
God of grace and God of glory, on your servant pour your power! In the name of our Savior. Amen.	I seek your will, O God. Have your way in my life this eventide. In the name of our Savior. Amen.

TUESDAY, NOVEMBER 23
(Read Isaiah 64:8–9)

(Morning)
O God, I thank you that you so awesomely have created me. I pray that I may
choose to follow your will in everything I attempt to do this day.

(Evening)
O God, I rest in my certainty that you are still at work in shaping me.
Almighty God, help me to treasure and follow the insights
that will keep me cooperating with your plan.

The well-known hymn "Have Thine Own Way, Lord" says "Thou art the
potter, I am the clay. Mold me and make me after your will." A worthy
sentiment, indeed, but I am not passive and inanimate like clay. I suppose
that is why Adelaide Pollard added that she was "yielded and still." Isaiah
must have shared the same yieldedness: "We are clay and you are our potter." God, it takes willingness to part with many things I hold dear if I am
to yield to the shaping of your hand in this finite vessel.

(Morning)
Gracious God, help me to live in glad expectation of your
handiwork in my life, knowing that your will is my true fulfillment.
(Prayers of Intercession)

(Evening)
Dear God, the world I live in constantly encourages me to
stubborn resistance to your will. Help me to moisten my spirit,
that this clay may yield willingly to the work of your hands.
(Prayers of Intercession)

As Jesus taught his disciples I pray.
(Pray the Prayer of Our Savior.)

(Morning)
With your infinite power you sustained
me through the night. I thank you,
God. In the name of our Savior. Amen.

(Evening)
I rest in your peace this night. Give
me a calm spirit as I yield to your
will. You neither slumber nor sleep.
In the name of our Savior. Amen.

WEDNESDAY, NOVEMBER 24
(Read Psalm 80:17–19)

(Morning)
I thank you, God, that your hand has been upon me
in spite of my waywardness and neglect to do your perfect will.

(Evening)
I thank you, God. In the darkness of the night, I rejoice in the light of your
countenance. Grant that peace and joy may penetrate the walls of my resistance.

The Israelites made mistakes, willfully disobeying directions from you,
the God of creation. These recorded declarations by the prophets, ordained
by you, were willfully ignored. As they suffered from their errors and sought
restoration, God, you were already waiting, more willing to restore than
they were to request restoration. I, too, have made costly departures from
your will for my life. I need to shed my shame and gladly receive your
gracious restoration. This could make the difference in my life. Praise God!

(Morning)
Most gracious God, open my eyes to your grace and mercy this day,
that I may bear to see the reality of my transgressions.
(Prayers of Intercession)

(Evening)
Help me to accept your restoration and keep my vow
never again to turn away from you, O God.
(Prayers of Intercession)

As Jesus taught his disciples I pray.
(Pray the Prayer of Our Savior.)

(Morning)
I am not ashamed of the gospel of
Jesus Christ. I know its power. In the
name of our Savior. Amen.

(Evening)
O God, restore my soul, may every
fear of failure be cast aside. In the
name of our Savior. Amen.

THURSDAY, NOVEMBER 25
(Read 1 Corinthians 1:3–8)

(Morning)
Thank you, God. Great is thy faithfulness, O God, my Savior.
Morning after morning, new mercies I see!

(Evening)
Thank you, God, for a beautiful Thanksgiving Day! I pray that each and
every day, my life will be a continuous paean of praise and thanksgiving!

Our nation's day of thanks hearkens back to the day of the Puritan forebears. As they feasted, so do we. God, as they thanked you for physical
survival and sustenance, so do we. Indeed, this appears to be the sole focus
of our thanks. But the Puritans' rejoicing was about a far more significant
blessing—that of spiritual freedom. The apostle Paul, in today's reading, is
also giving you thanks for the many spiritual gifts you gave to the Corinthian
Christians. He was deadly serious. Those new Corinthian Christians needed
those spiritual gifts. As a matter of truth, nearly two thousand years later,
the need for spiritual gifts is no less. My sincere thanks for the spiritual
gifts I see and possess.

(Morning)
I thank you, God, for the beauty of this earth. Enlarge my heart
and mind to use wisely the endowment of your spiritual gifts.
(Prayers of Intercession)

(Evening)
I acknowledge your greatness, O God, but I seem reluctant to give you
the thanks and praise. Stir my soul to give thanks in everything!
(Prayers of Intercession)

As Jesus taught his disciples I pray.
(Pray the Prayer of Our Savior.)

(Morning)
As the day unfolds, I pray that I will be
open to receive your grace. In our
Savior's name. Amen.

(Evening)
As the shades of night close in on my
tired frame, I pray for rest. In our
Savior's name. Amen.

FRIDAY, NOVEMBER 26
(Read 1 Corinthians 1:9)

(Morning)
God Almighty, I thank you for your marvelous creation
and the way your handiwork has shaped my frame. In gratitude,
I lift my heart in unceasing praise.

(Evening)
God Almighty, drop your still dews of quietness till this fervor
inside of me stops and I can sleep peacefully.

As a lifelong member of a congregation in the "free church" tradition, I have experienced a great deal of contentiousness. Free churches are like that; they have no ordained official to dictate policy and eliminate endless debate. Lest we give up on the manifest inefficiency of the processes of spiritual democracy, the apostle Paul reminds us that it was you, loving God, who called us together, and you can be depended upon faithfully to sustain and use us according to your creative will. I will follow with faith and hope the assignments that you give to me, not looking for success but remaining faithful to what my hands find to do.

(Morning)
Dear God, as the days are fewer before the new millennium,
I am especially grateful for each and every day given to me.
(Prayers of Intercession)

(Evening)
Grant that with the passing of this day, I may find peace and rest.
Free my mind of the pressures that have disturbed me this day. So may it be.
(Prayers of Intercession)

As Jesus taught his disciples I pray.
(Pray the Prayer of Our Savior.)

(Morning)	(Evening)
Success is failure turned inside out. I pray for faith. In the name of our Savior. Amen.	I learned so late when night came, how near you were, O God. In the name of our Savior. Amen.

SATURDAY, NOVEMBER 27
(Read Mark 13:28–33)

(Morning)
God, I lift my eyes to the hills this day. I thank you for eyes
and ears and for a voice to praise your holy name.

(Evening)
God, this day has been a blessing. I pray that my thoughts
and dreams will be in tune with your perfect will. So may it be.

Creator God, the threat of the end of the world was a reality for all of us so long as the Soviet Union and the rest of the world were at odds. Nevertheless, most people lived as if they had limitless time to clean up their lives and settle their moral and spiritual obligations. But even some teenagers, who hardly expect to reach twenty-one, seem to care little about carefully preparing for the end of their world. Your child, Jesus, urges us to remember that nobody is here forever, that nobody knows the day or the hour when his/her world will come to a screeching halt. Just as responsible adults carry insurance against catastrophe, so must I be spiritually alert and prepared for a sudden end. Without even the thought of old-time fire and brimstone, I must face realistically the fact that eternity is a long time to regret my unreadiness.

(Morning)
God of love and compassion, strengthen me and empower me
to prepare my spirit to live as if the end may be this very day.
(Prayers of Intercession)

(Evening)
O God, give me courage and energy to be thankful
in the living of these days. Grant peace on my spiritual pilgrimage.
(Prayers of Intercession)

As Jesus taught his disciples I pray.
(Pray the Prayer of Our Savior.)

(Morning)
Your mercies are never exhausted, O God. In the name of our Savior. Amen.

(Evening)
Be still, my soul, and enjoy the rest that comes in sleep. In the name of our Savior. Amen.

SUNDAY, NOVEMBER 28
(Read Mark 13:35–37)

(Morning)
Dear God, forgive my procrastination to seek your will in this short time of preparation for life this day. Give me strength, I pray.

(Evening)
Dear God, help me to realize that the distrust in the world is a panic effort to resist your transforming love. In spite of opposition, help me to trust.

Jesus offers a compelling metaphor for watchfulness. It is as if we were on a typical job, under a typical boss. Whatever we do in the boss's absence, we are sure to be hard at work while the boss is watching. Surely no naps and no unexcused absences from the premises are permitted. God, Jesus reminds us that nobody knows when the end of the world will come, and the "Boss" will hold us to our accountability. On the other hand, everyone has her or his own end and day of reckoning. Indeed, we are all being watched.

(Morning)
O God of love and compassion, grant me courage to face
the doubts and fears of this unfriendly world. Free me
to love you and those whose lives touch mine until the end of my life.
(Prayers of Intercession)

(Evening)
O God, I thank you for the opportunity to study your Word.
I pray to be an ambassador of your love to the world.
Grant me courage to be prepared for life everlasting.
(Prayers of Intercession)

As Jesus taught his disciples I pray.
(Pray the Prayer of Our Savior.)

(Morning)
Grant us wisdom, grant us courage to face these days. In the name of our Savior. Amen.

(Evening)
Your ways are beyond our understanding. Let peace abide this night. In the name of our Savior. Amen.

MONDAY, NOVEMBER 29
(Read Isaiah 40:1–5)
(Sing "O Come, O Come, Emmanuel")

(Morning)
Voice of comfort and Mender of broken hearts, your gentle whisper
has called me from a night of slumber. As I walk softly in the earth realm,
may I share your message of consolation to all whom I will meet.

(Evening)
Voice of mercy and Mender of broken hearts, today I have met the wounded of
spirit, the downhearted, and the wandering. I pray that my actions of healing
toward them will be their reminder that your promises of comfort are sure.

Wonderful Word of life, I sing of your promises and live in this powerful
hope. As this season of Advent comes again, let me see more of your beauty
in my sisters and brothers. Let me be a living testimony that you are the
Day Star of my life. Your promise that "blessed are they that mourn for
they shall be comforted" is so sustaining for many in this time of forced
gaiety. Help me to remember that you sent your child, who was born to die.
Let me live in the power of Jesus' life, death, resurrection, and return. Despite the situations I am facing now, you have promised me comfort. I live
with this constant and consistent belief. All praise to the God who continues to come!

(Morning)
Promise-keeping God, hear my petitions for those
who don't have hope this day and for those who are struggling
to hold on to the little hope that remains in them.
(Prayers of Intercession)

(Evening)
Blessed Assurance, you have held me in hope all day long.
I pray for those times when I forgot to pray
and for all those who are sleepless because of their lack of hope.
(Prayers of Intercession)

God will not put any more upon me than I am able to bear! It's a promise!

(Morning)	(Evening)
I am a promise and a possibility! I will lift my voice and call out this reality to others all day long! In the name of Jesus. Amen.	Hope of the penitent, into your arms I commit my spirit. Restore me in the night watch, I pray. In the name of Jesus. Amen.

TUESDAY, NOVEMBER 30
(Read Isaiah 40:6–11)
(Sing "Standing on the Promises" or another familiar song)

(Morning)
Covenant Keeper, I awake in the glorious power that your love
is everlasting and your truth will endure for me, even again today!
What a tremendous way to start my day!

(Evening)
Covenant Keeper, in you every promise has been kept. Through you I have been
enabled to keep my word today. Wherever I have failed, please forgive me.

Sure Foundation, I am so tired of living on the premises and not dwelling
within the safety of your promises. I am keenly aware that in you are only
"Yes" and "Amen." Your word cannot lie. Your promises have never failed.
You are a promise-keeping God. I recite the words. I pray the creeds. I sing
your songs of matchless praise. And yet, I continue to forget. Forgive me.
Help me this day to join with that heavenly host, gathered in the eternal
abode, and sing with conviction, "Glory in the highest to my God and my
Sovereign. I'm standing on the promises of God!" Even so, let it be!

(Morning)
For others, just like me, living outside your promises, I pray.
(Prayers of Intercession)

(Evening)
Today, I have recalled your many promises to people of the living Word. For
those who continue to need your strong, unfailing reassurance, I pray.
(Prayers of Intercession)

**Blessed Assurance, Jesus is mine!
He has already come and dwells in my heart!**

(Morning)
Let my every step be taken with faith
in your Word. May the words of
comfort hold me all day long. In the
name of Jesus I pray. Amen.

(Evening)
Where I have faltered, hesitated, and
stumbled today, please gather these
steps into your bosom of love and
grant me rest to do differently tomorrow. In the name of Jesus I pray.
Amen.

WEDNESDAY, DECEMBER 1
(Read Psalm 85:1–2)
(Sing "Precious Memories" or another familiar song)

(Morning)
Memory-making God and Holder of hope, I thank you for the gift of yesterday.
With the advent of this new dawn, help me to make memories worthy of you.

(Evening)
Memory-making God and Holder of hope, it has been a long
and trying day. I remember both the good and the ugly.
Let every memory become a stepping-stone to better tomorrows.

"Precious Memories, how they linger. How they ever flood my soul." Some of my memories I would like to forget. Some of my memories I wish I had never made. Some of my memories are of horrible things I have done. I could become depressed. I could live in a state of defeat. I could be filled with despair. But I recall your steadfast love. I recollect your ready forgiveness. I remember your gift of great salvation. These are precious memories. Let me never forget how you came into my life. I open the treasure chest of my life to allow you to be in every memory I make today.

(Morning)
This day I will pause to listen to your quiet, still, and calm voice.
For those who need to hear you today I pray.
(Prayers of Intercession)

(Evening)
You have spoken sweet peace to my soul when I have stopped to listen.
For those who may have missed you today I pray.
(Prayers of Intercession)

**Just think of God's goodness to you! Though storms may sweep,
God is more than able to keep!**

(Morning)
Giver of dreams, speak to me and through me today. In the name of Jesus I pray. Amen.

(Evening)
In the stillness of the midnight, let your promises unfurl and sweeten my dreams. In the name of Jesus I pray. Amen.

THURSDAY, DECEMBER 2
(Read Psalm 85:8–13)
(Sing "There Is Something about That Name" or another familiar song)

(Morning)
Love-maker God, your tender and gentle stirrings have called me to another day's beginning. Help me to return love to you in all that I say and do today. Love, through me, even the unlovable.

(Evening)
Love-maker God, let me to your bosom fly. As the sun greets the moon and night begins its watch, let my actions of the day bless all those whose lives I touched for you today.

Tender and gentle God, I pray that love and faithfulness will meet in my actions as I move into this day. I am so aware of the tensions, the ambiguities, and the stresses in my own life. It is difficult not to get caught up in the commercial activities of this holy season. As I strive to be loving, I can recall so many times and situations where I failed. Forgive me. Restore to me a right spirit. Cleanse my heart. Heal my spirit. And allow the advent of your sweet and holy Spirit to descend upon me afresh and anew today. Let me be reminded that all I do is to be a reflection of you and an act of your love on your behalf.

(Morning)
Righteous One, help me to live the life I talk about this day!
I pray your tender ministry for . . .
(Prayers of Intercession)

(Evening)
Peaceful Sovereign, I have tried to be a peacemaker this day.
For those who need your abiding ministry I pray.
(Prayers of Intercession)

After I have done all that I can, help me to stand firm on your Word.

(Morning)	(Evening)
Jesus, you love me. This I know! Help me to live like it this day. In your name I pray. Amen.	Let righteousness and peace kiss each other as the moon meets the sun and ends another day. Restore me. In Jesus' name I pray. Amen.

FRIDAY, DECEMBER 3
(Read 2 Peter 3:8–9)
(Sing "What a Friend We Have in Jesus")

(Morning)
Ancient of Days, you have ordered the dawn and given me breath.
With my eyes, I behold your beauty in the earth. With my mind,
I recall your promises. And with my life, I will bless you this day!

(Evening)
Ancient of Days, I have encountered many today who have not
acknowledged your presence. I pray that my life has been
a witness to your living in me this day.

Jesus, I will never forget what you have done for me. Jesus, I will never forget how you set me free. Jesus, I will never know how you brought me out of the dominion of sin. Jesus, I will never forget. No, never! How can I forget? Your mighty outstretched hands of mercy have reached me, touched me, claimed and restored me so many times. Your gentleness and kindness have restored my brokenness on countless occasions. I cannot forget. I will not forget. You restore my soul with your tenderness. What a friend you are!

(Morning)
Faithful Friend, many are in need of your embrace today.
I lift them before you in prayer.
(Prayers of Intercession)

(Evening)
Covenant-keeper, all of your promises are for whoever will believe them.
For those who cannot receive them, I pray.
(Prayers of Intercession)

It may be a long time in coming, but God's promises always come true!

(Morning)
Steadfast Lover, let your promises
grant me hope and boldness in this day.
In Jesus' name. Amen.

(Evening)
Forgiving God, I have done what I
could do today. At times, it was not
so good. Forgive and restore my soul
in the night. In Jesus' name. Amen.

SATURDAY, DECEMBER 4
(Read 2 Peter 3:10–15)
(Sing "Holy! Holy! Holy!" or another familiar song)

(Morning)
God who comes, thank you again and again for the gift of this day.
My soul cries "hallelujah" for the advent of new possibilities.

(Evening)
Spirit of the living God, fall fresh upon me. Melt and mold me.
Fill me, so that I may be of use to you tomorrow.

Living, you loved me. Dying, you saved me. Buried, you carried all my sins away. Rising, you have freed me forever. You are coming back again! What a glorious day! I know your advent is soon. I want to be ready when you return. It will be the awesome day of your coming. Hear my solemn confession of the sin within me. Change me. Turn me in a new direction. Transform my thinking. I desire to live a new life in Christ. I offer my heart as a manger for your abode.

(Morning)
Too many people are yet crying out, "No room"! I lift them in prayer.
(Prayers of Intercession)

(Evening)
Too many are stuck, star-gazing. I lift them in prayer.
(Prayers of Intercession)

Am I really living a holy and godly life, worthy of being called Christlike?

(Morning)	(Evening)
Transforming Fire, touch my lips and my life for the living of this day. In Jesus' name. Amen.	Darkness of growth, enfold me with your gentleness. Hold me close. In Jesus' name. Amen.

SUNDAY, DECEMBER 5

(Read Mark 1:1–8)

(Sing "Fix Me, Jesus, Fix Me!" or another familiar song)

(Morning)

Open my eyes, that I may see glimpses of truth you have for me.
Open my eyes, illumine me, Spirit divine.

(Evening)

You have opened my eyes, and I have seen you in many today. Now assist me in
carrying them in my heart and in doing what you would do.

Illuminating Spirit, I have been baptized with water. Baptize me with your
refining fire. Change my heart, help me to love. Change my mind, and
teach me how to serve. Change my actions, and let my motives always be
pure. Help me to do the right thing for the right reasons. Confession of my
sin is essential, for I want to see your face in peace. I live in a wilderness
place. Often I feel as strange as John must have looked. People look at
themselves as the standard for right. People have set themselves up as the
absolute truth. When I deny their reality, I sometimes feel like a voice crying in the wilderness. Forgive me for the times I fall into this delusional
trap! Season of Advent, come quickly for the healing of this world.

(Morning)

God who comes, touch me. Let me be an agent of healing,
restoration, and wholeness today. I lift before you . . .
(Prayers of Intercession)

(Evening)

God, who has been with me all day, for those I have met and their needs, I pray.
(Prayers of Intercession)

Be ready when Jesus comes. He is coming again—real soon!

(Morning)	(Evening)
Speak to my heart! Silently now, I listen. In Jesus' name. Amen.	Thundering Quiet, I fall content into your awaiting arms. Rock me gently. In Jesus' name. Amen.

MONDAY, DECEMBER 6
(Read Isaiah 61:1–4)

(Morning)
Sustainer of us all, flood my heart
with the knowledge of your reality during this day.

(Evening)
Sustainer of us all, thank you for this day.
Use what has been to ready me for tomorrow.

Almighty God, you know and understand the real world in which we live; all glory and honor be yours. We confess that we see the problems and do not turn easily to you for the answers. It is your desire that we hear the good news that you want us to be healed in our brokenness. You are mighty!

(Morning)
Powerful God, open my heart to the presence of your Spirit
in the meeting of my needs this day.
(Prayers of Intercession)

(Evening)
You who provide the answers, let my life bring praise to you.
(Prayers of Intercession)

Take on the mantle of praise instead of a faint spirit.
(Pray the Prayer of Our Savior.)

(Morning)
Open my mind and my heart to the role you have identified for me. In Christ's name. Amen.

(Evening)
As I lie down to sleep, Creator God, fill me with your Spirit. Let my hours of rest be used to renew your Spirit in me. Let me awake with a fresh yearning to serve you in my real world. In Christ's name. Amen.

TUESDAY, DECEMBER 7
(Read Isaiah 61:8–11)

(Morning)
God of justice, as I awake I give thanks for this day. Guide me to be faithful to your promises. Use me to further your just will.

(Evening)
God of justice, you who have covered me with the robe of righteousness, I rejoice. Thank you for this day.

Planner of all that is, I praise your promise of salvation to all who choose to return your love for us. The prophet offers a hymn of praise to the work that you do, O God. Your righteous order and proclamation of greatness will come forth as the earth brings forth its shoots and as a garden grows. Almighty God, help us live as the doers of your justice to all, as the lovers of justice to all, as the proclaimers of your greatness.

(Morning)
Loving God, help me to see your way of justice in all I do today.
(Prayers of Intercession)

(Evening)
God of all, use me to end violence and wrongdoing. Grant me your love of justice and your hatred of injustice.
(Prayers of Intercession)

**"God will cause righteousness and promise
to spring up before all the nations."**
(Pray the Prayer of Our Savior.)

(Morning)
You, O God, sent your Word to show the way of truth. Thank you for Christ Jesus, who comes to teach even me. In Christ's name. Amen.

(Evening)
Now this day is done. As I prepare for sleep, infuse me with your truth of justice. Encourage my entire being to be filled with your entire love. Thank you for your continuing guidance, for I have not arrived at perfect righteousness. In Christ's name. Amen.

WEDNESDAY, DECEMBER 8
(Read Psalm 126:1–3)

(Morning)
Great is your name, O God, and great are your deeds.
Fill my day with shouts of joy.

(Evening)
Great is your name, O God. You have done great things for us. We rejoice.

God, you love laughter. You plan for our days to be filled with joy. This psalm celebrates being brought back from captivity in Babylon. It must have seemed like a dream too good to be true. Laughter and shouts of joy filled the air. Even other nations could see the great things you did for this people. Israel praised you, God! Praise! Praise God. That is what we are to do. This book, in the middle of our Bible, can be the center of our lives. We have only to pray these psalms, to be encouraged, and to receive your blessings.

(Morning)
Joyful God, help me to find and express the joy you have for me this day.
(Prayers of Intercession)

(Evening)
There is blessing all around. Loving God,
keep me from taking myself so seriously.
(Prayers of Intercession)

**"Then our mouth was filled with laughter,
and our tongue with shouts of joy."**
(Pray the Prayer of Our Savior.)

(Morning)
Thank you for sending this Word to teach and remind me of the eternal joy of loving you. Thank you for the blessings of laughter. In Christ's name. Amen.

(Evening)
Wise and wonderful God, you know that when I seek joy, I find it. Let your Holy Spirit bubble through my being as I come to take rest, so that I awake with a hymn of praise to you. In Christ's name. Amen.

THURSDAY, DECEMBER 9
(Read Psalm 126:4–6)

(Morning)
Giver of life, all praise to you for what I have, what I am,
and what I am becoming as your child.

(Evening)
Merciful God, you are here with me in the weeping and shouts of joy.

Merciful God, the poet prayed that you would restore Israel's fortunes. The Negeb is the desert to the south of Judah. Its dry riverbeds became filled after the winter rains. This is the prayer—to be renewed like the watercourses in the Negeb. To be filled to overflowing with your blessings.

(Morning)
Sustainer God, thank you for your constant presence in my day.
Help me to remember you in all of my moments this day.
(Prayers of Intercession)

(Evening)
Provider God, thank you for meeting my needs
in your perfect way, in your perfect time.
(Prayers of Intercession)

"Those who go out weeping . . . shall come home with shouts of joy."
(Pray the Prayer of Our Savior.)

(Morning)
In the midst of weeping, my tendency is to forget that this experience can result in the seeds of joy. I can only see the pain and frustration of the moment. Strengthen my faith. Help me lift my eyes to Christ Jesus. In Jesus' name. Amen.

(Evening)
Most gracious God, as evening turns to night and night becomes day, give fruit to the seed sown in my life this day. Open my eyes and heart to the joy that comes from serving you. Turn my weeping into the knowledge of your presence. In Christ's name. Amen.

FRIDAY, DECEMBER 10
(Read Thessalonians 5:16–24)

(Morning)
Creator of this day, as I arise I rejoice in this day. Make my life one of
unceasing prayer. I give thanks for each moment of today.

(Evening)
Creator of this night, guide me in seeking your will through my love of Christ
Jesus. "Rejoice always, pray without ceasing, give thanks in all circumstances."

Holy, perfect God, you who are able to do all that you ask of us, thank you
for your wisdom. In your knowing each of us, you have given us models of
perfection for which to strive. May we learn to rejoice always, to pray
without ceasing, to give thanks in all circumstances. This is your will for
us. Guide us in our living, so that we do not quench the Spirit or despise
the words of the prophet.

(Morning)
Loving God, help me to discern your message,
your truth in all that I will see and hear this day.
(Prayers of Intercession)

(Evening)
O God, the Source of truth, help me to hold on to what is good,
to abstain from every form of evil.
(Prayers of Intercession)

"May the God of peace . . . sanctify you entirely."
(Pray the Prayer of Our Savior.)

(Morning)
It is easy to see what is required of
today's Word. What is hard is handing
my will over to you each moment of
the day. Please guide me in my
moments. In Christ's name. Amen.

(Evening)
As I prepare to rest, wise and loving
God, let your promise of faithfulness
fill my heart. In Christ's name. Amen.

SATURDAY, DECEMBER 11
(Read John 1:6–8)

(Morning)
Amazing and faithful God, over and over you have shown
your love and your wisdom for us.

(Evening)
Amazing and faithful God, you sent John as a witness.
So, too, use me to witness for Christ.

Dear God, how many words confront us each day? We read them, we hear them, we say them. How easily our minds let them dance, without thought, through our being. Sometimes we are stopped short in our saying them when we hear a child repeat our thoughtless words. Please take our words and use them as witness to testify to the light which is our beloved Jesus.

(Morning)
Instructor God, teach me the words you would have me use and share.
(Prayers of Intercession)

(Evening)
Instructor God, help me to live my life according to your Word.
(Prayers of Intercession)

"John the Baptist was not the light, but he came to testify to the light."
(Pray the Prayer of Our Savior.)

(Morning)
Words are so important. They can wound or heal, build up or tear down, clarify or confuse. You sent Jesus to be the living Word. Fill me with your Word, so that my life reflects Christ. In Jesus' name. Amen.

(Evening)
As I review this day, I find that my words did no harm. If they did, show me clearly. Prepare me to repair that harm. Thank you for sending your Word. In Christ's name. Amen.

SUNDAY, DECEMBER 12
(Read John 1:19–28)

(Morning)
God, as John's testimony made clear who Christ is,
may my life also be a clear testimony of who you are.

(Evening)
God, please take my life. Use me to further your will.

Redeeming God, John was certain of his role. He came to prepare the way. He was the forerunner of the Messiah. He does not describe himself. He does not explain his role. He does not try to persuade this group of his importance. He does not read hidden agendas into their questions or his answers. His message was simple: repent, become cleansed. Among you stands the Savior.

(Morning)
God, help me to know my role. Let me be sure of who I am.
(Prayers of Intercession)

(Evening)
Loving God, thank you for never tiring of my seeking
to define myself in your way.
(Prayers of Intercession)

**"The one who is coming after me;
I am not worthy to untie the thong of his sandal."**
(Pray the Prayer of Our Savior.)

(Morning)
You have one role for each of us, to love you with all our heart, mind, and soul. You want us to be your child. May we want that too. In Christ's name. Amen.

(Evening)
Day's end has come. Did I fulfill your role for me? Renew me so that I may be better ready for that role tomorrow. In Christ's name. Amen.

MONDAY, DECEMBER 13
(Read 2 Samuel 7:1–16)

(Morning)
Holy Spirit of truth and grace, grant us wisdom,
that we may discern your will for us.

(Evening)
Holy Spirit of truth and grace, you have been trustworthy
throughout the day; guard us now throughout the night, we pray.

O God, we are at times beset by strife—even in our churches, our work-places, and among our families and closest friends. Just as David's family was torn apart by betrayal, violation, rape, and murder, our lives also are thrown into turmoil by conflicts. Grant us discernment, we pray, so that we are not diverted or distracted by faulty advice. Restore our faith, O God, that your will will finally prevail, that you are always with us, and that you are good—all the time.

(Morning)
Let us praise God, who is our rock and salvation,
our very help in times of trouble.
(Prayers of Intercession)

(Evening)
God's steadfast love endures forever.
(Prayers of Intercession)

Strengthened in the knowledge that you do deliver us from evil, I pray.
(Pray the Prayer of Our Savior.)

(Morning)
O God, be with me throughout the day. Bless me with the assurance of your presence in the face of adversity. Bless my seeing, my hearing, and my doing, and guide me in your way everlasting. In Christ's name, I pray. Amen.

(Evening)
My refuge you have been, and my refuge you will be. Enfold me in your love throughout the night, even as you have kept me throughout the day. Awaken me tomorrow with hope and faith renewed. In Christ's name. Amen.

TUESDAY, DECEMBER 14
(Read Psalm 89:1–4, 19–26)

(Morning)
Steadfast God, make us faithful, even as you are faithful.
Holy God, make us righteous, even as you are righteous.

(Evening)
Steadfast God, thank you for being with me today.
Guard and bless me now, and enfold me in your gentle love.

God, you seek as your servants those who seek your will and way. Just as you called David to serve you, despite his sins and family conflicts, you call us. Just as you anointed him with oil, anoint us with your Spirit, that we may be wise and strong for your sake. Just as you sent him Nathan to challenge and correct him when he went astray, so send us sisters and brothers who will speak the truth to us in love. Lead us in the way of your righteousness, and save us when we love earthly power more than your holy power of justice and truth. May your power flow in us and through us, for in you is the way of truth and life.

(Morning)
Let us praise God, the Maker of heaven and earth, the Womb of all life.
(Prayers of Intercession)

(Evening)
O God, you know our needs before we do. Hear now my prayers for all those
whose names and cares I lift up to you.
(Prayers of Intercession)

Holy and mighty God, I pray for the coming of your reign.
Maranatha! Come, Jesus.
(Pray the Prayer of Our Savior.)

(Morning)
God of time and space, God beyond all time and all space, be with me throughout this day. Set my feet in the path of your love. In Jesus' name. Amen.

(Evening)
O God, you are the rock of our salvation, the ocean which bathes and cleanses us. May your healing waves wash over us throughout the night, that we may awake, refreshed and renewed by your Spirit. In Jesus' name. Amen.

WEDNESDAY, DECEMBER 15
(Read Romans 16:25–27)

(Morning)
O God, you strengthen us according to the good news of Jesus Christ.
Renew my commitment to you and to your reign of justice, freedom,
and love, for which Jesus lived and died and lives again.

(Evening)
O God, thank you for the love and hope with which
you have sustained me this day.

Dear God, for those who live amidst violence and poverty, the Bible's words of justice and liberation may seem like a distant dream; for those who live amidst comfort and privilege, they may seem mysterious or irrelevant. But in Jesus Christ you send us hope, which overcomes our cynicism and despair, our refusal to understand and to care. In Christ we know that you stretch out your mighty hand to the poor and the powerless, the captive, and the oppressed. Give us the willingness to heed your will, we pray, and the courage to obey.

(Morning)
Conquer my doubts and fears, so that I may obey you
with boldness and faith throughout the day.
(Prayers of Intercession)

(Evening)
Thank you for reminding me today that after everything else
passes away, justice, love, and freedom will endure.
(Prayers of Intercession)

O God, I yearn for the coming of your will and reign on earth as in heaven.
(Pray the Prayer of Our Savior.)

(Morning)
Dear God, help me to see, to understand, and to do your will for me today. In the name of our Savior, the Christ. Amen.

(Evening)
Dear God, thank you for the gift of Jesus Christ, who leads us in the way of courage and compassion. In Jesus' name I pray. Amen.

THURSDAY, DECEMBER 16
(Read Luke 1:26–33)

(Morning)
Holy God, even as you favored Mary with your messenger Gabriel,
favor us with your presence, we pray.

(Evening)
Holy God, thank you for being with us,
for helping us to know your work in our lives.

Dear God, when you send us new ways to serve you, we often fear them, as Mary did. We wonder how they may be possible or what others might say. Help us not to fear the news that you are with us. Instead, help us, with Mary, to dare to accept the inconvenience of having Jesus Christ in our lives. Make us bold to seek God's liberating reign, both in our lives and in the world.

(Morning)
Grant us wisdom, grant us courage, and make us unafraid to do your will.
(Prayers of Intercession)

(Evening)
The yoke of your presence is easy, O God, and the burden of your will is light.
Thank you for favoring me with your Spirit today.
(Prayers of Intercession)

**O God, thank you for the courage of Mary and of Jesus,
her son, whose prayer we pray.**
(Pray the Prayer of Our Savior.)

(Morning)
Dear God, this is the day that you have made; let me rejoice and be glad for the opportunities for service which you set before me today. In Christ's name I pray. Amen.

(Evening)
I rest now in your presence, O God. Be with me through the night, that I may awaken to a new day to love and serve you and bless your holy name. In Christ's name I pray. Amen.

FRIDAY, DECEMBER 17
(Read Luke 1:33–38)

(Morning)
God of amazing grace, we thank you for your Holy Spirit,
which makes all things possible.

(Evening)
God of amazing grace, thank you forging new possibilities for us this day.
The impossible has become possible with you as our helper.

Dear God, we believe; help our unbelief. You send us your messengers, and we doubt them. You remind us of your power, and like Mary, we object, asking, "How can this be?" You ask for trust, and we respond with doubt. Quench our doubts and overshadow our fears with the mighty power of your Spirit. For we know that with you, nothing is impossible. Help us to see the signs of hope in our midst. Help us to be signs of hope for others, so that we may bear witness to your healing until the coming of the new heaven and earth, for which we yearn.

(Morning)
Overshadow our fears and fill us with your power, that we may know and trust
in your presence in our lives.
(Prayers of Intercession)

(Evening)
Thank you for your presence and grace and for blessing us with your favor.
(Prayers of Intercession)

May your power flow in us and through us as we pray to you, O God.
(Pray the Prayer of Our Savior.)

(Morning)	(Evening)
Like Mary, we are your servants; let it be to us according to your Word. In Jesus' name. Amen.	Another day is gone; bless us, that we may rest in the shadow of your power. In Jesus' name. Amen.

SATURDAY, DECEMBER 18
(Read Luke 1:46–55)

(Morning)
Gracious God, my soul magnifies Jesus,
and my spirit rejoices in you, my Savior.

(Evening)
Gracious God, you have done great things for us; holy is your name.

Holy and merciful God, in Mary's song you have given us a vision for the righting of our relationships with one another. Your Word is both of judgment and of hope. There is a common goal of justice and reconciliation, but different paths are set before people of different stations. For the proud and rich and mighty, it is simplicity and humility; for the poor lowly, it is to be lifted up. Give us courage and hope, we pray, that the powerless may find power and that the privileged may let go of their privileges, toward the creation of a new heaven and new earth.

(Morning)
Let me magnify you and praise your name,
seeking your reign of justice and freedom.
(Prayers of Intercession)

(Evening)
Thank you for your vision of new possibilities.
Bless us as we seek rest in the knowledge of your power and grace.
(Prayers of Intercession)

**Give us all the bread we need and save us
from both poverty and excess, I pray.**
(Pray the Prayer of Our Savior.)

(Morning)
Gracious God, blessed be your power
and majesty. Guide me this day
according to your vision of justice
and freedom, I pray in Christ's name.
Amen.

(Evening)
Blessed God, thank you for the peace
that comes from entrusting our lives to
you. With you, all things are possible.
In Christ's name. Amen.

SUNDAY, DECEMBER 19
(Read Luke 1:54–55 and Romans 16:26)

(Morning)
Creator God, as you remembered our forebears
by speaking to them, speak to us, we pray.

(Evening)
Creator God, thank you for your prophets
and for all through whom you have spoken to me this day.

Gracious God, you spoke to Israel by sending them prophets who brought words of judgment and hope. So, too, throughout history and throughout our lives, you send us prophets who comfort the afflicted and afflict the comfortable. But we confess that at times, fearing change, some of us fear to give up our comfort and others fear to give up our misery. Forgive our complacency and paralysis; move us beyond guilt and despair, that we may be believers and doers of your Word, proclaiming your reign until it comes

(Morning)
All glory be yours, O God, for you are worthy of our trust and praise.
(Prayers of Intercession)

(Evening)
Thank you for the comforts and challenges
you have placed before us today, O God.
(Prayers of Intercession)

May your realm come, as you proclaimed it through your prophets.
(Pray the Prayer of Our Savior.)

(Morning)
God of our fathers and mothers, be with us and guide us in your way of truth everlasting. In the name of our Savior I pray. Amen.

(Evening)
God of peace, give us peace to accept this day, comfort our disappointments in the knowledge of your surpassing will, and grant us rest so that we may meet tomorrow's challenges. In the name of our Savior I pray. Amen.

MONDAY, DECEMBER 20
(Read Psalm 148)

(Morning)
O God, the Mother who gives birth to the dawning sun, I praise you as I begin
this week. Filled with anticipation, I ask you for guidance in preparing my
mind, soul, and body for the birth of the Christ.

(Evening)
O God, the Father whose hands protect me through the night's deep slumber, I
give thanks for the vivid and hidden blessings I have encountered this day.

My hands begin, O God, motionless in a moment of praise for you, joining
with the hands of simple carpenters and shepherds who became the agents
of your vision. My mind begins, O Creator, open and hungry in a soft moment of your revelation. My soul begins, O Sustainer, glistening in the
light of truth which is your promise. I come, O God, ready to receive the
hope that will inspire me beyond the birth of that promise to its fulfillment
in seeking justice and offering compassion with all the gifts I have to offer.

(Morning)
God of love, may my mind, body, and soul be opened
and filled with a love that seeks you and lends your mercy to all.
(Prayers of Intercession)

(Evening)
God of justice, grant rest to all the tired souls of the world, teach each of us
your gentle mercy, and teach us to heal one another through word and deed.
(Prayers of Intercession)

Praise Yahweh from the heavens; praise Yahweh in the heights!
(Embrace your family and friends.)

(Morning)	(Evening)
As my body awakens, may I come to know the light that brings hope to the dim world of the forsaken. Teach me strength, and teach me justice. In Christ's name. Amen.	Though my tired eyes find rest, my soul still longs for your presence and my hand still longs to touch your face. Teach me peace, and teach me pa-tience. In Christ's name. Amen.

TUESDAY, DECEMBER 21
(Read Isaiah 61:10–11)

(Morning)
Mysterious and glorious God, I greatly rejoice in you. I face your dawn dressed in your joy, your love, your legacy, and your promise. I greet you in the warmth of the sun and the freshness of the winter air. I long to know you in other ways, great God. I greatly rejoice in you. But I greatly thirst for more of you.

(Evening)
Mysterious and glorious God, I greatly rejoice in you as I conclude this day. As I have wandered through this small world, I have searched for a piece of you that would fit into the palm of my hand. I long to know the whys and hows of this society and world.

O God, even as I praise your name joyfully, my eyes fill with tears, for I know that the path to Bethlehem eventually leads to Golgotha. I look to the discord in Serbia, the chaos that haunts Israel, the iniquity in my own society, the often unseen violence in my own neighborhood, and the hurt I have inflicted on others, and I wonder where you are. When will you cause righteousness and praise to spring up before all the nations? This hurting world craves you, O God. Will you not come to us? I praise your works, O God; they do not go unseen, but so often I feel that you do. Yet I ask for light to see your righteousness, and I ask for the strength to preserve it.

(Morning)
I speak of the citizens of a hurting world, so that they might know your love.
(Prayers of Intercession)

(Evening)
May you watch over the sleeping earth, O God, whose seas and skies are filled with the joys and fears of your many people.
(Prayers of Intercession)

**So Yahweh will cause righteousness and praise
to spring up before all the nations.**
(Embrace those who suffer oppression both at home and abroad.)

(Morning)
O God, I hunger for you, and this world aches for your gentle touch. May we know your tears as we have known our very own. I praise your mysterious name. In Christ's name. Amen.

(Evening)
May my eyes close only in rest and never in apathy or denial. I long for you, O God. May your face be both the soft light and the soothing darkness that usher in my dreams. In Christ's name. Amen.

WEDNESDAY, DECEMBER 22
(Read Luke 2:22–33)

(Morning)
God of my rising, today I prepare for the fullness of your presence.
I arise and open my heart to wait for you. I wait for you to soothe my eyes,
for they have burned and longed to see you since I first heard your name.

(Evening)
God of my resting, tonight I come, my eyes still searching. I search
the past events of the day and of my life, so that I might see
your Word live in my actions and the works of others.

O God, how often I have felt like Simeon. How long your people have searched for the light of your salvation. We have walked along busy city streets, quiet country lanes, our hands shoved into our pockets or grasping gnarled walking sticks. Now we approach you as Simeon approached the Christ child, receiving a mere glimpse. We share the briefest of moments with you, O God, but in those moments you bring us the peace you brought Simeon—the peace of your light and of your touch.

(Morning)
May we take your peace into our arms and praise you, O God.
May we spread it throughout this world of discord.
(Prayers of Intercession)

(Evening)
Help me to take your people in my arms, O God. Help me to find your peace in
each of them. And may their souls know infantlike peace.
(Prayers of Intercession)

**My eyes have seen your salvation, which you have
prepared in the presence of all peoples.**
*(Embrace those hurt by racism, sexism, homophobia,
and other acts of hatred.)*

(Morning)
Dear God, I have opened my eyes today. I look outward and onward, beyond my small self, beyond my broad world, for you. In Christ's name. Amen.

(Evening)
Dear God, on this night I turn my eyes inward, turning from the wide expanses of the world to the still silence of my own soul, in the hope of finding you. In Christ's name. Amen.

THURSDAY, DECEMBER 23
(Read Luke 2:34–5 and Isaiah 62:1–3)

(Morning)
God of wonders who awakens, I come filled with the breath of a December morning. I come to you in wonder, for I feel as if I am standing on the cusp of something too beautiful to be named.

(Evening)
God of wonders who puts to rest, as you wrapped your Word into the garments of flesh to become the most human of humans, wrap me in a garment of your Word, so that I might always be enveloped by your presence.

The weight of incarnation is so heavy, O God. We wait for you—a God who is human. A God who suffers and dies, on the cross and yet a thousand times more. A God comes into this world. A God who is cruelly berated, beaten, raped, and abandoned. A God who will be lynched, who will suffer from AIDS, whose body will be eaten away by cancer. You come, O God, and you bring us a portion of something totally unlike what we know. But when you come, you become like us. Your presence is so human and yet so divine—so gloriously sad, so wrenchingly beautiful—that it will pierce our very souls. We awaken to your presence, O God. We await your becoming.

(Morning)
God with us, be with us still.
(Prayers of Intercession)

(Evening)
Your name is my evening prayer, O God, as I remember the names of the many others who long for freedom, comfort, and peace.
(Prayers of Intercession)

A sword will pierce your own side, too.
(Embrace mothers whose children are in pain.)

(Morning)
O God, this day of your creation gives birth to more of the beautiful moments of my life. Show me your face in the faces of my neighbors. Help me to remember that those faces make up those beautiful moments. In Christ's name. Amen.

(Evening)
O God, I have been visited by you so many times today. I have found so often that your loving face is revealed in many different emotions. You have brought all the laughter and tears of life to my door. I pray for the strength to heal the hurting and to sing with the joyous. In Christ's name. Amen.

FRIDAY, DECEMBER 24
(Read Psalm 148 and Luke 2:29–32)

(Morning)
O God of beautiful days, I am ready to meet the glorious face of your creation.
I begin today praising your gift of time, and I measure the gifts
of each minute as I approach the gift of the Christ.

(Evening)
O God of beautiful nights, I give thanks for today and thanks for tomorrow.
Today is a day of preparation, but it is also a day of living in its own right.
Give my soul rest, that I may know the in-between moments.

On the eve of birth, O God, a million things come to mind: the preparing, the waiting. As I find my way from chore to chore, help me not to lose sight of the child of God who plays among the mess of wrapping paper. Rather, let me play with that child. Let me celebrate with the child and with the earth and heavens and with all the souls of creation. Let us celebrate in the preparing. Let us celebrate in the waiting.

(Morning)
All over the world, O God, there are those who have nothing
to wait for—no matter the season, the religion, or the culture.
Help them to forge hope out of nothingness.
(Prayers of Intercession)

(Evening)
Although the wait seems to near its end, O God,
there are others for whom the wait seems eternal. Help them
through their sicknesses and powerlessness. Bring them healing and grace.
(Prayers of Intercession)

A light for revelation.
(Embrace your own waiting.)

(Morning)
Today, O God, I sit on the threshold of a new day. In front of me is the birth of the Christ. So close, so soon, it seems. Help me not to forget this day, O God. Help me to remember all of your creation, all of your gifts. In Christ's name. Amen.

(Evening)
Throughout this day, O God, I have striven to be patient in my wait for your revelation. It draws even nearer, and my tired eyes force themselves open. Do I dare try to meet you at dawn, O God? Thank you for teaching me to love my day of waiting, O God. Help these approaching hours to be loving ones as well. In Christ's name. Amen.

SATURDAY, DECEMBER 25
(Read Galatians 4:4–7)

(Morning)
Creator God, This is the day of birth! The day of joy! The day of song!
Among us today comes God. Among us today we find the Christ!

(Evening)
Creator God, your peace guides me through the year. I praise you in thanks
and in astonishment, for your love flows beyond belief.

O God, you have come to me today! For so long I have feared your departure. I have watched your birth and death and return, only to see your ascension. I have waited for your return, fearing that you no longer can hear my prayers. Today you have returned to me. Today you have returned to me as a beautiful, innocent child—a child who will grow, just as I have grown; a child who will change the world forever, just as I will change the world forever. You are among us today, O God. You fill every crevice with your light and every recess with your splendor. The Christ has come and dwells among us!

(Morning)
Though I feel your presence deep within my soul, there are many who are
longing on this Christmas day. Hear them, O God, and help me to hear their
cries along with the joyous chiming of bells.
(Prayers of Intercession)

(Evening)
Though this day of celebration nears its end, guide me daily to remember your
love. Guide me always to remember your people.
(Prayers of Intercession)

**"So you are no longer a slave but a child, and if a child
then also an heir, through God."**
(Embrace those who have no one to embrace them.)

(Morning)
I bid you welcome into this world, living Christ! I welcome you in love, and I welcome you in thanks! I give you praise for a day in which we may strive to shape your world as you have envisioned it. In Christ's name. Amen.

(Evening)
How beautiful this day has been, O God. Help me to paint tomorrow with the beauty of your presence. May your incarnation forever find expression through the actions of your church and through me. In Christ's name. Amen.

SUNDAY, DECEMBER 26
(Read Luke 2:36–40 and Psalm 148:13–14)

(Morning)
Sweet God of justice and passion, though Christmas has passed,
I continue my praise. I awake to see a morning inhabited by your Spirit.
I awake to continue, my path illuminated by your light.

(Evening)
Sweet God of justice and passion, I do love this world!
Help me to carry that love in a way that is malleable and generous.
Help me to give it to each soul I meet.

O God, I know that your greatness does not end with one action; nor does it end in the temple with a pronouncement of redemption. It does not end with a birth or with a death. That is the miracle of your story, O God. As the baby grows into a child, filled with wisdom and your favor, teach me to grow in my knowledge of you, so that your presence may grow within my soul. Teach me more as the days continue into the new year, O God of truth. Forgive my impatience and my ignorance. Forgive the hurt I have caused, and help me to bring comfort to those I have injured.

(Morning)
Who are my neighbors, O God, that I might bring them healing?
(Prayers of Intercession)

(Evening)
Help me to bring your presence into a crying world.
(Prayers of Intercession)

Hallelujah!
(Embrace all you meet.)

(Morning)
O God, I ask to continue on the path of the Human One. I ask to be an instrument of peace in a violent world. I ask for your revelation to extend from my soul to my hands. I ask for the strength to work for your beloved people who live in cellblocks, shanty towns, and cardboard boxes. I ask for strength, O God. In Christ's name. Amen.

(Evening)
O God, I give thanks for this day. I give thanks for its blessings and for the strength you have granted me. Help me to bring food to those who hunger and water to those who thirst. May my searching never cease, O God. May my scope instead widen. Nestled in the name of the Christ and in the name of the created, I pray. Amen.

MONDAY, DECEMBER 27
(Read Jeremiah 31:7–14 and Sirach 24:1–12)

(Morning)
God of all my life, I come before you in the brightness
of this day with thanks, eager to hear your Word.

(Evening)
God of all my life, with your wisdom help me to know all
that I have experienced today and appropriate it into your tomorrows.

Spirit of dance, of song, of salvation for all peoples, gather us together. Hold us in the power of your love, not as a scattered community but as one led back to offer you praise in songs from the heart. Comfort us in the mournings of our lives. Help us to trust in your goodness. Fill us with the joy of living in this time into which we are chosen as your own.

(Morning)
God of compassion, strengthen me with your goodness, that I may hear and
respond to the cries of those seeking to quench their thirst and need.
(Prayers of Intercession)

(Evening)
Giver of life, water our spirits, that we may be refreshed for the days ahead.
(Prayers of Intercession)

Grain, wine, and oil—food for our bodies, seeds of spirit sown for all.

(Morning)
Open me to the harmony of spirit within, that I may be in tune with the needs and desires of others. I pray that my path not be diverted from you this day. In the name of the Christ. Amen.

(Evening)
Lift the weariness of my aching body and overloaded mind, that I may sleep restfully. Free me from any disharmony of this day. In the name of the Christ. Amen.

TUESDAY, DECEMBER 28
(Read Psalm 147:12–20)

(Morning)
God of my awakening, I praise you.
All of my being reaches out to you and to your world.

(Evening)
God of my resting, your teachings have worked actively within me.
Use me, send me. Make me to move with your Spirit.

Praise to you, awesome God, who in strong blessings protects all of your creation. You continue to watch over your children, giving food of the finest quality. You scatter that which impedes our way toward your peace. You bring not destruction but healing to all creation. The wind of your Spirit blows and flows into our lives. Our praise is always in thanksgiving for your Word of life.

(Morning)
My beginning and ending are in you. Grant me to know this in my whole being.
(Prayers of Intercession)

(Evening)
Word of my life, bless me with the love to reach out and touch others.
(Prayers of Intercession)

Blow, fresh wind, and flow, new waters of peace.

(Morning)
Speak your Word, great God, beyond the gates of my life arena, to melt away the coldness of the world which has not heard or seen you. In the name of the Christ. Amen.

(Evening)
Awesome God, settle me into rest. Soothe away the hurt of unfulfilled dreams. Renew my strength for tomorrow's journey. In the name of the Christ. Amen.

WEDNESDAY, DECEMBER 29
(Read Ephesians 1:3–14)

(Morning)
Creator of all things, bless my life today.
Create a desire in me to love in Christ's name.

(Evening)
Creator of all things, at the close of this day,
find me holy and flawless, blessed with the Word of truth.

Gracious God, in the core of our being, you secured our redeemed lives through the promise of Christ. Transform us with your spiritual blessing. You have gifted us with grace. Christ Jesus is the profoundly human and divine presence of that grace. How generous of you to take us as your own children! Your pleasure with us enfolds itself as we search for Christ in the paths and avenues of this world. We present ourselves as part of your plan and purpose. Dare us to risk and be Christlike.

(Morning)
God of all gifts, gather the gift of myself into a presence of thought,
word, and action for your will.
(Prayers of Intercession)

(Evening)
In and through your beloved Child, Jesus Christ, blend me,
great God, into the heart of your waiting people.
(Prayers of Intercession)

Gifts of forgiveness and grace in redemption and Christ Jesus.

(Morning)
Holy One, choose me for holiness of Spirit in these last days of the century. I pray for vision of your world ever becoming. In the name of the Christ. Amen.

(Evening)
In restful sleep, I long for your new vision to be revealed. Thank you for blessing me in all ways. In the name of the Christ. Amen.

THURSDAY, DECEMBER 30
(Read Ephesians 1:11–14)

(Morning)
Holy Spirit, place your mark upon me,
so that all of my life is lived in praise and glory.

(Evening)
Holy Spirit, the hours of the day have passed into history.
Work your salvation in me to become a hope for the future.

Great God, how you gather your people for a new century, a new time unfolding. I am filled with gratitude for including me in your history of redemption. As one of your people, show me to the walkways of truth. Enrich all with continued blessings in Christ. Increase our boldness to believe that we are inheritors of your love and closeness. Guide us to offer expressions of love, hope, promise, and freedom in Jesus Christ to all of creation.

(Morning)
God of promise and possibility, accomplish in, with,
and through me your wise counsel and will.
(Prayers of Intercession)

(Evening)
Increase my belief. I offer myself for others.
(Prayers of Intercession)

The origin and source of love is Christ.

(Morning)
Praise to you, God, for your gift of redeeming love. In the name of the Christ. Amen.

Evening)
How can I ask for anything more? Still I beg, through the power of the Holy Spirit, to work your saving purpose in me and all peoples of the world. In the name of the Christ. Amen.

FRIDAY, DECEMBER 31

(Read John 1:1–18)
(Sing "Morning Has Broken" or another familiar hymn)

(Morning)
Morning Light, let my day begin with the promise of your Word
to lift me from any shadow of spirit.

(Evening)
Evening Light, with joy and celebration I turn myself over to you.
As day turns into night and the promise of a new century begins tomorrow,
may I rest in the future of the world becoming.

Consecrated to your Word-become-flesh, who continues to live among us,
guide us from beginnings to endings to newness of life. Free us to sing
with joy and celebration of your grace, affirmed and revealed in your child,
our Savior, Jesus Christ. Help us to search our hearts, that we may serve
humanity in the light of the One who is the true Light. In Jesus do we see
your face, your grace, and your love.

(Morning)
Receive me as your child, O God.
Grant me openness to accept all your children.
(Prayers of Intercession)

(Evening)
Send a brightness of light to enter into the new century.
I pray for courage and tenacity to carry this light for you.
(Prayers of Intercession)

**Sing "Many Gifts, One Spirit" or a song of celebration
of the gift of the Light of the World.**

(Morning)
God of new beginnings, carry my life
this day as evidence of your grace and
truth in Jesus Christ, in whose name
I pray. Amen.

(Evening)
Great God, close this day for me with
a prayer of belief in new beginnings.
Thank you for your heart of love in
Christ Jesus, in whose name I pray.
Amen.

Contributors

Brenda Eatman Aghahowa, D.Min., is a lecturer in professional and technical writing at Chicago State University in the Department of English, Speech, and Modern Languages.

Robert S. Alward, D.D., is pastor emeritus at Glenview Community United Church of Christ. He lives in Marco Island, Florida.

Christopher Atwood is pastor of Brecksville United Church of Christ in Brecksville, Ohio.

Geoffrey A. Black is the minister for church life and leadership in the Office of Church Life and Leadership, United Church of Christ.

Ronald S. Bonner Sr. is the assistant to the president for Affirmative Action/Equal Employment Opportunity for the United Church of Christ. He is an ordained United Church of Christ minister.

Linda E. Boston is a parish pastor living in Chicago. She is an ordained minister in the Evangelical Lutheran Church of America.

Norval I. Brown is pastor of Fourth Street United Methodist Church in Aurora, Illinois.

Lawrence A. Burnley is an administrator in the United Church Board for World Ministries, United Church of Christ. He is an ordained minister in the Christian Church (Disciples of Christ).

Lynn Calvert is a registered nurse. She is a member of the United Methodist Church.

Marie Antoinette Carlson is the minister at Christ United Methodist Church in Elmhurst, Illinois.

Janette Chandler-Kotey is the associate pastor and minister of music and the arts at the St. Paul United Methodist Church in Dallas, Texas.

Leona J. Cochran is a chaplain at Trinity Hospital in Chicago, Illinois. She is a member of the United Church of Christ.

Valerie Bridgeman Davis is a professor of religion at Huston-Tillotson College. She also serves as copastor at the Banah Full Community Church in Austin, Texas. She is a member of the Church of God.

Pamela Canzater Cheney is the associate minister at Lakewood Congregational Church in Lakewood, Ohio.

Ruth C. Duck is a professor at Garrett-Evangelical Theological Seminary. She is a member of the United Church of Christ.

Anthony Earl is a pastor living in Chicago, Illinois.

Vera Jo Edington is a diaconal minister of Christian education at the Olympia Fields United Methodist Church in Olympia Fields, Illinois.

Jacqueline Ford is a lab and systems support specialist living in Chicago, Illinois. She is a member of the United Methodist Church.

Stephen A. Gifford is minister of evangelism for membership growth for the United Church Board for Homeland Ministries, United Church of Christ.

Brandon L. Gilvin is a student attending Hiram College. He is a member of the Christian Church (Disciples of Christ).

Deborah Grohman is in ministry in Indianapolis, Indiana. She is a member of the Presbyterian Church (USA).

Clark Harshfield is retired and living in Long Beach, California. He is a member of the United Church of Christ.

Linda H. Hollies, D.Min., is the director of the United Methodist Conference Center in Grand Rapids, Michigan.

Joan Clifford Hutter is a writer and editor for *The Chautauquan Daily.*

C. Nozomi Ikuta is minister for liberation ministries in the Division of the American Missionary Association, United Church Board for Homeland Ministries, United Church of Christ.

Teruo Kawata is a retired United Church of Christ minister living in Hawaii.

Valentino Lassiter, D.Min., is pastor of East View United Church of Christ and college instructor at John Carroll University in University Heights, Ohio.

Hector E. Lopez is the conference minister for the Central Pacific Conference of the United Church of Christ.

Jose A. Malayang is the general secretary for the Division of Evangelism and Local Church Development of the United Church Board for Homeland Ministries, United Church of Christ.

Leah F. Matthews is the acting minister of biblical and theological foundations in education in the Division of Education and Publication, United Church Board for Homeland Ministries, United Church of Christ.

Jacqueline W. McGlen is a clinical social worker and licensed minister. She is a member of a Neo-Pentecostal Charismatic Church in Maryland.

Ella Pearson Mitchell, Ph.D., is a retired professor, prolific author, and preacher living in Atlanta, Georgia. She is an ordained minister in the American Baptist Church.

Anita Moore-Hackney is a retired educator living in Silver Spring, Maryland. She is a member of the Presbyterian Church (USA).

Richard E. Osburn is the senior pastor of Forest Grove United Church of Christ in Forest Grove, Oregon. He has joint standing in the Christian Church (Disciples of Christ) and the United Church of Christ.

Maria de Lourdes Porrata is minister for community empowerment for the American Missionary Association of the United Church Board for Homeland Ministries. She is an ordained minister in the United Church of Christ.

Gailen Reevers Sr. is the pastor of Lincoln Memorial Congregational Church in Los Angeles, California.

Daniel F. Romero is the conference minister of the Southern California/ Nevada Conference of the United Church of Christ.

Paul Hobson Sadler Sr. is minister of evangelism for African American and Native American Indian church development, United Church Board for Homeland Ministries, United Church of Christ.

Daniel Sather is pastor of Faith United Church of Christ in Cincinnati, Ohio.

Don C. Skinner is a retired United Church of Christ minister and chaplain emeritus at Allegheny College in Meadville, Pennsylvania.

James A. Smith Jr. is the former minister for higher-education relationships in the Division of Education and Publication, United Church Board for Homeland Ministries, United Church of Christ.

Kenneth B. Smith is the former president of the Chicago Theological Seminary.

Peg Stearn is minister at First Congregational Church in Guilford, Connecticut.

Deborah Streeter is a United Church of Christ minister living in Carmel, California.

Eric Thorsen Jr. is an administrative assistant at the West Michigan Conference of the United Methodist Church.

Maren C. Tirabassi is a poet and prolific writer. She is the pastor of Northwood Congregational Church, United Church of Christ, in Northwood, New Hampshire.

Prospero I. Tumonong is the treasurer and director of administrative services at the West Michigan Conference of the United Methodist Church.

Peggy Way is a professor at Eden Seminary in St. Louis, Missouri. She is an ordained United Church of Christ minister.

Wayne Wilson is a graduate of the Howard Divinity School in Washington, D.C. He is a member of the United Church of Christ.

Elizabeth Yeats is an educator in the Friends General Conference in Philadelphia, Pennsylvania. She is a member of the Society of Friends (Quaker Church).